A FOOT IN THE BUCKET

GOING GREEN IN THE HILLS

by

JENNY GREEN

First edition published in 2015
By Read Fox Books

A CIP record for this book
is available from the British Library

Distributed by the Author
'The Old Police House'
Clifford
Herefordshire HR3 5ER
nellhound@outlook.com

ISBN-978-C-9932564-1-7

Printed in the United Kingdom
by Powerprint
Oxford Chambers, High St,
Llandrindod Wells
Powys LD1 6AG

First printing 2015

For Gordon
my three girls
and my late father, H.J.W.

ACKNOWLEDGEMENTS

To give one's time is the greatest gift anyone can give to a friend, thus I say 'thank you' to Gill McHattie who said 'If you don't do something with this, I will' and she did; proof-reading, suggesting and getting the ball rolling. To Gordon who designed the cover, titled all the stories, and whose practical advice, encouragement, unbelievable tolerance when computer generated hysteria was about to take over and whose loving support enabled this book to reach publication. To my daughter Liz who juggles ten balls in the air at the same time but who found time to deal with 'computer things' that were beyond me. To Emma Van Woerkom who patiently guided me through the intricacies of officialdom, and to the many friends, some in The Hay Writer's Circle, some not, whose encouragement (and I suspect impatience in the face of my lackadaisical attitude and inhibitions) I say 'Thank you.'

Except for the two 'G's' all names have been changed

CONTENTS

WHY DID YOU BUY IT

Somehow the elegant visions of Elizabeth Barrett Browning and other Victorian ladies gracefully lowering themselves onto velvet button-back chairs, patiently composing their letters and poems in an exquisite hand is not my scene. The leisurely hours spent at a delicate rosewood desk will never be mine, for chaos followed me around close as a shadow during my years as a 'townie', and apart from the fact that its causes became vastly different when we adopted the country life it stayed with me. As soon as I became reasonably proficient at one aspect of daily living I'd take on another, so between the doing and the learning there was precious little time for standing and staring in the time honoured country manner.

Roses round the door, strawberry teas on the lawn, and the careless tossing of hay on the end of a pitchfork to while away a balmy summer afternoon are many people's dreams. Fortunately they were never ours. Had they been, the reality would have been disillusionment a hundredfold, for however far removed our lives may have been from the general idea of rural living it was a way of life which we deliberately chose, based on a philosophy which we believed could only enrich our existence and give a point to our labours. And a great bonus which we could never have anticipated was to find ourselves in the many humorous situations we would otherwise not have encountered.

Gordon, although town bred was an inveterate wild-fowler and amateur ornithologist who escaped to the marshes of the Dee estuary on every possible occasion to immerse himself in the soul of the great wilderness which is the inseparable companion of all those places where sea birds thrive. Not so I. Farmland surrounded the home of my youth, yet I lived in a state of almost total non communication with everything it offered. Seasonal delighted expressions at the way in which nature produced new generations of animals, birds, insects and plants were the only acknowledgements of the forces that separated my interests from those whose livelihood depended on these very things, and I grew to adulthood caring little, other than that from these sources came my daily bread.

While our children were young and impressionable we were determined to expose them to the maximum amount of culture

1

available, so in 1966 as the large shipping company for which Gordon worked as a graphic designer was moving to Southampton we thought it would be a good idea to live within walking distance of the city.

Local shops were comprehensive and Gordon enjoyed his two mile walk to work down by the Solent each day, generally overtaking the slow-moving rush hour traffic. Every Thursday I would walk the mile into town to whiz round Sainsburys collecting more or less the same thing each week for I was already into the healthy food regime. Never did any ready-made meals or sugary drinks find their way into my trolley, so no time was spent lingering or pondering. Thus food shopping was easy and quick consisting almost entirely of things with which to make other things. Of course every so often Mr Sainsbury would move the stock about so I'd come across something I didn't want where I was expecting to find porridge oats, which took up a bit more time until the new map had impinged itself on my psyche. But shopping was normally a speedy affair, and with my purchases I'd walk to the park behind the store, hop onto a bus, and within a few minutes I'd be home.

Everything was very convenient. We saw no need of a car for trains to everywhere were numerous with plenty of economy offers during the school holidays. Buses were frequent, and sitting on the top deck was always a rewarding experience, giving views of all the hidden things behind hedges and beyond buildings. Over the years we visited museums and art galleries, theatres and concert halls. We brass-rubbed in ancient churches until our knees complained and when at home listened to tortuous practice on a variety of musical instruments. We toured Roman dig sites and poured over ancient volumes in atmospheric cathedral libraries learning the ways and customs of civilisations that had thrived without knowledge of the technological dawn. Sorties on a quick train to London produced wider harvests. It was enjoyable, instructive and frequently exhausting. It was all very, very urban.

During the latter half of the 1960's however, under all this mind improving, murmurs of unrest were making themselves felt, and all our diversions and occupations whilst being stimulating and enjoyable, didn't seem to be getting us anywhere. It was at this point that we realized that 'getting somewhere' for us, meant getting closer to the fundamentals of life. We were, in short, disillusioned with the

2

trend of a society proud of its ability to spend and throw away, mindlessly dancing to the tune of the advertisers with their constant reiterations that to buy is to live.

All around us people seemed to be greedily reaching out for what was jubilantly proclaimed to be a higher standard of living, the birthright of all, but with suicide and mental ill health increasing alarmingly it seemed that the pickings were hardly worth while. Our involvement with community activities in the city only reinforced our view of this sad decline of human happiness. We became convinced that this frenzied pattern of living was taking people further and further away from the one thing that our ancestors knew about and valued above all others......the land.

An old saying, which all countrymen understand only too well, 'no foot, no'oss' and we were very much aware of a new dictum with similar but much more sinister implications...... 'no land, no life', and could anyone who'd read it not be disturbed by Rachael Carson's warning in her book 'The Silent Spring'?

As children of the thirties and forties, memories of wartime Britain remained vivid. Neither of us looked back in horror to a childhood where junk food was unknown and television was unavailable except for those living in the southeast, and our small weekly ration of sweets was something to anticipate with delight every Saturday.

The house in Wallasey on the Wirral peninsula where Gordon lived with his parents and two sisters had been severely damaged when a land mine destroyed the house opposite, and their house had to be demolished causing them to seek temporary shelter. The inhabitants of that dormitory suburb suffered severely from air raids when German bomber crews mistook the parallel roads leading down towards the Mersey for slipways, and repeatedly jettisoned their bombs on this almost entirely residential area.

At my childhood home in a Cheshire village a good part of the lawn had been turned into a vegetable garden, chickens roamed the small orchard, and because my father's business required him to be mobile he was in the enviable position of retaining his car throughout the war. At weekends he would frequently drive to the military hospital in Chester to return with two or three recuperating soldiers or airmen, and I remember those Sunday afternoons not for the faces of those brave men but for the crutches and heavily bandaged limbs and

3

heads, whose owners were taking their ease on deck chairs in the garden or by the drawing room fire before returning to hospital, and at some later date to duty.

Maybe, deep in my psyche were then laid the foundations of my attitude as to how life should be lived. The look on my parent's faces when news came that friends had been killed in an air raid on Wallasey; the wounded soldiers and airmen indulging in unaccustomed normality as they enjoyed crumpets, or strawberries freshly picked; the delight of lingering over the sweet counter on a Saturday morning. And then later, when the Americans set up an army base not far away, the joy of catching oranges and sweets as they were hurled from a passing troop lorry to the accompaniment of 'Hiya kids.'

All this, and much, much more I think, paved the way many years later for my decision to agree with Gordon that there was more to life than being a consumer. Keeping up with the Jones's held no interest.

We read widely. Books about noise, pollution and population occupied much space on our bookshelves. Paul Erlich and Ralph Nader, amongst others caused us to consider whether our masters at Westminster were more than slightly deviating from the truth when they allayed with soft words and persuasive phrases any facts which might cause the populace to think the familiar values and established patterns of life could not happily jog along for ever.

The food offered in the shops was not so much the produce of soil as of chemicals. A quick glance at almost any packet, jar or bottle revealed words not normally in the average woman's vocabulary. Animals were being regularly dosed with goodness knows what in order to fatten them more quickly. Anything that grew was a sure bet for liberal doses of pesticide, fungicide and herbicide. Some farmers were saying that their fields could produce crops only by applying more of these very things. Like the Cheshire Cat the age of organic traditions was beginning to fade, and just as the grin of the Cat remained for some time after the rest of it had vanished so did our politicians subdue the voices in the wilderness, continuing to declare that all was well with our world. It was blindingly obvious they didn't read the same books that we did.

During this period of revelation our two eldest daughters were spending more and more time at a riding school deep in the heart of

4

the New Forest. Each Saturday morning they would drive off with my friend and her two girls to apply themselves as enthusiastic pupils and willing general helps, returning in the evening to talk incessantly about the spirit of this horse and the cleverness of another and grumble about how hard they had worked as opposed to anyone else. The whole thing sounding more akin to a stint of hard labour rather than a pleasure for which we were actually paying. Exhausted by these horsey activities, they would soon be overtaken by sleep, yet at some early hour the following morning they and their cronies would repeat the pleasures and tribulations of the previous day.

Gordon was tired of senior management being unable to see ahead let alone around corners, frequently making demands for work which required much thought and careful execution to be delivered pronto. All around him colleagues were being moved to London or made redundant. He was in line for the former but elected not to move, whereupon the company decided that Gordon outside London was better than no Gordon at all. He could they told him, carry on working where he was.

Then unexpectedly our concerns became more urgent. Louise aged 11, Angela 9 and Jessica 5 walked the short distance to school alongside barely moving traffic, inhaling exhaust fumes. Seven months after starting primary school Jessica had an asthma attack, then a few weeks later another. These increased in frequency, and after a dreadful attack one evening which culminated in her being rushed to hospital where she was immediately placed in an oxygen tent, we knew that a move to 'somewhere' had become a necessity.

The ball was now in our court and we had to get down to some really serious discussion. So discuss we did, drinking far too much coffee as we talked into the early hours with vague ideas becoming definite plans, until something that seemed to be a better idea pushed the preceding one out as not being that good after all.

The girls were enthusiastic about country life although the thought of leaving their friends was a drawback, but we said that friends could come to stay, that new friendships would be forged, and promised that we'd make up in other ways for what they were losing. Gordon would earn an income and work on the property as we had no illusions that anything we bought would not need working on, and I would go into food production in a big way.

5

The tax threshold in 1972 was £1,300, petrol was thirty-three pence a gallon, and meticulous workings-out on the costing of general living suggested that if we could find a property at the right price we could eliminate our mortgage. With reduced overheads and producing most of what we ate we could live as well on less than half our previous income. But there was a risk. Was Gordon going to be able to make a living as a freelance graphic designer whilst living so far from where the action was? A decision had to be made and we talked long and hard, then made it.

So it was that in 1972 Gordon handed in his resignation and the scene was set. Two years before The Good Life appeared on our television screens, we were about to throw away not only our security but also all we had known in a search to prove the meaning of the phrase 'the quality of life.'

***

'How on earth did you find it?'

We couldn't count how many times we heard the question that first summer, and we became adept at gauging what the questioner really thought about our migration to the backwoods and our choice of abode.

Visitors generally fell into two categories. The roses-round-the-door types who were horrified at the revelation that there were still in Britain houses not blessed with the usual variety of sanitary objects, and the enthusiasts who fell in love with our funny little house, and saw nothing strange in the fact that some of our personal arrangements were a little less than perfect. Our guests were given an inkling that all was not as glossy as it might be when they drove into the yard of the farm below, to discover that the lane was no more and the rest of the quarter-mile journey had to be completed up a stoney pot-holey track. At this point they had to make a decision to either continue on four wheels, praying that the suspension and everything else would still be attached to the chassis if, and when the journey was completed, or to get out and walk.

The enthusiasts cheerfully saw the house quite delightful as it was and frequently expressed their envy. The idea of living in shabby

6

chaos in such an environment was something they would gladly have tolerated if only they could have thought of a way to earn a living.

The 'roses' people would enter the house anticipating all the usual accoutrements of the country dwelling as portrayed in 'Ideal Home', but the first step over the threshold put paid to those fancy ideas.

Treading warily over the flagstone floor of the big kitchen which gave them their first interior view, their eyes would scan uneasily across the not very level ceiling, then pass down the walls on which several layers of paper had taken leave of the one beneath, then, with noticeable jarring they'd come finally to rest on the ghastly cooking range, resplendent with two ovens and a frontage of blotchy tiles, its' colour suggesting that in the gay history of Tironnen someone had aimed at it large quantities of damson juice and blood.

This was always too much for the 'roses' people. Suspecting (correctly) that more horrors awaited their inspection, they would stand open-mouthed for several seconds before hastily transferring their eyes to the comparative safety of the ceiling. At this point we would usually discern a little gulp, a sure sign that a massive effort at composure was taking place, then a weak smile which transformed itself into a far too enthusiastic beam of delight considered by its' wearer genuine enough with which to confront us.

'How on earth did you find it?'

But we always knew they were really saying 'Why on earth did you buy it?'

TIRONNEN

The rightness of our decision to move there seemed to be reinforced by the endless sunny days, and enthusiastically we put some semblance of organization into the house to facilitate a modicum of daily running. But the best thing we did was to roll a large log up the yard to a suntrap at the foot of the ash tree. We would sit there daily tucking into lunches of cheese and biscuits, fruitcake and fruit, drinking too many cups of coffee and planning our future as we tossed thoughts and ideas around. 'What do you think about this?' Gordon would say, and my invariable reply would be, 'hold on', as I switched on the kettle, put mugs on a tray and a minute later carried the steaming drinks outside to where Gordon had preceded me to the log and was mulling over his latest idea. We'd stay much longer than was necessary, talking endlessly as we looked towards our pretty house and the magnificent panorama of the Brecon Beacons beyond. The newness of it all produced endless delights and fresh topics of conversation, and the joy of being on our hillside surrounded by vast stretches of hills and valleys utterly intoxicated us. How fortunate we were.

***

The search for a house had begun the previous spring, and in reply to enquiries estate agent's brochures fell through the letterbox in great numbers. For one reason or another nothing seemed suitable. Properties were either too big or too small, with too much land or not enough, frequently too close to civilization or too expensive. Practical reasons and personal choice condemned all but a few to the waste-paper basket and those we pondered over didn't whip up much enthusiasm. Nothing seemed right, although we couldn't always give sound reasons for rejection. Maybe it was because such a momentous change was taking place in our lives that with a sense of sureness 'our house' would turn up we had no hesitation in discarding them.

Spring passed and there were times when my confidence waned a little. Summer still found us pouring over details of one 'desirable' residence after another, consigning brochure after brochure to the

8

waste bin, then one Monday morning I opened a batch of brochures from an agent in Brecon announcing a multiple auction in August.

I quickly skimmed through each sheet of print, lingering a little over one particular piece before passing on to the next, then starting again with the first one to concentrate more fully on the details. I examined the next one, then the third which I read and then read again before putting it under the others I was holding. I finished reading and examined again the one to which I'd already paid greater attention. There was no picture, but in green lettering larger and bolder than the rest of the printed information was one word......Tironnen.

I murmured the word several times, wondering what it meant. It was a beautiful word, soft and clinging as though it didn't want to let go. A word without aggression or harshness, and it permeated my mind, as still gazing at the sheet of paper I put it on top of the others and placed them on the hall table whilst I scurried through the house with Hoover and duster, regaining some sense of order after the weekend.

Time after time I was drawn as by a magnet to lean over the hall table to read the particulars of the house with the lovely name, and by midday I'd placed the paper under the globe in the centre of the table as though security was needed to ensure the details would not vanish to leave me bereft after all the waiting months. That evening as we sifted through the day's mail Gordon agreed that not only was it the only property we'd heard of that sounded worthy of further investigation. It had the right number of rooms, five acres of land and numerous outbuildings. It sounded perfect. The next day I phoned the agent.

'It'll probably make between nine and ten thousand,' he said, and hope sprang within me.

I relayed this information to Gordon who had evidently given the matter some thought during the day, for when he arrived home that evening he announced, 'You'd better go and see it then because I won't have any spare time for several weeks.

This suggestion had no appeal at all. I was confident that I knew the sort of house we both wanted down to the last nook and cranny but to be the only one to see it......that was rather an alarming prospect. What did I look for? Short of the thing actually falling down while I was there how did I know its condition.

9

'I'll write out a list of questions and all you've got to do is look round carefully and write down the answers. It seemed simple enough.

During the next ten days things looked more promising all round. We received several more possible brochures, yet still the farmhouse high in the Welsh hills had that extra 'something' which in my mind made it already more than just a building. The agent's descriptive sheet was now pinned to the notice board in the breakfast room. Goodness knows how many times in the course of a day I passed it, yet every time I did so one lilting word reached out, beckoning me. Bright green print demanding my attention..........I'm here ....waiting....Tirronnen.

Angela and I travelled by coach to Brecon where the agent met us and straight away we drove west towards the village of Pontbrynnach, turning off the main road after several miles to begin climbing through twisting narrow lanes until the council road suddenly ended and we turned into an immaculate farmyard. Passing across the front of a neat freshly painted house we started climbing again, this time bumping over a rough steep track, banked high on both sides and allowing no view of what lay beyond. Dog roses, brambles and honeysuckle massed the right-hand bank while on the other, cropped grass marked the edge of a small wood. After a while the banks became lower and we passed through a five-barred gate and there it was...... My heart sank.

About three hundred yards further on and considerably higher, a great barn of a building stood like a fortress on an outcrop of land. A high forbidding grey wall faced us, unrelieved by any window or door, and as we bounced up the uneven track the massive wall regarded us dourly. We reached the yard still without any idea of what the rest of the house might be like. Surely, I thought, there must be windows somewhere. Before I had time to ponder this serious disadvantage, a beautiful dark-haired woman appeared, proving that at least there was a door, and smilingly introduced herself in a quick lilting voice as Carys Pritchard.

We followed her up some steps which rose to an enclosed courtyard (mysteriously referred to in the agent's blurb as a rear-forecourt) thereby lopping off several feet from the height of the west wall and producing proportions more pleasing to the eye. A wide, heavy oak door was open to admit us to a large high stone-flagged

10

room, airy and cool and very welcome after the bright heat in which we'd sizzled during so many hours of travelling. Immediately opposite was an important looking door, panelled and delicately ornamented by thin strips of wood. It struck me as slightly strange to find such refinement in an old hill-farmhouse but I didn't dwell on the incongruity and looked around me. To the left of the door a staircase rose to turn by a large window before vanishing from sight. On our right a dreadful grate-cum-cooker flanked by roughly built cupboards commanded our attention.

Through the imposing door by the stairs was another equally large room, the funereal feel and smell telling us as we entered of its infrequency of use. This was endowed with a fireplace of unbelievable proportions. Made of house bricks, and built higher than it was wide, it leaned forward into the room with quite a gap separating it from the wall at the top. The monster riveted my attention for several seconds, and the thought flashed through my mind that while scarcity of cash might conceivably have suggested house bricks as a viable material, and lack of knowledge about fixing a fireplace to the wall accounted for its lopsided appearance, that horrible shape was a deliberate choice on someone's part. My imagination was stretched to the limit as I tried to appreciate the satisfaction of its creator as he regarded it at the end of his labours. I gave up and turned my attention to the floor. This, I realised was suspended, and again I was puzzled as this seemed a remarkable extravagance. In the centre of the south wall was a window of normal Georgian size but seeming very small as the only window in such a large room. I leaned into the deep recess of the three foot thick wall, the better to see the glorious view which stretched from the Black Mountains on the border and across the Brecon Beacons and Fforest Fawr, to the distant Carmarthan Fan, beyond which lay the beautiful wooded lowlands of west Wales.

Looking down I realized that the house was built on a promontory, not noticeable on our approach, and the field below sloped down steeply towards the valley. The window may have seemed disproportionately small but the sky was big and nothing prevented the light from this big sky flooding the room.

The staircase, which reversed its' direction half way up, reached a small square landing. Four doors similarly fashioned to the imposing one below opened onto bedrooms two of which were quite small, the

11

other two much larger and not of the most pleasing proportions. A fifth door, tongued and grooved to denote less importance admitted us to the attic stairs which were very rickety, having suffered much from uncountable years of fierce weather blowing through the unboarded eaves to work unmolested destruction. This roof space had obviously been divided into two rooms although the low wattle and daub walls were now almost non-existent. I shone my torch into the apex of the roof bringing into focus each pair of intersecting beams and the stout pegs that held them together, truly tested for strength over more than two centuries. The massive framework looked as though it held the whole house together in a vice-like grip, and I marvelled at the people who had built this place and fashioned this roof out of the huge timbers on a site so remote and high.

Downstairs once more we inspected a small room off the main living room. This was referred to by Mrs Pritchard as the dairy and was used as a kitchen. It was without the benefit of piped water although like the rest of the house it did boast electricity. The back door was open to show the magnificent view whilst the smells of summer from a small bed of annuals wafted in. Then returning to the living room we passed through a low panelled door, and treading carefully down winding stone steps entered a cellar. But this was no ordinary cellar. It was small and low with several narrow insets in the walls, arched at the top as though their purpose was to hold a statue, which could hardly have been the case, and the ceiling also arched in a pleasing curve like a bodega. A narrow channel led from a solid block of wood like an old tree trunk about thirty inches high, to a gutter which ran along one side of the wall. Through an arch was a replica of the first room except for the absence of the wooden block and gutter, and it was without astonishment that I heard Mrs Pritchard remark as we climbed the steps and went outside 'and at the back there used to be a wrought iron balcony running the width of the house but gone long before my time.' This was indeed a house of surprises and I mulled over the functional aspects of it and how they seemed, in many instances to have been startlingly overruled.

Was hill-farming in 18th century Wales so prosperous that doors would be panelled and unnecessarily ornamented? Why would a busy farmer allow much needed manpower to build rooms far in excess of normal height? I couldn't believe that a wine cellar came into the category of 'things a hill-farm cannot be without' (at this point the significance of the block and drainage system in the cellar escaped me) and what was all this about a wrought-iron balcony? I began to think that the only connection Tironnen had with farming was that in recent times farming families had lived there.

I walked to the top of the garden, looked back down its length and was delighted by what I saw. The Brecon Beacons formed a magnificent background to a pretty whitewashed stone house with a bright blue door, small interestingly curved windows either side and two more above, just as I had pictured it those countless times when I'd read and re-read the brochure pinned to the notice board at home. The house was built back to front. The front door in the north wall looking into the hill, thereby protected from the fierce south westerlies we came to know so well. On the western side ran an L-shape of outbuildings, including a great two-bay barn with massive doors accessed from the yard. I wandered about poking nosily about in the buildings and decided that whatever stock we wanted to keep could surely be adequately housed within them. That evening I phoned Gordon.

'It's gorgeous. The right number of rooms, the right size, lot's of outbuildings, and the view is glorious. They use a pokey little room as a kitchen but we could easily turn the living room into a kitchen-cum-dining room and......'

'Just a minute,' interjected my spouse, 'You're racing off at a tangent about irrelevancies. I asked you to note certain things, so can we start on those? How about the floors? Were the upstairs floors level or not?'

I thought for a moment. I hadn't filled in any of the questionnaire I had been given, but through the rosy haze surrounding my view of everything connected with the house I seemed to see the upstairs floors being reasonably firm and flat underfoot. 'Yes, yes, they seemed pretty straight to me.

'The architraves.....were they level?'

My mind's eye swept without hesitation to the important looking door by the stairs. Without doubt that was level, likewise the cellar door and the one leading to the kitchen. I transported myself back to the square landing and realised that I'd been so eager to see what lay beyond that whether the architraves were straight or not had escaped me.

'I'm not sure......I don't remember.'

'It's no good not being sure. I gave you a list of questions to answer as a guide to the condition of the place. What on earth were you looking at while you were there?'

'But it's all so fascinating' I protested. 'You see, it's not a farmhouse at all. I think it must have been a hunting lodge, in fact I'm absolutely certain of it.' I realised as soon as the words were out of mouth that the fact of my certainty was, whilst possibly interesting entirely irrelevant, and would not be lost on Gordon.

'That's beside the point. If you think it's that good, find out what matters or else forget it.'

***

The following afternoon Angela and I went back to the farm where unexpected tea and cakes awaited us. It seemed, on second inspection that the upstairs floors had quite a slope to them. In fact it was a very obvious slope and I couldn't imagine how I hadn't noticed this the previous day. I clutched my notebook and jotted down various details. I took photographs outside from every angle, although it never occurred to me to take any of the inside. House, outbuildings, land, view.......snap, snap, snap; and all the while I wondered about the history of Tironnen.

***

'That's no help at all.' Gordon put down the notebook containing my compilation of apparently useless information.

Suitably chastened I volunteered 'They were living in it.'

'Which tells me' said Gordon, 'that it has four walls, a roof, and that the floors are able to withstand the weight of furniture.'

I sifted through the bric-a-brac of my mind for un-rosy memories and grasping the first that occurred perked up. 'The stairs to the attic were rotten.'

This was received in silence, and then Gordon asked, 'Was it nine thousand the auctioneer said it might fetch?'

Glad of a change of direction I nodded. 'Nine to ten.'

Knowing my propensity for seeing what I wanted to see, my long-suffering husband took the bull by the horns. 'Well, put your money where your mouth is. Is it worth that much?'

There could only be one answer to that. The little house on the hillside was so suitable in every way. Everything about it was 'us', and I knew without doubt that if Gordon saw it he would endorse that. Tironnen would be a challenge and we'd never shirked a challenge. Yet I also knew that if the bids went anywhere near nine thousand we'd be out of the running. Even to my enchanted eyes and in the full knowledge of our inventiveness, resourcefulness and general thrift, a liberal dose of spare cash would be necessary to anyone living in and wishing to improve Tironnen.

'No' I muttered.

'What then?' he replied. 'Eight and a half? Eight?'

I took a deep breath. 'Eight.....no more than eight,' and after pausing a moment whined 'But I wish you'd go and have a look.'

'Look love' said Gordon gently, 'I shall be happy in any house that you're happy in but it wouldn't necessarily work the other way round would it? You've a good idea of what we want and if you're so sure it'll suit us all, then let's see what we can do.'

We tried to imagine what the other people who had decided to bid would be like. A house of such character and potential would attract a lot of attention but with all those outbuildings and a five-acre field it might not be the ideal holiday home. Having to get out of one's car to open and close three farm gates before reaching one's front door would probably deter quite a few. Living in the middle of a field wasn't everybody's idea of bliss either, and so we went on, putting forward reasons, sensible and ridiculous, why others might not be in competition with us, and the agent's figure of nine thousand became just possibly a shade on the high side.

Having decided to bid, another problem loomed large. We would determine a figure that we felt was right and if Gordon went to the auction he would go not one pound above it, and if the house was knocked down at a fraction more I would be furious. On the other hand if I went, I'd think as the bidding reached our stated figure, that just a fraction more might secure it, and as fractions have a habit of compounding themselves Gordon would be furious.

We pondered this dilemma for a while until he mentioned it to a friend who was also our solicitor.

'Simple' said Norman. 'Meg and I don't know that part of the world and we'd enjoy a day spending someone else's money, so we'll go along and bid for you.'

So the die was cast. We arranged a bridging loan from the bank manager and all we could now do was wait.

***

We'd never bought a house by auction before, and not being present ourselves couldn't even taste the excitement and tension as the prospective buyers and onlookers packed themselves into the large room set aside for the auction in the Bear Hotel. I mooned between house and garden all morning in a state of nervousness, unable to concentrate on anything, looking at the clock with idiotic frequency. In my mind's eye I followed Norman and Meg as they drove through prosperous Wiltshire, across the Severn Bridge and into Wales.

What if they were late? Had a crash. Got lost. I must have been a pain in the neck because although I had the sense to keep my hysterical imaginings to myself I was very jittery. The successful result of this day would be our commitment to a new life towards which we had planned for so long. Yet now, with the possibility of the signing and sealing only a few hours away my heart thumped wildly. Either we would succeed in our endeavours or we would fail and I didn't want to fail. Yet there we were, with three children, about to throw away a regular income and all that was familiar to us.

Four years ago we had been sitting with visiting friends in a Southampton pub, a building used by Henry V as his courthouse before setting sail for France to win his victory at Agincourt, and in this historic setting we had watched the journey of spaceship Apollo to the moon. 'A great step for mankind.' Indeed it was, and now in our own small way we too were taking a great step.

Were we mad? Some of our friends certainly had reservations. Should we have had them too?

The hands on the ship's clock in the hall announced the fatal hour and as I stared at it, my thoughts miles away in the hotel at Brecon, I wondered absently why it was that I'd never before observed the name

16

of its maker.......Christie & Wilson, Glasgow. Louise and Angela and their friends were cleaning bridles, chattering and giggling in the garden. I wandered into the playroom where Jessica was lying on the sofa reading, recovering from the effects of last night's asthma attack. I felt sick.

***

Gordon answered the phone.

Waiting at the foot of the stairs trying to catch the gist of the conversation it seemed to me that Norman was giving a grand build-up......to what? I returned to the playroom. The tack cleaning had finished and a crowd of youngsters were exhibiting their acrobatic prowess on the exercise bar outside. I heard the sound of the receiver being replaced and seconds later Gordon was by my side.

Our lives were now, for better or worse, linked with Tironnen......The Land of the Ash Tree.

NEXT TO GODLINESS

Not owning a car ourselves, a good friend had offered us transport should our move transpire. So on a warm dry day in September two adults and three children climbed into his camper van with one eager dog, Dylan, one furious cat, and a teddy bear almost as big as its asthmatic owner and certainly much fatter. Removers would arrive with our goods and chattels the next day.

Of the journey I have no recollection at all. Nor have I any of our arrival at Tironnen and certainly none of Gordon's impression of his latest acquisition. Probably this last spot of amnesia was just as well, for after a brief exploration of the upstairs he would quickly have realized that the place we had bought was......shall I say, somewhat in need of a good dose of T.L.C.

Maybe the shock to his spirits was mitigated by the warmth emanating from the fire in the plum-coloured grate which kind Mrs Pritchard had thoughtfully lit to lessen the chill of the empty house. But he kept his thoughts to himself.

He and John brought garden chairs in from the van, then decided that they may as well empty it of all the other paraphernalia after which they could settle down for a relaxing cup of tea. I unearthed a kettle, teapot, drinks for the children, mugs and some biscuits, and pouring water from a large jug (again courtesy of kind Mrs Pritchard, for water had to be collected from a spring a hundred yards downhill) made a very welcome cuppa.

Eager to be exploring their new surroundings the girls gulped down their drinks, then thrusting hands into the biscuit tin each grabbed a handful of biscuits and set off with Dylan, and I was left with a question on my mind which I was finding difficult to formulate. We chatted about the superb view, the glorious old pasture, how wonderful our crops would be on our south facing slope and how the outbuildings could be adapted to house the various animals we would acquire. We vocalized at length on how the 'dairy' would be divided to make a bathroom and a shower room and how the room in which we were sitting would become the kitchen with our old oak table resplendent on the flagstone floor. I visualised the hooks in the great central beam, which had in former years held great hams and sides of bacon, soon holding various chattels suggesting the sort of industry appropriate to the life of a smallholder, although at the time, apart from my enormous copper jam pan, I hadn't a clue as to what these might be.

The size of the two main rooms, the pulling away of a scrap of wallpaper in the window recess to reveal the pinkish-grey stone beneath, the wide oak boards in the room overlooking the valley and the fascinating cellar, all came under enthusiastic discussion but nothing was said to indicate what Gordon really felt. I suspected that he was buoying himself up by looking at the positive side of things and I became aware that I was doing just that myself, as I thought about the inside, the outside, the outbuildings, the land, of what we had taken on, and worse, what we had left behind.

What had we done?

But really I meant what had I done!

Shaking with apprehension, longing yet dreading an answer to the question I was too terrified to ask, I skirted the issue knowing that if a deathly silence followed I'd know that things were a lot worse than I'd allowed myself to think.

'It wasn't just the suitability of the place that got to me it was the ambiance,' I said. But a deathly silence didn't follow.

Everything it seemed was alterable, renovatable or buildable. It would just take time and as Gordon had to earn a living, the alterable, renovatable and buildable activities would have to be attended to as and when it was possible. This could take quite a long time.

Everything to make the house as we wanted was achievable....in time. Probably with a little more expenditure than had been anticipated, but......in time.

Ingenuity of the highest order would be required to attend to some of the more unusual challenges, but with time......There was nothing to be despondent about.

Suddenly the architraves upstairs didn't seem quite so lop-sided or the floors so sloping and I breathed a sigh of relief. What John really thought I don't know and never did find out but as Gordon spoke he nodded and interjected several 'Oh, yesses' and 'definitelys' and was a buffer of encouragement on the certainty of everything being absolutely wonderful......in time.

The girls returned from their foray. They'd been up the hill behind the house via an ancient and much overgrown cart track and they marched through the door bearing pieces of wood for the fire and a bunch of cow-parsley which Jessica put in a jam jar she'd found on the wall in the yard. Already the place was beginning to feel homely.

'Food,' I said. 'I think food is in order' and began undoing the straps of the picnic basket. The deep windowsill became a sideboard and after everyone had eaten to their satisfaction John said it was time to bid us farewell. We wandered down to the gate at the lower end of the field, waved him off and then climbed up to the top of the meadow the better to view our estate. Way, way below us sporadic traffic passed in and out of view behind the trees lining the A40 and I thought of the noisy roads of the busy city we'd left just a few hours ago where the sound of traffic never stopped. Now the only sounds were those made by us and the birds around us.

Life was going to be very different.

***

That evening, before our sleepy children retired to their beds of blow-up mattresses and a put-u-up, Gordon said 'There's something I'd like you to see. Come outside.'

Puzzled, they followed as we walked round to the back of the house from where we overlooked the valley. One solitary light shone in the distance on a hill on the opposite side of the A40, then headlights appeared, to vanish after a few seconds leaving just that one acknowledgement of habitation. For although our near neighbours were only a few fields away on either side, no lights gave away their presence, hidden as they were by the wooded hill on one side and rolling pastures on the other. A thin wisp of whitish smoke almost luminous against the blue-black sky, was the only intimation of their whereabouts.

Jessica rubbed her eyes. 'Why are we out here? I'm tired.'

'Look around you' said Gordon. 'Look above you. What do you see?'

'Oh yes' cried Louise 'Isn't it wonderful. All that sky and all those stars. They're so bright and the sky is so dark...... and so big.'

20

'And it's always been there. It's just that when we lived in the city there were so many lights on the ground from buildings, street lamps and traffic, that we couldn't see it. Just think, twenty-four hours ago we couldn't have seen this.'

We walked round to the front of the house, which was really the back as it faced into the hill, and looked above the darkness of the fields to where the stars twinkled and then silently we wandered round to look out over the valley again, letting the immensity of what we were seeing engulf us.

Some days later our neighbour called to introduce himself.

'I expect you'll be getting rid of the privy' he observed.

'We most certainly will' we said heartily.

'Don't want to be seeing the stars then?' Was there a touch of pity in his voice?

Perhaps he had a point.

***

Yes, life was going to be very different and just how different was immediately apparent. After our successful bid for Tironnen our solicitor had held back £50 against the installation of water that the vendor had said he would implement. However this hadn't been done, which somewhat annoyed us. So Tironnen had neither bath nor tap and overnight the taking of a bath became a luxury, something to be anticipated with longing when we made arrangements to stay a night or two with friends. But this had nothing to do with cleanliness however, for we had only been in the house a couple of days before Gordon decided that the operation of washing could be accomplished with more thoroughness and ease than by using of a bowl of water.

There are two processes without which the neo-peasant cannot survive......thought and ingenuity. Sometimes more is needed of one than of the other. But they travel side by side from one year to the next, an invaluable and necessary replacement for money and a sure method of guaranteeing that the way repairs and renovations are accomplished are unique in the extreme.

So when the master of the house announced that we should have a shower it was a normal and serious statement to be acted upon with all speed. The fact that the spring providing our water was one hundred

21

yards down the hill with nothing linking it to the house did not beset him with problems. He disappeared outside and I judged by the sound of things being thrown about that he was searching for something in the barn. After a while he reappeared carrying a number of old wire cloche supports and a vast amount of crumpled black plastic recognizable by sight as the cover of our urban compost heap.

'Do you know what that is?' I asked

'Of course I do. But it's plastic and the only plastic we've got and we need plastic' he replied.

'It hasn't been washed' I observed frostily.

'By the time we've all showered it will be' he replied in a manner suggesting that the subject was closed and any further interruptions would not be tolerated. So the plastic was spread out on the floor, a fascinating study for a biologist who would, no doubt, have been able to identify the various dried creatures and other things adhering to it. I thought about making another protest but didn't. There were more important things to think about than the previous function of our shower curtain. Something out of nothing was writ large in our philosophy and you couldn't get more 'something' out of less 'nothing' than a shower out of a former compost cover.

Gordon, who was very enthusiastic about the whole thing, shaped the cloche wires so that they formed a square on which he draped the plastic, which he then secured firmly with twine. This arrangement was then carried through to our future bathroom and suspended by means of a rope fixed to one of the many meat hooks that adorned the ceiling. He then made a square shallow box of wood, lined it with more plastic, and setting a stout length of tubing into one corner placed it under the curtain. We all trooped out to look and admire. We were very impressed.

I put a small metal table in the shower base on which to place a bucket, and made a hole in a piece of soap which I threaded with a length of cord and hung from a nail in the frame.

Later, I reflected that the previous night I'd attended to my ablutions with a flannel and a bowl of water, and now, here I was, red plastic mug in hand, gaily pouring water over myself from a yellow bucket on the little table in front of me. I watched the water that flowed by the natural gravitation of the floor along a channel towards a length of tubing which was pushed through a seemingly tailor-made

22

mousehole in the old back door. The little house was really moving into the twentieth century.

I looked around me at the materials and construction which made up Green's instant genuine rustic shower circa '72 and burst out laughing, for whichever way I looked, from the rope holding it to the ceiling, down the now faintly ponging curtains, to the mousehole drainage system......this was progress. Maybe not a mod con, but quite definitely a con.

DRIVEN TO EXCESS

Many years ago a very disparaging article appeared in a national daily about life in Australia. Some days later a letter appeared from an immigrant hotly defending the country of his adoption in which he said that there was nothing about Australia that a Marks and Spencer's and a Sainsbury's wouldn't put right, and I fancy that the man who delivered our Land Rover from London had much the same sentiments after he'd surveyed his destination.

'Nice place you've got 'ere. Bit lonely though' as he scanned the hills for some sign of two-legged life. 'Wouldn't mind living in a place like this, wouldn't mind at all. Course, the missis likes a few shops close   by and she dun 'arf enjoy 'er bingo; she'd want that too. She likes lots of company does the missis, lots of company' He dwelt silently for a few moments, no doubt picturing these amenities on our hillside, then unexpectedly said, 'Yes, very nice, very nice.'

Pausing for a somewhat longer period to consider the pros and cons of rural Wales however, his next statement suggested that already the pros were beginning to make less weight.

'Course, we like to go to the pictures. Do you 'ave a cinema round 'ere, and pubs? I expect you've got pubs.'

We could help him there.

'Oh yes, pubs in the village and there's a cinema in Brecon which is pretty up to date with what it shows.'

'Brecon? Well I've just driven through there. It must be a good ten miles away. That's a fair way to go to the flicks isn't it? Sort of becomes a major excursion doesn't it?'

His initial enthusiasm for country living was rapidly losing momentum. 'And where's the village with these pubs then?'

Not being interested in this chitchat Gordon had wandered off to examine our new acquisition. 'Well,' I said 'you see that hill covered in trees? No, not that one, further to your right. Yes, well, if you look down to the valley on the left-hand side you can just see a road.'

The man strained into the distant unfamiliar wooded terrain seeking the spot I indicated.

'Follow that along a bit and there's the village.'

'Not exactly on the door-step is it? I mean, it's not exactly what you'd say was a stone's throw away is it? Not convenient like.'

He regarded me with a mixture of amusement and pity, unaware that these sentiments were reciprocated, and turning to where Gordon was standing by the Land Rover said 'Well, just not convenient is it?'

I was sorely tempted to say 'convenient for what?' but laughed instead and enquired of him, 'tea, coffee or homebrew? Gordon......tea, coffee or homebrew?' Whereupon we all trooped inside.

He obviously enjoyed his drink for he downed two more in rapid succession and declining our offer of lunch, rose and said he must be on his way.

'I'll be glad if you'd run me to the main road and I'll get a lift from there.'

'I'd be glad to' replied Gordon 'But I don't have my licence yet.

The man looked at him unable to believe what he'd heard. Then he slowly sat down, picked up the glass he'd just emptied and studied its interior for some seconds. He then quickly tipped the remnants of liquor down his throat, noisily smacked his lips, heaved an enormous sigh and paused from further activity whilst seeking strength to continue some sort of conversation with these people who were obviously raving mad.

'Do you mean to say that you're living in this God-forsaken hole miles from anywhere with that bloody great thing out there and you can't even drive it?'

'That's right' I said brightly, 'But we'll soon learn, and don't worry, our neighbour is going into Brecon and he said he'd hang on until you were ready.' The man sprang to his feet. 'Right. Where do I find him?' and when directed, hurried from the house and down the track as though he couldn't wait to leave behind the awfulness of fields and trees, hills and streams and the half-crazed people who chose to live among such alien things, his sanity no doubt held together by the beckoning vision of the congestion of life in SE13 or wherever it was he called home.

Oh well, each to their own.

We walked round our Safari Land Rover a dozen times, climbing in and out like a couple of kids in a playground, thrilled at its obvious strength and durability, and indeed our ownership, because once we had decided on our move it was clear that we'd have to have our own transport. Gordon had booked driving lessons and two weeks before

25

our moving date took his test.......and failed! He was mortified and puzzled. Being a very thorough person in everything he undertook he thought he'd done his test correctly. His instructor had harboured no doubts about his passing and was furious.

'That's marvellous; you've let me down. What the hell happened?'

'Well, I was told I should've covered the brake at every intersection even though I was on the main road. I didn't know that.'

'What?' fumed his instructor 'He's failed you on that? I didn't know that either!'

But that was the only reason given and it seemed that there was no arguing with the examiner. Gordon didn't pursue the matter and for a short while we were pretty downcast by this news but common sense came to the fore.

'The girls will be picked up at the end of the lane for school so that's not a problem.'

'I can walk to the village if it's important.'

'If we need to go further afield it'll have to wait.'

'Unless there's an emergency in which case we'll just get a taxi.'

Any problems were not insurmountable.

Gordon phoned the test centre in Brecon and booked a date for a test a few weeks hence. So, shortly after we'd moved in, the one-year-old Safari Land Rover we'd ordered duly arrived. After several trips to get used to driving it, accompanied by our helpful neighbour from the farm across the fields, Gordon passed his test. It was rather different from the previous one, as he had to give hand signals while changing into 2nd gear on approaching every junction, at a time when Land Rovers had crash gears for 1st and 2nd, and the three-point turn in one of Brecon's narrow streets became a six-point turn.

He arrived home very relieved.

Hurrah; we were mobile.

So much depended on his being able to drive but it was as well he didn't know just how much and how soon. The girls were thrilled at the news when they arrived home but their pleas for 'just a short drive' fell on stony ground as the light was already going, until eventually relenting Gordon drove them a mile or so to the crossroads on the common then down onto the A40 and back. The Land Rover exceeded all their expectations.

'Tomorrow' announced Gordon, 'We motor.'

26

The forecast for the following day was not good, in fact it was awful, but that Saturday morning in November was surprisingly warm, and although the grey sky suggested the forecasted weather it was not unpleasant. So after breakfast, parents, girls and dog piled into the Land Rover and we were off, looking forward to viewing some of the area about us. At first the delight of driving in our very own vehicle meant that initially we noticed little. Taking a steep right bend at a nearby hamlet, our attention turned to the clusters of houses and distant farms on the hills, some of which were soft and rolling, others very steep, and all the while leaves fell gently around us from the gloriously coloured autumn trees.

Climbing ever higher we left the trees and houses behind and soon found ourselves approaching a cattle-grid that marked the beginning of the army firing practice range. A very large notice announced:

DANGER
DO NOT ENTER THIS AREA
WHEN THE RED FLAG IS FLYING

after which came some dire threat, which I can't remember. Probably 'or we'll send you to the Tower and chop off your head.'

Well, something like that.

But no red flag was flying so we continued on our way and I observed many of the ancient cart tracks still visible whilst the ruins of scattered farms, long since abandoned, brought vividly to mind thoughts of the people who had lived in this bleak isolation. It must have been such a hard life. But that was then and we were very much in the now, driving over desolate shell-shocked moors in our serviceable, roomy, child and animal friendly Land Rover.

With pocket money to be spent we were persuaded to take a trip to Brecon, so instead of turning up the lane to Tironnen we passed it by and turned down towards the main road where the Land Rover really got into its stride, racing along at a breath-taking fifty miles an hour. No sluggard this!

'I don't think we should hang about here' I said as we pulled into a parking space, 'That sky looks ominous and we're not dressed for a downpour.' So we settled for half an hour in which the girls could do a bit of shopping and we could make a perfunctory exploration of the

27

town. At the appointed time we all met up, and while leaving the car park exchanged comments on the girl's purchases and the impressions we'd formed during our short sojourn. It was then that the first large drop of rain splattered onto the windscreen, then after a few seconds another then another. I wondered if raindrops were heavy because the way these large drops splashed out like a sunburst hitting the windscreen suggested that they were being hurled from on high and you can't hurl something that is light. 'What a stupid thing to think about' I said to myself. 'What on earth does it matter,' and turned my thoughts to recall the excellent greengrocers in the market hall and decided it would do us very nicely until our own produce was available.

It was nearly lunchtime when we arrived home. The rain had become incessant and a strong wind had blown up. By mid-afternoon dark clouds were sweeping across the sky at a rate of knots and we watched from the window as the rain was driven almost horizontally across it. In the distance we could just pick out the blurred headlights of cautiously moving traffic on the road below. Gordon voiced the feelings of us all when he said, 'Well, I'm glad I don't have to go out in that. I think it's going to get a lot worse.' I drew the curtains, laid the table and after our evening meal we settled down to occupy ourselves in various ways enjoying the warmth emanating from the hideous plum-coloured range.

But even though the walls on the south and west sides of the house were more than three feet thick the storm gathering outside made its presence known with rattles, bangs and creaks; a multitude of unfamiliar and ominous sounds both within and without. It was very alarming. Common sense dictated that a house which had suffered such gales for nearly three centuries was hardly likely to collapse about our ears, but none the less it was scary.

At about eleven o'clock, just as Gordon and I were finishing our evening drink, Jessica woke, barely able to breathe. The idea of calling out our new G.P. at this hour and in this weather was appalling but we had no choice. We had already met him courtesy of her asthma and had judged him to be kindness itself. He was also gloriously eccentric although we didn't know it then. In the storm he drove over from the other side of the valley, through the three gates, which Gordon had gone out to open for him, and racing the few yards from his car to our door entered, quite drenched. He studied his patient for a few moments, asked us some questions and gave Jessica an injection. Then he said 'Hospital.......now,' and after making a phone call to advise the hospital of our impending arrival, departed to brave once more the tempest outside.

By this time Louise and Angela were awake, and while I wasn't happy about leaving them there wasn't much I could do. I explained that Jessica was very ill and that we didn't know how long we'd be but they were quite untroubled. Indeed being on their own with the storm raging was viewed as quite an adventure. I just hoped all would be well. I rushed around collecting necessities while Gordon wrapped Jessica in a blanket, covered her with his waxed jacket then I guided his steps towards the Land Rover by shining the torch.

Our journey began. I held Jessica close as we rolled down the track, splashing through the water which was racing down from the hill. Through the open gates we reached the lane below where, because of the high banks the headlights just about charted our course as long as we moved at a snail's pace. Once we reached Pontbrynach the street lights helped a little although the rain was as heavy as ever. After a short while we turned off the main road and began to climb, gently at first along back lanes, then after a few miles we joined the Cardiff road where the incline became more pronounced. We knew we were in for a pretty hairy trip for between us and the hospital at Merthyr Tydfil lay the road across the high moorlands of the Brecon Beacons.

The wind grew even stronger as we drove, lashing the rain against the windscreen where Gordon had his face pressed to the glass, desperately trying to follow the line of the road as it twisted this way and that, ever going higher and higher the wipers fighting a loosing battle against the onslaught. Every so often as we negotiated a right hand bend I could just make out the shape of the steep-sided hill round which we were travelling. Streams of water were racing towards us and once or twice I caught a glimpse of bubbling white foam that had built up as the torrential rain poured down the hillside onto the road.

Gordon was very tense which wasn't surprising. Jessica was sleeping the sleep of exhaustion and at some stage I pressed my face to the nearside window. I didn't expect to see anything so I don't really know why I did it but as I strained into the blackness a

29

frightening truth came to me. I knew that the hillside rising on my right was sheer for the road had been cut into it. Therefore the natural downward progression of the hill on our left was also sheer. It was then that my heart stopped. There was nothing there!

Just at that moment a car coming from the opposite direction rounded a bend, its headlights confirming what I'd already guessed......that our wheels were a couple of feet away from a sheer drop.

They showed something else as well.

There was no barrier.

No wonder Gordon was tense. He must have been aware of this all the time. A wife and desperately sick child as passengers, the night as black as pitch, the mother of all storms raging and an unfamiliar road. Indeed, the worst of all possible routes to negotiate, would be enough to unnerve anyone, let alone someone who barely twenty-four hours ago had passed their test. Oh, and two potential orphans at home.

I closed my eyes. 'Please, please let us get safely to the hospital', but I didn't know to whom or what I was supplicating. They were just words and I suppose I thought that silently repeating them represented positive thinking...... if I thought at all. It was something to do as we crawled slowly forward. The mantra droned on in my head interspersed with wonderings about how far we'd come and how far we had yet to go to reach the summit when I heard Gordon say with what sounded like relief in his voice,

'I think we're at the top Jenny. We're on the flat and there should be a building on our left. Can you see anything?'

I squinted through the driving rain and it seemed that in the dark quite a large area appeared to be a different sort of blackness from the rest. It had to be.....it just had to be, and yes, a faint glimmer of light told us that we had reached The Storey Arms, the highest pub in Wales, hostelry for generations of walkers, but for us confirmation that the worst part of our journey was over. I put my hand on Gordon's shoulder, a small gesture to let him know I understood how anxious he'd been. Now he could relax a little, for as previous studies of local maps had shown The Storey Arms marked a remarkable change of terrain, and we knew that from now on our progress was down a moderate incline sided by fields and woods all the way to the valley below and our destination.

30

The storm had abated not one jot when an hour later we made our return journey across the Beacons. We were now driving close to the hillside, well away from the sheer drop which had accompanied the upward climb and caused such tension, and although visibility was still non-existent Gordon was fairly well at ease for he knew where he was; more or less!

Our little girl remained in hospital for several days, although it was the following day, well, later that day really when we all visited her and Gordon and I saw what had been invisible to us only a few hours before. How dependant we had been on Gordon passing his test but little had we known just how much and how soon and under what conditions.

***

For several months Jessica was in and out of hospital. She was a happy child, entertaining and funny, loving to be with friends but never at a loss when she was on her own, reading, drawing and writing stories being her favourite forms of enjoyment and she made the best of her hospital stays. Her consultant was convinced that the asthma was psychosomatic and assured us that the latest medication he was about to prescribe for her was having excellent results with patients around the U.K so it was arranged for the district nurse to call at her school twice weekly to give her an injection of this latest magic. But after two weeks nothing had changed and we were even visited by a health visitor who came to check that we weren't ill-treating her.

Our G.P., Gavin, who by this time had become a friend, was at his wits end with this child who reacted so strangely to all known palliatives, and as he lived several miles on the other side of the valley we felt we were helping a bit if, when Jessica had an attack coming on we could take her down to the village surgery which was more or less in the middle.

Early one Sunday morning we were all gathered in the consulting room and after administering the appropriate remedy the usual reaction occurred: all signs of wheezing immediately vanished. It was the same every time. As soon as the injection was administered the asthma disappeared. Well, on this particular morning, Gavin looked at his patient who was weary from the attack but now able to breath easily, and said, 'I think the only thing now is for our little Jessica to go to the asthmatic school.'

I was horrified and glancing at Gordon I saw the same reaction. How could our compassionate doctor say such a thing in front of her? If going away from her family was a probability surely we were the ones to tell her rather than for her to hear such a brutal announcement from him. I was stunned. I didn't want to be in the surgery any longer and took Jessica out to the Land Rover where I settled her on the back seat. She was very subdued although that was to be expected after an exhausting attack. Gordon and Gavin followed deep in conversation and out of the corner of my eye I saw Gordon nod his head as though in approval. What, I wondered, was going on. I turned to join them ready to demand an explanation but Gordon held up a hand to forestall my wrath.

'There's a reason. Go ahead Gavin' and he explained that as Jessica's reactions were so unusual he had conferred with colleagues, and bearing in mind the consultant's psychosomatic theory it was decided that a jolt might be the answer; thus the announcement in her presence about the asthmatic school. In other words, shock tactics.

I pondered on this. It seemed terribly cruel but could it work? I walked a few steps back to where my daughter was sitting and as I put my head through the open window, she asked in a barely audible voice 'What's the asthmatic school?'

I thought quickly. This was a question I didn't want asked but if there was any validity in the shock tactic approach then it must be followed through and my answer must be as forthright as Gavin's original statement.

'It's where they'll help you to get better. Like a boarding school really, without the long holidays.'

How I hated myself as she looked at me with tears welling in her eyes. I climbed in and put my arms round her but couldn't say anything. I'd said enough.

'Let's get home' I called out, and bidding our good-byes we drove away in deep thought, I with a weeping child in my arms.

By the time we arrived in the yard however, a change had come over her. She had perked up a bit and almost as soon as we entered the house demanded some toast and honey. Then more. And from that day on things gradually began to get better. Sometimes she would be wheezy for reasons we could understand, other bouts seeming to occur for no reason at all, but the attacks lessened in their ferocity and frequency and the stays in hospital became a thing of the past. Thoughts of the asthmatic school were put on hold and very slowly a little weight began to cover her thin frame. Occasionally a visit to our doctor was necessary but as the years passed to teendom, on the rare occasions it was necessary a quick puff of her inhaler would be enough to sooth the contracting bronchial tubes.

Many years later, long after we had moved from Tironnen, we drove up that steep, winding road across the Beacons, and although it was a glorious summer day, in my imagination I could hear the wildness of that awful night and see Gordon having just passed his driving test battling his way through the sheeting rain as we pressed our way through the blackness.

THE SECRET ROOM

There comes a time, when even to a slovenly mind such as mine, the disadvantages of carrying on normal daily living in a house that has suffered the ravages of nearly three hundred years of battering by the elements makes every job just too irritating and time consuming.

Tironnen had in its later years been used as a stable and then as a grain store and general maintenance had not been much attended to. Large dollops of concrete and yards of brightly coloured baling twine were obviously the mainstays of repair, so the wind and rain had lashed unchecked under the eaves and through the stonework playing havoc with floorboards and window frames. The floorboards sloped every which way so that furniture met the skirting boards at floor level in the usual way but rose like the leaning Tower of Pisa so that a gap of several inches separated the top of the object from the wall. It was not very convenient.

I once saw on television a young woman telling how she painted pictures on cobwebs, and when asked where she found them replied that she hunted around in outbuildings and neighbour's garden sheds and other such places. Now, if I were a painter of such artistic whimsies I'd be home and dry from the collection point of view. No traipsing around dark outbuildings or dusty sheds in the cold, poking behind this and that and chancing a blow on the head from some dislodged implement. For the dedicated cobweb enthusiast I can heartily recommend the leaning furniture method as a quick and comfortable means of obtaining the finest examples. More ordinary mortals such as we, however, are not always so appreciative of such things and with no remorse or further thought for the industrious spinner, we put floor levelling at the top of our list of things to be done.

Louise slept in one of the two small bedrooms at the front of the house overlooking the garden and the sheep scattered hill that rose steeply to the north. The floors of both rooms inclined towards the central beams and any piece of furniture placed against the inner wall had to be levelled by having books of suitable thickness judiciously inserted under its front half as a precaution against the bric-a-brac which usually finds a home on the top of chests and dressing tables sliding forward every time anyone moved in the vicinity. Wardrobe doors mysteriously opened, silently forming a barrier across the already crowded little rooms and carpets surreptitiously moved centre-wards to gather in inconvenient folds.

Thus floor levelling assumed priority and with it the almost complete demolition of the two bedrooms where the girls slept. We began work at the door of Louise's room pulling off layers of wallpaper and removing any rough and loose pieces of plaster. It was only later that I thought I should have kept the wallpaper. Some were obviously Victorian and possibly Georgian and would have told much about the history of the house, but at the time I gave it no thought. We wanted to progress but I very much regret not having saved some.

After a while I left to see if the dough which had been left to rise was ready to be kneaded into loaf shapes, and Gordon continued working his way round to the short outer wall on the side of the house above what was traditionally known as the dairy and which would eventually become a bathroom and shower room. This protruded from the main body of the building as a small single story with a steeply pitched roof. It was at this point that he came across a narrow piece of vertical wood, which struck him as rather odd. Why would there be a piece of wood rising up from the floor of this room in a two foot thick stone wall, the other side of which was the roof of the dairy? Pulling off more wallpaper revealed more wood.

'Jenny' he called, then after a pause to ensure he had my attention, 'Jenny, there's something strange up here' which interesting remark had me scraping frantically at my dough covered hands, wiping the remainder down my trousers and leaving a trail of sticky wholemeal bits in my wake as I hurriedly made for the stairs. By the time I arrived in the bedroom Gordon had pulled away more paper and the lath and plaster beneath to reveal a panel of solid oak, and our excitement knew no bounds as we tore at the flimsy covering wondering what we'd find.

Within minutes we were gazing at a tiny door, no more than four feet high. Its six panels mimicking in miniature the doors in the rest of the house and as perfect as the day it had been hung, for this little gem had never known the embellishment of paint or stain and the warm honey colour of the oak door stood proudly representing all that was good and honest.

35

Now to find a hidden door in one's house is no everyday occurrence and we contemplated the diminutive entrance like a couple of star struck kids for quite some while, until bursting with curiosity Gordon lifted the iron latch and effortlessly pushed it open.

Inside there was enough daylight coming through chinks at the gable end of the dairy roof and through gaps where a few slates had broken or slipped, to dimly light a small garret measuring about eight feet by six into which four wooden steps descended from the door. The pinky brown stonewalls rose about four feet high at the sides but although the roof was quite steep it was only possible to stand upright in the centre. There was no evidence that a proper window had ever existed, but four large stones set squarely into an aperture on the eastern wall opposite the steps suggested that the early morning sun might at some time have found its way in. Cobwebs liberally decorated the beams and rafters and judging by the multitude of small twigs, straw and feathers that were heaped there, the top of the walls had obviously served as the des res for generations of many feathered families.

It was one of the most exciting moments of my life. To stand in that little room which had been hidden for we knew not how long was to rub shoulders with the past, yet the initial thrill soon gave way to an uncomfortable feeling of unease.

Whose past? Someone must have called this room 'theirs', and have confided their secrets and shared their dreams with its intimate smallness.

It was said that Tironnen encompassed a ghost within its walls, although no one we'd spoken to had actually seen it, but we'd been told that many years ago a young servant girl had either fallen or jumped from the iron balcony, being killed as she met the ground below. Was it she who had been consigned to this most humble part of the house, in which to store her few possessions and to which she would drag her tired body after the interminable day? In the dimness I pictured her, sturdy and strong, although perhaps not strong enough to withstand with ease the torments of her arduous life, forever fetching and carrying in the service of her betters.

My mind's eye saw a cot set against one of the longer walls onto which she would sink to grasp a few minutes of solitude before sleep obliterated her weariness. Doubtless, sometimes she had crept to this

36

private place to think and dream. This would be where she visualized how her life would run, the long span of years ahead holding hope, laughter and the unshakeable belief of youth through the ages in her ability to overcome whatever trials might occur. But there must have been times, I said to myself, when only despair and resignation were her closest companions. Thoughts of her life only made tolerable by infrequent visits to her family and the place she would always call home, from where she would return with a heavy heart.

Here she would sit in the stolen minutes when she thought she would not be missed, to admire a trinket, a love token from a nearby farmer's boy perhaps, or to pass proudly through her fingers a brightly coloured ribbon newly bought from a visiting tinker down in the village. I pictured her fondly placing these treasured objects in a rough box set aside for such personal possessions and when she had done, pushing it from sight under the cot.

'What a super annexe it will make for Louise.' Gordon's voice was very much a thing of the present, the suggestion equally so.

I pulled myself together. What on earth was I doing, allowing myself to indulge in such silly thoughts?

'It'll need a lot of work on it' mused Gordon. 'But can't you just see it with a polished floor and a dormer window overlooking the Beacons?

'Yes' I agreed, 'It would be lovely'.

I could just see it. The thought of Louise ensconced here, surrounded by all the paraphernalia of the modern teenager, a great deal of which tended to be on the noisy side, was not unattractive. Having two doors instead of one to separate us from intrusions of electronic sound was something worth considering, yet it was with a sense of relief that I heard Gordon continue, 'But with the roof and the water to attend to and so many other things ...... after all she'll have a pretty room. She doesn't really need more space, does she?'

I nodded in agreement. It was best to close up this tiny room for the time being, to let the disturbed secrets settle once more, to shut out the light from the opened door and leave the atmosphere dim and still, letting the past keep company with itself again.

We made enquiries from our neighbours but the only response we got was one of amazement. Many folk had in the past had connections with Tironnen and we found several elderly people who

37

recalled their parents and grandparents telling them stories about the house, but nobody knew about the sealed up room. Of a ghost there has never been a sign but I still get maudlin when I think about the young girl who would have lived in the garret, and nostalgia mingles with delight when I recall the morning I first set eyes upon it.

THE HORSE SALE

'We are' said Gordon staring hard at me 'Only going to look'.

In order to reinforce this statement and at the same time let it be known just who had the last word, he glared equally hard at our three daughters.

'Of course we're only going to look' I retorted irritably. 'Whoever suggested that we were going to do anything more than just look? Nobody to my knowledge has said that they're going to do anything more than just look. Anyway, what more is there to do I might ask. I wish you'd stop holding us up when we want to be on our way.'

It was a bright, sharp Saturday morning in mid January as we bundled into the Land Rover, rolled down the track, spirits high with the anticipated pleasure of the bustle of the market place and the thrill of our first horse sale. We fastened the bottom gate which led from our empty field and drove by the side of the wood and through the ford then out onto the narrow lane, turning in the direction of our destination, Abergavenny. I picked up the sale catalogue and idly turned the pages. It didn't mean very much.

'Lot 15. Grey mare 3 yrs. 14.3.hh. Property of Mr l. Jones of Nantwitch.'

'Lot 16. Grey gelding. 8 years. 15.2.hh. Property of Mr B. Phillips of Longtown.'

Few descriptions offered more information so the catalogue wasn't exactly compelling reading to an un-horsey person like me, and anyway if when we arrived all five hundred equines proved to be identical, what did it matter.....we were only going to look.

The general chat ensured that the journey passed quickly, and having parked the Landrover, we found ourselves in the throng of people who for one reason or another were gathered together for the auction. Here I thought, everyone had the same thing in common, interest in the horse, whether to buy, to sell, or as in our case just to look. We decided to go our separate ways then meet later by the main gate. The girls set off together, Gordon went his way and I stayed where I was to take in all about me.

Horses and ponies of all shapes and sizes and in varying conditions of physical well-being and mental alertness stood in the pens. There were old horses and foals, most of which would end up supplying a pet-loving public with a suitably disguised meal for dogs and cats or feeding the lions in safari parks. It seemed a rotten end for an animal which had served someone faithfully for years or, as in the case of the foals, hardly had any life at all. I turned my attention to other things.

Small gatherings of people were grouped about the pens many of which were still empty. This was the meeting place of all and sundry, with everyone seeming to know everybody else, and knowing exactly what they were about and what was going on. Next to me two farming types leaned on the metal rails of a pen ponderously weighing the good points against the bad of a showy chestnut horse, all the while goading the owner to voluble argument over each point of criticism.

Just beyond them a small animated woman imperiously commanded a young boy, who was standing at the head of a large black horse, to find his father. Her strident voice rose above the general buzz. 'Tell him I want to see the horse move' and when the lad remained silent and immovable by his charge, voiced even more shrilly 'Oh, for goodness sake get him, I want to see the horse move' at which the boy shot out of the pen and disappeared on his errand.

I wondered if there was some reason why I should choose to go in one direction rather than another but after glancing around and finding none I ambled up the nearest aisle. It was as I turned at the end that I saw her, although at the time I didn't know it was a 'her'. In the second pen along, a large pony, a great mass of cream-coloured shaggy winter coat, stood round-bodied and four-square in the little enclosure. A big man in a worn, bright green jersey groomed her with an equally bright green dandy brush, a fraying sleeve unravelling itself with every sweep of his arm. As I drew near he paused to break off a long strand of wool and dropped it on the floor before resuming the brushing.

I moved closer.

A dark grey stripe, starting at the withers, travelled the length of the pony's broad back to mingle dark shades with the long cream tail. The legs were well-boned and sturdy, their lower parts adorned with a number of horizontal grey stripes resembling football socks, which I thought very strange but not unattractive. The hooves were definitely of the serviceable sort. The pony's chest was broad, and attached to this capable looking body was a head festooned with protective winter whiskers which outlined the shape of the jaw with a fringe effect

40

reminiscent of a 1930's lampshade. I moved towards the pen. The man stopped brushing and glanced in my direction. I continued looking at the pony and threw a confident 'Good morning' towards the man.

'Morning' he replied. He appeared to be regarding me with the seriousness of one horseman to another and moved up to the pony's head and closer to me in order to move the conversation onto a more personal level. This seemed a bit dangerous so I studiously avoided his eye. Thinking that a fairly disinterested approach would send him back to his exercise with the dandy brush, I drew away and moved alongside the animal with what I hoped was a knowledgeable look as I appraised I knew not what, but Green Jersey still seemed to expect more than the salutations of the day. I thought perhaps I should say something horsey but didn't know anything horsey to say. My look of casual interest slowly turned into a riveted stare as I searched in vain for inspiration while Green Jersey remained immobile and unsmiling, now resting the brush on the pony's back, with no thought of his recent task stirring his brain. Perhaps, I thought, striking the pose of the silent uncommunicative type, if I could hang on a bit longer, someone else would come to distract his attention.

As if in answer to a prayer, a voice at my side boomed, 'Well, if it isn't George Thornley. Not seen you here for a while. Selling today then?'

Green Jersey's face broke into a smile as he acknowledged the speaker, but my relief was short lived. 'Nice to see you Thomas. I'll be with you in a minute but I think this lady's interested in the pony, so hold on a while'. Panic took hold. Why didn't this wretched man get on with his brushing or talk to his friend or unravel his jersey so that I could make a dignified getaway? I took a step backwards as though to obtain a fresh aspect of the pony's anatomy when I was struck by a brilliant thought. If I bent down, pretending to attend to my shoe lace I would be out of his sight for a second, and in that crouching position I could move along a bay or two before rising and mingling with the crowd. So I bent down and was just about to creep off when a pair of muddy brown boots appeared around the pony's hindquarters. My heart sank. Without a doubt, somewhere in a direct line above the boots would be a bright green jersey, so I remained rooted in this unedifying position. A loud voice confirming my fears asked 'What do you think then?'

41

The old adage better remain silent and be thought a fool than open your mouth and remove all doubt, flew through my mind, but did I have any choice? For certain Green Jersey and his buddy had got the measure of the situation and were already chuckling quietly to themselves. Frantic for inspiration, my eyes shot back to the pony and came to rest on a level with its belly. I thought it somewhat indelicate to be staring at that area indefinitely but held out as long as I could, feeling very foolish and alone amongst all this know-how, while the prospective salesman waited for me to rise and pronounce on my observations. It was only then, while my eyes were scanning this bare underside that I realized I was looking at a mare.

This was it. This was the point at which enlightenment was mine, when I could at least pretend to be on equal terms and converse about 'this mare', throwing in a 'she' with a savoir faire which I felt had been missing from my life till that moment. I stood up and confronted the waiting man...... and the weight of my ignorance descended on my shoulders once more. You can't carry on a conversation just saying 'she' you idiot. You've got to say 'she is something' or 'can she something or 'does she something'. I moved towards the pony's head and looked at her. From under a lustrous cream forelock and ornamented by long cream lashes, gazed two beautiful large oval-shaped eyes. I patted her head and she licked my hand. No clever words were needed now, no fine phrases or technical jargon to impress Green Jersey. I'd lost my heart and it didn't matter what anyone thought. 'She's lovely' I said, and walked away.

***

I strolled up more lines of pens stopping from time to time to look at different horses but only seeing the lovely head of the cream coloured mare. Chestnuts and bays were there in plenty and a sprinkling of greys and blacks, yet all I could see were the two great brown eyes with their long lashes. I wondered if Gordon and the girls had seen her and whether she'd made the same impression on them as she had on me. They didn't seem to be anywhere about so I spent a pleasant half-hour looking at the interesting things displayed on the many saddlery stalls but I had very little clue as to what most of them were for. I wandered into the auction ring, pushed my way through the

42

crowd and up the steps to a space a few rows from the front. Horses and ponies came in, were paraded round the ring whilst the auctioneer gave a résumé of their virtues and accomplishments, then were taken out to meet their destiny, good or ill.

'Lot ninety-four' announced the auctioneer.

A young boy came into the ring leading a large cream pony with a dark stripe the length of its back, horizontal lines on its legs, a bewiskered face and the great oval brown eyes which had bewitched me just an hour before. Green Jersey appeared on the dias beside the auctioneer where they conferred for a few moments.

'Now ladies and gentlemen' began the auctioneer, 'We have here a fine dun mare, cob type, 14 hands, six years old and a real good doer I'm told. She's had a foal and is sold now as a sound pony'......his speech quickened. 'Can we start the bidding at a hundred guineas? Thank you sir' as he indicated towards the back and bids came thick and fast from all sides. The boy kept walking round the sawdust-strewn ring with the pony in tow. She didn't seem very pleased at having to perform this way, and jerked her head back now and again in protest and I wished with all my heart that I could buy her but we'd only come to look.

The voice from the dias kept coming at me.

'One hundred and twenty-five guineas, one hundred and thirty guineas'

The mare had stopped and the boy pulled on the halter. A man in a white linen coat stepped from the side and prodded her with a stick.

'One hundred and thirty-five guineas; one hundred and forty guineas......' There was a pause and the auctioneer repeated his last call. 'One hundred and forty guineas, any advance on one hundred and forty guineas?'

The bewiskered face loomed before me, with its deep brown pools, film star lashes and velvet muzzle. 'One hundred and forty-five guineas I'm bid, any advance on one hundred and forty-five guineas?' Another pause, then, 'Going......going......gone.' Down crashed the gavel on the desk before him and the auctioneer looked towards the successful bidder.

'Your name madam?'

All was quiet while he waited for the response but there was none. Then I felt a nudge on my arm and a voice whispered in my ear. 'Your name luv, he wants your name and where you live.'

I brought myself up with a start and murmered 'Green, Tironnen, Pontbrynach.'

'I can't hear you.'

With great effort I raised my voice. 'Green, Tironnen, Pontbrynach.'

Through a haze I saw the auctioneer write in a book in front of him. The boy led the pony outside and Green Jersey stepped down from the dias to follow them.

Recovering my senses, I thought, but that's not the owner. That beautiful creature belongs to the Greens, and my mind went blank except for one word, rapidly flashing on and off in my mind's eye like neon lights. GORDON!!! Oh, my God!

I left my seat and climbed down to leave the ring with apprehension flooding every crevice of my being. Trying to keep my voice steady I gave the woman in the office the details she required, wrote a cheque with a quavering hand and went outside. The sharp January air did nothing to alleviate the nervous chill which enveloped me, and with dejection as my sole companion I moved off in a daze not wishing to get anywhere or ever see anyone again.

'Mum, mum'.

I turned to see Louise hurrying to catch up with me.

'It's jolly interesting isn't it? Gosh what's the matter, you look awful.'

I told her what I'd done. 'Ooh, I wish I'd been there but it's wonderful, where is she, what number is she, gosh, I must go and find her'. She shot away, turning after a few excited steps to call out 'Whoever thought we'd go home with a pony?'

'Who indeed,' I thought as the neon lights flashed faster and brighter. I passed round the back of the auction ring and leaned against an iron rail. In the distance I could see Louise fussing over the pony. I turned away and wallowed in my misery.

'You look as though you've lost a pound and found sixpence'. Gordon breezed towards me full of cheer. 'I didn't want to stay here for long so I went into the town and found an excellent second-hand bookshop. I bought two books on early twentieth century farming, one

44

of which looks brand new and both are full of lovely old photographs. A great find. I'm really pleased. I left them in the car, you'll love them.'

My normal enthusiasm for such a purchase was absent and solicitous as always Gordon took my silence as a sign of weariness.

'Shall we be going home now? It's getting on a bit.' My Waterloo had arrived.

'Not yet. There's something I want to show you.' We sauntered up the lane between the pens.

'Have you enjoyed yourself? Seen anything interesting?'

'Oh, this and that,' I replied, trying to fend off the inevitable.

We walked on a while then stopped. Louise re-appeared and Gordon turned to me and said 'What was it you wanted to show me?'

'This.' I indicated the pony.

'Bessie' said Louise. 'That's her name.'

'Very nice'. Gordon was obviously rather puzzled but still in a safe world. 'Yes, very nice, a lovely colour. What an interesting stripe along its back.' A ray of hope flickered on the horizon but was instantly dimmed by the brilliance of the neon lights. We stood looking in silence.

'Right' said Gordon, rubbing chilled hands together in a business-like way, 'Let's find the other two and we can be on our way'.

'What about the pony?' piped Louise.

'Well, it didn't get here by itself did it? Presumably someone will also take it away.'

'Yes' prattled our daughter, 'the man said we should speak to Mr Edwards who drives that dark red lorry over there and he'll take her as far as the common.'

There was a pause which lasted about a week.

'What man? What common? What are you talking about?'

'The pony'. Louise sighed loudly and impatiently and flung her arms over the animal's back. 'That's what I'm talking about' and leaning her head on her outstretched arms she gazed up at her father with an expression of rapturous delight and uttered the inevitable words 'She's ours.'

***

The journey home was not the chatty affair that the outward one had been. Gordon's fury at my irresponsible behaviour lessened as the miles passed but he was convinced that the chances of my purchase being suitable, well, alright at best, were far outweighed by the probability of it being a pig in a poke. My own confidence was waning fast, my mind full of nagging doubts. Perhaps the pony was totally unfit for our purpose. Perhaps she was unfit for any purpose. Perhaps she bit or kicked. In my innocence I didn't know what else a horse was capable of. Maybe all we could do would be to have her put down and I became more morose and crotchety by the minute as I contemplated the possible result of my impetuosity.

Late in the afternoon we all trooped down to the common to wait for the lorry which was bringing Bessie to her new home. In the distance we saw it turn off the main road and vanish into a dip before appearing over the brow of the hill to where we waited. Mr Edwards drove onto the short roadside grass, let down the back of the lorry and after untying the mare led her down the ramp.

'That's a real good pony you've got there' he said, standing back a little to admire her. 'A real good pony. You could have done a lot worse than get a pony like that.'

His speech did me a power of good but my ego had a long way to go before it was back to normal. He held out the halter which Angela quickly took. She secured the loose end and having thereby provided herself with a makeshift bridle, vaulted onto the pony's back. Having had no exercise that day, Bessie was quite exuberant but soon settled down and we all strolled home behind her as night slowly fell. The girls had put plenty of straw in one of the stables as we didn't want to leave her in a strange field on her first night and she immediately found the hay net hung up to welcome her. They fussed and hovered and admired but I stayed out of it, unaccustomed diplomacy suggesting that in the current jargon I kept a low profile, this reinforced by the sheer terror of peering over the stable door and seeing a white elephant.

The following morning we turned Bessie out and watched delightedly as she went down on all fours and rolled over and over on the grass, got up, shook herself, galloped off down the field with great abandon then turned to race back alongside the track. Stealing a few sideways glances at Gordon, I could tell he was impressed but this

46

was not the time for me to make any observations about our acquisition. But someone else had also been observing the new arrival. While we watched our neighbour appeared. Inspecting his sheep in the next field he had observed the activity and walked up the hill.

'I heard you'd got a pony.' It didn't surprise us that he'd heard. He joined us leaning on the gate and looked at Bessie as she thundered towards us head on to veer round, a vision of flying hooves and splattering mud. He watched in silence, and without taking his eyes off the pony produced a pipe and tobacco from his jacket pocket and proceeded through the lengthy ritual of poking, patting and puffing. I began to get anxious. He always had several horses on his farm and was considered locally to be a good judge of horseflesh. Was he about to negate the praise of Mr Edwards the previous day? I couldn't wait any longer, and trying to keep my voice level and sound as casual as possible enquired 'What do you think?'

He didn't hurry to answer but continued looking down the field at Bessie who had now come to a standstill, and with head held alert, nostrils flaring, was surveying her surroundings. The tobacco in the pipe was patted a bit more, the pipe puffed, and finally contemplatively sucked while I shuffled from one foot to the other, hardly able to bear the waiting yet dreading what I might hear. Our neighbour then removed the pipe from his mouth to pronounce judgement.

'You've got a real good pony there. Good chest, plenty of bone and plenty of spirit. A real good pony. Yes, very tidy, very tidy'.

After suffering agonies of regret for my recent misdemeanour and the humiliation that could be the likely outcome of it, I rejoiced at these words. Vindication was mine. I could feel my head swelling with pride and was just about to bestow on Gordon a self-satisfied smirk when our neighbour turned to him, his expression holding just a hint of admiration for a townsman who was able to select an animal with such valuable qualities, and said, 'You're a shrewd one aren't you, choosing a pony like that'.

47

THE PLOT THICKENS

Life in the country produces its own special problems and for anyone hoping to have a fair degree of independence whole attitudes have to change. As 'townies' we might frequently have found ourselves irritated when plans to clean a bike, mow the lawn or go for a walk were thwarted by bad weather. Such things, however, were relatively unimportant and could easily be slotted in at some other time, but when your lifestyle for the year ahead depends on doing certain jobs at a given time the weather governs all, and if something has got to be done......it's got to be done.

For instance, the yard around the numerous outbuildings was cobbled which was very picturesque but hard to keep clean and tidy once livestock was installed. I found that the quickest and easiest way of cleaning it was during a downpour when attired in an all-engulfing old mac, wellies beneath and sou'wester above I could brush and sweep letting the deluge do most of the work for me. I didn't have to hike buckets of water from the enormous iron tub in the yard. However if I'd planned to do indoor work that day it had to be pushed on an hour or so whilst I happily sloshed around outside.

And so it was with the vegetable garden, for although the inclination to get down to any serious work was not very evident that first autumn, time waits for no man and if we were going to eat the following year preparation had to be attended to without delay. The first thing was to decide where to put it. Apart from a few trees on the periphery and the wood at the far end, there wasn't a square yard of our meadow which was in shade. Being on a south-facing slope it wasn't going to lack for sun so it was a question of putting it where it would be most convenient. Then one morning, listening to the radio while I was ironing, I heard a man speaking about the benefit of growing plants in a micro climate and how even a few inches below the normal level of the ground could raise the temperature several degrees. This sounded very interesting and he sounded just the person who could help us. I'd missed the beginning of the programme and had no idea who was speaking, but there were ways and means of finding things out so I phoned the County Council working on the theory that whilst I couldn't see any obvious connection, maybe they

48

could put me in contact with someone whose finger was on the gardening pulse, and that is exactly what happened.

What a coincidence that the person to whom I'd listened on the radio was Mr Elwyn Griffith, horticultural adviser for Breconshire no less, and he would be delighted to come and advise us. So he did, and within minutes had his finger on the very spot or rather he stood on the spot and expansively indicated that we should site our garden in the slight dip north-west of the barn in order to make use of the micro-climate which it encompassed. All this excitement suggested it was time for another coffee under the ash tree and we consulted books, drew diagrams and discussed for far too long, thoroughly enjoying ourselves. I was to be in charge of this. Gordon would help with the heavy work and I couldn't see that keeping a vegetable garden going was anything I couldn't cope with.

I could see it all......the dozens of neat rows where no weed saw more than a brief glimpse of daylight. Massive brassicas, legumes fat and luscious, things growing up and things hanging down, the whole horticultural array causing every visitor to gasp with admiration and envy, while they questioned me on my methods.

'It's just a matter of getting the ground right and putting the seeds or seedlings in,' I could hear myself saying, in a tone of voice which implied that getting the ground right and putting the seeds in had precious little to do with it. Rather it was an inexplicable mystique, the rare gift of one in total communion with mother earth that was at the core of my success, and my guests would marvel at my modesty and obvious oneness with the land. Ah yes, how many times my mind's eye beheld our vegetable garden in all its glory. And why not? Hadn't I produced abundant salad crops in an urban garden? This enterprise held no terrors for me.

Looking back, it seems that the true facts about growing all our vegetables for twelve months of the year must have been rather slow to take root in my brain. I remembered the wartime days when the lawn of my childhood home was turned over to cabbages, beans and whatever else my father wanted to grow but how they got there was something of a mystery to me. Yet the population of the whole nation had rallied to the cry of Dig for Victory, and I reckoned I could do as well as anyone if I put my mind to it and my back into it. What escaped me though, was that 'anyone' didn't have to cope with an area nearly the size of a tennis court, which is what we'd worked out was necessary to keep us fed with an abundance of fruit and vegetables for twelve months. There was also the preparation of this harvest for storage, one way or another, plus time spent on even minimal housekeeping. And although common sense dictated that animals would take up a good part of my daily doings I really had no idea of what I was taking on. Ah, how blissful is ignorance!

So our garden was going to occupy a mighty large space and our neighbour agreed to plough that part of the meadow for us. We watched as his bulky blue tractor crawled painstakingly across the green meadow, leaving in its wake great clumps of churned up red soil, the foundation of bountiful and nutritious harvests.

Visions kept flashing before me. Indeed, more than visions. I could taste the succulent beetroot, crunch the emerald sprouts and relish the sweetest peas. I dreamed on and our neighbour finished ploughing and went home. We put a fence round the raw earth to separate it from the meadow below and the triangular paddock above and gazed at this potential fount of family health. At this point the familiar vision should have appeared. It didn't, at least not for some while and when it arrived was rather blurred at the edges. Then even this went and I was faced with stark reality.

Had I really imagined that I could cultivate all this on my own? It was enormous, and all I had were two hands a few old tools and 364 days. Of course there was always optimism but weighed against my ignorance the scales didn't go down much in its favour.

Our plan was that the waste from our animals and the house should provide all the nutriment for the garden but events had begun to happen in the wrong order. The garden was beginning to take shape before the arrival of as much as a single hen, let alone anything whose waste would make a significant contribution. Likewise our kitchen rubbish, deposited in splendid isolation in the centre of one of the three compost bays we'd optimistically erected, had more the appearance of the outgoings of a bedsitter occupant who habitually eats out than a serious attempt at the beginning of an organically inspired vegetable garden.

So that first year we reluctantly decided that chemicals should come to our aid and in spite of my initial distaste I thoroughly enjoyed distributing these miracle powders, tossing out a measured amount,

50

first this side then the other as I walked leisurely up and down, up and down. It was as though I had been overtaken by a slower, more agreeable age, the very nature of the activity inhibiting any thought of hurry. The blue, warm windless day contributing to the unaccustomed air of serenity and I wondered if it was just coincidence that the size of our garden seemed a little less daunting. The following year we were heaving tons of rich heavy steaming muck off a trailer and there was nothing serene about that, and I looked back with a rather muddled sense of nostalgia at my first gardening year when I lived in the leisurely age of chemicals.

It was at this time that I remembered the name of an author, one of whose books on vegetable growing I'd once briefly encountered on a library shelf. I had replaced it at the time as it didn't seem to be what was required but that was years ago and now an all-embracing-horticulture-for-the-serious-minded type book was just what the new back-to-the-land-me needed. I was convinced that my thirst for knowledge of things that grew and stuff that caused things to grow would be appeased once I and Mr. Shewell-Cooper's book got together but when we finally did, the more I read the more my spirits sank.

'To know that you do not know is the beginning of all wisdom' spoke Socrates, and one thing was certain....I didn't know. It might not have been quite so bad had it not been for two things. One, there were an incredible number of elementary facts it would be useful to carry in my head, and two, that I am the possessor of a memory which, when called upon to store any new information, baulks at the idea with the force of a rodeo horse. I lay claim to being the only person in the world who has planted potatoes with a manual of instruction travelling up the rows with them. Still, if Socrates was right at least I had wisdom on my side.

With the first seeds sown I was in the garden daily, yanking out any weed that had the temerity to trespass, and peering for the signs of life which the rational side of me said would surely come, always accompanied by the nagging doubt that in a few weeks time I'd still be looking at virgin soil. Well, the weeds came alright, but so did everything else... hundreds of varied green shoots eagerly bursting from the ground, some it seemed almost growing as I watched, and I learned a lot. Quickly.

51

Our first harvest saw us with enough peas to feed an army but the beetroot didn't last long into the new year, so I made additions to my lists of 'seeds sown, where, and when' and noted the quantities as well. Unfortunately keeping orderly books doesn't suit my temperament and elaborate details bore me, so even as I wrote down what most serious gardeners would consider essential information, I knew my notes would either get lost in the general confusion of my life or I'd give up on the idea. Successive years would just as likely yield enough peas to feed an army and not enough beetroot to see us beyond Christmas. It's just the same preparing food for the freezer.

The enormity of my duties periodically coincided with an excessive surge of pride in the crops I'd produced and I'd spend days in the kitchen, submerged under great piles of this and that, blanching, rinsing and bagging, until the big chest freezer we kept just for fruit and vegetables was bursting. The effect of this enthusiasm was invariably accumulative, so I'd begin a mammoth bake of pies, cakes, rolls and anything else I felt inclined to make, and the small freezer kept for 'ready mades' was soon filled too.

At the beginning of this operation everything would be neatly labelled but before long the neatness would be anything but, as the idea of all this labelling had absolutely no appeal at all. I'd tell myself I'd remember what's what and proceed with haphazard storing, trying to ignore the fact that on a nearby shelf sat Rosemary Hanbury-Tennyson's superbly written book on freezer management. I knew it was a thoroughly good book because I'd read through all the do's and don'ts when I'd first bought it. The organizational abilities of the writer astounded me and I always hoped, for her sake, that many copies had landed in more willing hands than mine.

Not labelling packages does occasionally call for bouts of quick-wittedness and a cool head, not to mention a sense of humour. But really awful disasters are few thank goodness, although when they occur are guaranteed to be recounted for years to come by a family with scant concern for my feelings, and the Case of the Great Soup Drama of '74' will be with me to my dying day.

Friends were expected for a couple of days and would be arriving in the early evening. It was a perfect late spring day and we carried the refectory table outside and set it under the blossoming damson tree. So welcoming it looked, groaning under plates of home-made goodies, and pretty too, as from time to time delicately shaded pink petals fell from the branches above, dislodged by a gentle breeze. In the centre I'd placed a large Victorian tureen of chilled tomato soup. I'd made the soup that morning but on tasting it thought more flavour was required, so delving into the freezer I pulled out a bag of bright red cubes which I tipped into the saucepan and absently stirred while reading the previous week's copy of the Brecon & Radnor Express on which I'd placed vegetable peelings. In the light of events I can only conclude that the Brecon & Radnor must have been riveting reading, for having stirred sufficiently I took no further interest in the soup and poured it into the tureen.

Our friends arrived. We talked about old times and caught up with bits of gossip while I put a few finishing touches to some of the dishes and enjoyed the appropriate noises of appreciation at the tempting array. I proudly announced that the only imports were flour and sugar and modestly accepted the utterances of praise at my cleverness.

'Now, do begin. You must be hungry after your journey, so help yourselves.'

'It looks wonderful' was the response and our guests began the feast while I hurried back to check on something in the kitchen. Seconds later when I re-joined them I was gratified to notice that all conversation had ceased. I assumed everyone was overcome by the sheer ecstasy of experiencing the flavour of 'real' food, although I did notice that our friends seemed to have some sort of muscular spasm in the region of their mouths but I thought it was probably an unfortunate habit they'd got into. Something to do with their life-style perhaps. Then Jessica began a weird dance round the garden, clutching her stomach and making dreadful noises through uncontrollable laughter.

'You've spoiled the soup' she chanted 'You've spoiled the soup.......those cubes you added weren't tomato at all, they were strawberry. You put strawberry puree in the soup!'

FOWL PLAY

Before retiring to bed I often used to pull back a curtain in the big kitchen and gaze outside for a few moments. On one such occasion the yard was drenched in moonlight, the whitewashed buildings standing out sharply, like frosting on a cake, and beyond the barn the ash tree on the bank was silhouetted razor-sharp against the clear sky. I slipped the latch off the door and going outside, stood on the forecourt by the gate. Everywhere looked quite magical. I opened the gate and wandered up the yard steeped in the enchantment of the place, then turning strolled back towards the pond that reflected the budding branches of the sycamore growing up from its damp edges. It was all so beautiful, so silent, and yet there was something wrong. This silence was just too sterile.

No animals dozed peacefully behind the beast-house doors. No feathered creatures gripped perches or lay in corners, heads tucked snugly under wings. Bessie was always about of course, but strictly speaking Bessie wasn't part of the yard, her presence being there by invitation only. No, a yard should be a centre of energy, a hive of hustle and bustle, a place of industry and gossip. Most definitely the domain of the hen. We'd talked about getting some hens ever since we'd arrived but not got round to it as getting some semblance of organization into our lives, the vegetable garden up and running and thinking about how we were going to earn a living occupied most of our time. Now, my senses outraged at the sense of deprivation on our doorstep I went back inside and renewed the subject with Gordon.

Anyone can keep hens. Just throw them a few handfuls of corn every day and let them scratch away then you'll have plenty of eggs. Some will wander off and three weeks later come back with chicks in tow.

This was the sort of thing we'd read in books and magazines aimed at instructing the uninitiated in the skills of poultry husbandry. Books written by people who knew, who'd done it all, who had experienced the delights of the newly hatched chicks and the sadness of finding the mutilated body of the hen caught by the fox. People whose confidence in their ability and knowledge made them want to share the secrets of success with the ignorant. And I just couldn't wait to see hens in the yard and get my hands on some lovely brown eggs. Every week I'd been buying eggs from a nearby farm and one day Mrs Stevens told me she was replacing her hens. She did this every year, she said. They were one year old and had a fair bit of life in them yet. Would I like some?

Oh, would I like some! 'Could we take them now?'

'Yes, but have you any boxes with you? I'm short of boxes.'

We hadn't, but undeterred, spread some sacks and newspapers on the rear seats and the floor of the Land Rover, popped in twelve fat brown hens and set off along the twisting lanes. Gordon drove very, very slowly although that didn't stop our passengers clucking disapproval as we gently swayed round corners. Some who had found themselves a perch on the back of the seats wobbled precariously, occasionally pitching off to land with a squawk among those on the floor.

Several elected to leave the safety of the floor and fly up to join the others on the seat backs, squawking with annoyance as they grappled for a foothold in the moving vehicle, but one, more adventurous than the others and evidently feeling quite happy about her surroundings, took a great leap for hen-kind to land on the back of Gordon's seat, and he drove home with a large brown hen clucking contentedly and periodically pinching his ear.

The yard sprang to life the minute we emptied the Land Rover of its bemused contents. The hens staggered around for a minute or so gathering their wits and getting used to having their feet on firm ground again. Oh, our yard did look nice. Our first twelve hens laid large brown eggs frequently but not always in the henhouse. Some of them laid in a nettle patch or on a sill in the barn and some chose places we didn't find until months later when rummaging in a patch of undergrowth for one reason or another. *Don't let them out before 10 a.m., instructed the books. Then they'll lay in the henhouse and you won't have to go hunting for eggs.* A number of our ladies had other ideas about starting work at such an early hour and would require keeping in nearly all day if we wanted to find all our eggs in the cosy nesting boxes we'd provided, so when I opened the henhouse door first thing I let them all wander off regardless of their ideas on working hours. But whenever I heard the shrill cackle of a job well done I'd race out of the house like a bloodhound on the trail to track down the whereabouts of the latest chosen laying spot. Sometimes I'd find it, sometimes not, but the last call of 'egg ready' was at about four o'clock and that particular hen never laid a minute sooner.

Fortunately, when one of them had found somewhere suitable to her requirements, she'd return there each day for many weeks until boredom with the furnishings set in and sent her scurrying off to look for surroundings better matching her present mood. It was all very domesticated and at last the yard was being lived in. Yet something was missing.

'A cockerel?' My neighbour at the farm below looked at me as though I'd taken leave of my senses. 'I don't know where you'll get one round here. People don't keep surplus cockerels.' This didn't sound very promising, and sure enough, a number of enquiries brought pretty much the same response. Then one day I was in the village store asking the shopkeeper to keep her ears open in case anyone mentioned the word 'cockerel' when a voice behind me said, "I've got a cockerel you can have.' Those words made my day.

'Really?' I said, 'You don't want him then?' which was stating the obvious but that's how my words of delight formed themselves.

'No, I do not.' A small plump homely looking woman spoke with such venom that I thought there must be something wrong with him. 'I'm fed up with having all these chicks about the place. The hens go off and there's no end to them. I'll be glad to have him away from the place for I should have cut his life short a long time ago. You're welcome to him.'

We arranged a time to call and the following afternoon drove over to her farm on the other side of the valley. After tea and biscuits in the cosy kitchen we were taken out to meet the unwanted bird. He was a large white fellow who peered at us with a degree of hostility which we later realised belied his true personality and we put him in a sack on the floor of the Land Rover.'

'He's fine' said Gordon, 'Just what we want.'

At this point her husband who had been standing nearby joined us, and in a deep sonorous voice observed pointedly 'A fine bird.'

'Yes, just what we want,' I echoed Gordon, who added 'He'll suit us fine.'

'I was just telling these people that I'm glad to be rid of him' said the farmer's wife, 'Such a......' but before she could go any further her husband interrupted with 'The market price is three pounds.'

56

'Three pounds?'

'That's right. Three pounds. A fair market price.'

We were too ignorant of fair market prices to dispute it but it seemed an awful lot. However, we'd come especially for the bird and short of saying we wouldn't take it, there didn't seem much we could do. Neither of us was very good at bargaining. We tried to look unconcerned as Gordon took the last two pound notes from his wallet and dug into first one pocket and then another in search of coins. I opened my purse, shook out the contents into the palm of my hand, then like Gordon, rummaged in my pockets, collecting together the various denominations of loose change which I invariably drop into them, all the while flashing smiles of confidence to the farmer and his lady whilst interjecting this undignified scrabbling with inane remarks.

'I thought I had more than this. It's funny how you can never find something when you want it.'

I climbed into the Land Rover looking for any stray coins which may have found their way under the seats, all the while aware that two pairs of eyes were watching every movement. Eventually we managed to cobble together the required amount, handed it over, and thanking them, leapt into the Land Rover before the farmer decided he'd charged us too little. We left the yard as quickly as possible in a state of shock.

Our neighbour at the lower farm was working outside as we drove up. We normally stopped and chatted but discretion warned us that this was an occasion when we should drive straight on up our track. However it was not to be, for Mrs Powell was slowly walking towards us. Ill at ease we stopped to pass the time of day. Then the sack on the floor began to shuffle about. Mrs Powell looked at it. We looked at it. We said nothing. After a pause our neighbour said, 'I've been to Hereford today. There were some fine cockerels in the mart. I would have got you one only I didn't know whether you still wanted one.'

Things were looking bad. Little did she know how interested we were in those fine cockerels at Hereford market.

Casually Gordon asked 'What were they going for?'

'Oh, about seventy-five pence mostly, although one or two got nearer the pound. Nice they were.'

The sack on the floor began to fling itself about in a way we could not ignore. Mrs Powell looked at it with undisguised interest.

'Actually, we've managed to find one' I told her with more bravado in my voice than I felt. 'He's just what we wanted, and he's very handsome' I added in a vain attempt to justify our costly stud bird.

She looked at us. More information was required.

'From Mrs Williams at Trecastle' I volunteered.

'At Dolmenyn?'

I nodded.

'Was her husband there when you bought it?'

'Yes.' Her eyes lit up. Further enlightenment was needed and she wasn't about to move until she had it.

'Three pounds' and we hung our heads at the admission.

She gazed at us in disbelief, then slowly a beam spread across her round face and she flung her hands upwards in a gesture of childish delight at having learned something so astonishing.

'Good-ness gra-cious' she chuckled, giving greater emphasis to her amazement by overly stressing all four syllables. 'Good-ness gra-cious.' By this time she was laughing so much she could barely speak. 'It's as well I didn't get one for you; I didn't know you wanted it stuffed and ready for the oven!'

***

The cockerel joined our maiden ladies with a degree of enthusiasm, which caused something of a stir and for a hectic hour or two indignant hens scurried as fast as they could in all directions, squawking and clucking at this intrusion into their well-regulated lives. Eventually the yard settled down to calm and order and as the days passed we waited for one of them to go broody, make a nest, and delight us with the sight of her little yellow chicks.

It didn't happen. We kept waiting and still it didn't happen and a telephone call to the farmer's wife from whom we'd purchased them elicited the information that our hens were a strain that in the interests of egg production had had the broodiness bred out of them and it was highly unlikely that motherhood would play any part in their lives.

58

They were happy, the cockerel was happy and as far as they were concerned we could wait forever.

Obviously what we needed were some good old-fashioned barnyard hens. Hens of no specified ancestry. Hens denied the benefit of modern science, and our postmaster came to the rescue. From him we acquired four white hens, which, he assured us, really knew their business. About the same time a bantam was offered, a funny little thing with iridescent starling-like feathers whose habit of streaking across the garden, screeching in the most alarming way may have been the reason she always looked so emaciated. She, however, came up trumps, for shortly after her arrival she disappeared, re-appearing in time for breakfast then going under cover again for the next twenty-four hours. Hurrah; we had a broody bantam, so we left nature to carry on unaided. Well, almost, because not having a bantam cockerel we needed to exchange the thirteen infertile bantam eggs for large fertile hen eggs, so it was necessary to find out where she had made her nest. This wasn't difficult as on the third morning of her broodiness she appeared on the ledge of the hayloft opening, screaming at the world before flying down for breakfast.

The hayloft was above two stables and access was by a ladder. I climbed up and saw at the far end of the wall close to the edge, her nest with its clutch of small white eggs. Back I went down the ladder to collect six eggs from the postmaster's fertile hens, which I exchanged for her own, and on returning from breakfast she settled down on these to await her happy event.

Well of course, nobody was about when it took place. Had we been, things might have turned out differently. We can only assume that when her first egg hatched, the occupant took its first hesitant steps to the edge of the wall and careered down through space to land on the straw beneath, followed by an hysterical parent who literally never looked back. The remaining eggs went cold and we found mother and child later, pottering about, quite unaware of any financial ruin they may have caused us.

They were also oblivious to a large grey cat sitting on the garden wall, a look of malevolence in its yellow eyes.

Claudius, Claudius Agrippa actually, so named because we acquired him ('him' not for long) at the time 'I, Claudius' was being shown on television and also because if he condescended to sit on your knee he'd spend the entire time gripping and pulling whatever garments you were wearing whilst purring loudly and contentedly. No one would put up with this for more than a few minutes so when you stood up or attempted to fling him off his claws would immediately find their way through however many layers of clothing were between them and one's flesh. So Claudius Agrippa, Claude for short, was not a welcome lap-cat.

There he was on the wall, eyes fixed on our hedge against starvation, and whilst three inches of chick isn't much of a hedge, more of a leaf really, this chick had to be guarded. I knew its parent would have hysterics should a predator approach but whether that would be enough to deter an assailant I wasn't sure. I had to do something about it. I hurried into the house glancing back as I did so to make sure Claude remained on the wall, grabbed my old leather coat from the back of a chair, and scrambling into it for protection against the razor sharp claws which I knew would shortly be employed in protest against me I hastened back to the yard.

Claude was as still and inscrutable as ever.

I sauntered over to the wall and casually stopped beside him. He rose slightly on his haunches and brushed against me, friendly and unsuspecting. I picked him up and began to walk across to where the chick was pottering and Claude stiffened. Sensing something was up he began to wriggle but I tightened my hold, and with my right arm round his lower half fixing his back legs firmly and my left arm across his chest encasing his front legs, I moved towards the chick. Claude was furious but I was determined. I was amazed that I got as close as I did.

I bent down, the bantam screamed and my grip on the cat became positively vice-like but I managed to thrust Claude's face within inches of the chick as it began to run away. My left hand made contact with his rear end and in a very measured voice I said 'THAT……..wallop……..IS…….wallop……..MOTHER'S, and at the last wallop I released my hold on the enraged feline which leapt from my arms with a banshee-like howl and fled towards the barn to nurse his affronted dignity.

One down, one to go. I set off in search of Grot also named for a very good reason.

Louise and I were in the village store one day when a young woman whom I knew only by sight was talking to the shopkeeper about some kittens she had and did Mrs Morris know of anyone who would like one? Overhearing this, Louise, who was inordinately fond of cats, nudged my arm which action the woman observed. 'They're lovely kittens' she enthused.

Mmmmm. Most kittens were lovely.

'Would you like one?' Accompanied by a winning smile.

Now there's nothing that annoys me more than someone who looks after their own interests in the guise of a generous offer.

'No' I said, turning towards a box of cough sweets on the counter and examining the wrappers with more interest than they warranted.

Louise again nudged my arm.

'Mum, please.'

***

Later that afternoon Gordon and Louise arrived back from a visit to the kitten-woman, our daughter not exactly joyful about her acquisition, in fact quite subdued. In her arms she cradled an orange duster out of which peered the small face of quite the most disreputable looking kitten I had ever seen. Issuing from its nose was a greenish slime which because it had tried to clean itself the kitten had managed to wipe all over its face.

Gordon raised his eyes to the heavens. 'We have a very compassionate daughter.'

'I had to' said Louise, 'She said she'd flush it down the loo.'

The horror on my face must have been apparent as I looked at this woebegone creature, although it wasn't just the state of the poor little thing that caused my reaction.

What a ghastly woman she must be, but I thought, how could anyone be prepared to do such a thing to an animal and also blackmail a young girl.

'We'll take him to the vet's this evening' said Gordon, adding reassuringly as he put his arm round Louise's shoulder, 'I expect he'll be able to sort him out.'

My idea of 'sorting him out' obviously wasn't quite as optimistic as our daughter's for as she and Gordon set off she waved and smiled happily from the window of the Land Rover. The vet'll put him down, poor little thing, I mused. Louise will be sad but there'll be half a dozen adverts for kittens at the vet's and she'll always know that she saved this one from drowning.

Fully expecting Louise to return with some exquisite creature whose rude health was obvious I made a cup of coffee, selected one of my current reads (generally two or three on the go) and settled down for a period of comfort and informed relaxation. Fifty minutes later I heard the sound of the Land Rover drive into the yard and when the engine died went outside to commiserate with my daughter and express delight at the beautiful kitten I knew she would be holding. But the face that looked out of the orange duster was the same as that which had departed earlier, just a little less disreputable.

I composed myself.

'Well, this can't be as serious as we thought.'

'We've got drops, and they have to be put in his nose twice a day and then he'll be alright.' Louise was obviously thrilled.

'Good' I said, thinking that this would be the sort of thing Gordon could do on one of those occasions when he got up from the drawing board, saying he needed to use different muscles.

'Did he say how long it would take to clear it up?' and before anyone could say anything, 'Just this one bottle?'

'The drops won't clear the condition' said Gordon, 'but they'll keep it at bay.'

'You mean..........?' I was having difficulty here, 'You mean..........?'

We simultaneously looked at Louise who was dangling a piece of string above the kitten's waving paws.

'I know he's going to get better' she said, 'because even though he's such a poor grotty little thing he's playing, and I know, I just know he'll be alright.'

'Is that what you're going to call him?' asked Gordon.

'What?'

'Grotty?'

'Oh, Dad.' Then after a moment's thought 'I suppose it is appropriate.' She held up the kitten with both hands. 'Would you mind being called Grotty?'

We were silent for a few seconds, then I mouthed 'For ever?........twice a day?'

Ye gods. Of all the kittens in Breconshire we had to have one that needed twenty-four hour nursing care.......Thank goodness I'd allotted the nose-drop business to Gordon!

However, as it happened Gordon held the kitten while Louise applied the drops and the little chap proved himself quite the most good-natured creature, not lifting a paw or making a mew while the drops were administered, After four days his nose began to dry up and his fur didn't get messy any more and with his milky-white coat and its black splodges dotted about his body and face he was really quite a pretty creature. Then we ran out of drops and something amazing happened. We went for several days without drops. Grot was fine. And lively. A few more days. Grot was still fine. And very lively. We never bought another bottle and apart from a visit to the vet to be neutered he never went there again. He certainly outgrew his unglamorous name, but Grot he remained.

***

Which brings me back to the newly hatched chick and my desire for self-restraint among our felines. Grot was sunning himself by the ash tree, far enough away not to have been disturbed by the earlier commotion. I scooped him up and walked towards the bantam and her chick. Being so much smaller than Claude, the wallops as I stressed 'THIS...IS....MOTHER'S.....' were decidedly less vigorous; just enough to impinge on him the connection between the chick and my displeasure. With fur so thick I doubt that either of them felt anything other than a loss of dignity but if anyone ever says that cats cannot be trained; well I know better for in all our years at Tironnen we never lost a chick to a cat.

Shortly after that, one of the postmaster's best whites disappeared. For days we didn't see her and I was convinced a fox had made off with her, so I was delighted when Jessica told me that while searching for a ball, she'd found the hen sitting in the base of an old tree. We all trooped out to see. The rotten trunk gave ample shelter and privacy and as she didn't seem inclined to leave it for food as the bantam had done we took corn and water to her, placed them solicitously within her reach and left her to continue her vigil.

Maybe this was where we went wrong for a week later, shortly before her eggs were due to hatch, this wretched creature possibly feeling the onset of rigor mortis, rose from her maternal couch, and finding life outside the tree more inviting than that within left it for good. Meanwhile our bantam proudly paraded about with her single offspring in tow, the sum total of my endeavours in six months of poultry management.

The following spring we bought eighteen one-year-old redundant battery hens which proved to be superb egg layers, well worth the forty-five pence each we paid for them, although collecting them wasn't a very pleasant experience. The sight of thousands of birds, four to a small cage, in long rows three tiers high, living such unnatural lives made us feel quite sick. We put them in cardboard boxes on the floor of the Land Rover and when we arrived home placed them in a disused stable into which I'd put plenty of straw, as I'd assumed (correctly) that these poor things wouldn't be able to stand unaided having spent their incarcerated lives propped up by either each other or the bars which divided the small cages. Removing them from the boxes was a bit of a messy job as these birds were programmed to lay an egg a day on the spot without first seeking out the natural comforts of a selected nest, and so hens and broken eggs were all jumbled up together.

We lifted out the eggy creatures and set them gently down on the straw, put in food and water and closed the door. After twenty-four hours most of them were scratching around as though they'd been doing it all their lives, yet still dropping eggs, with or without shells, some most oddly shaped, so I turned all but two out into the yard where they settled in with the hybrid-non-breeders, the postmaster's best whites and the screaming bantam. One of the two I kept inside was in a pretty bad way. Its legs were very weak and it just didn't have the strength to stand, so I kept the second one with it for company but after another two days these joined the others outside.

This sudden change in their life style played havoc with their insides. For the first week or so they pottered about, dropping eggs wherever they happened to be, then suddenly, as though a switch had been turned off egg production ceased. They gave their attention to the twice daily hand-out of corn and spent their time looking for a variety of tasty morsels in between. Exploration was new to them and the dung heap in the yard proved a treasure trove. But none of the battery hens ever had the joie-de-vivre of the others. Their long months of confinement had taken its toll, but they had nearly two years of normal life after they came to us, and had they been aware of it, I'm sure they'd have been proud to know that their previous imprisonment was part of the grand plan to supply the public with the cheap food it demanded.

Then all at once things began to happen. Two of the postmaster's best whites were found on nests in the barn, one among a pile of junk and the other between some bales of straw. I picked up each protesting lady, her clutch of eggs and most of the nest and transported the lot to rough coops within the confines of a small exercise yard and with sustenance to beak, left them with no choice other than that of remaining where they were.

From time to time we were given a hen or two, which was nice because it meant a great variety of colour in the yard, and as summer continued we found hens all over the place sitting on eggs, the most popular spot being a bed of nettles, the high plants giving them protection from wind and rain, and keeping them hidden from any marauding fox. On the odd occasion I'd put them in coops but mostly left where they were. I wasn't very systematic about it.

In spite of my lack of method our flock grew and I always enjoyed watching the mothers parade with their chicks, showing them how to scratch up the soil in the never-ending search for tit-bits, or teaching them the skills of dust-bathing. Any hen who ventured too close would be rushed at with screams of rage and any chick which strayed into another family would be summarily sent running. One way or another they survived and had a good life but I wouldn't like to return to this world as a chicken.

The yard was still empty when I took an occasional late night meander up towards the ash tree, but not entirely quiet, for behind the closed doors of the hen-house I would hear the soft cluck of a drowsy hen and knew that in the morning all the bustle and gossip of a busy street would begin again. Our yard was no longer silent and sterile.

POST MORTEM

Having sold a large family house in Southampton and paid off the mortgage we had a little nest egg in the bank which we would use to employ builders to attend to a few major works on the house, but also to enable us to enjoy a few weeks doing some minor jobs ourselves without having to do anything regarding earning. However, shortly after our arrival a request to Gordon for some graphics arrived from a former contact and a few days later came another. This was encouraging.

As the weeks passed and more work arrived, Gordon found it was a good idea to do the graphics in the morning and work on the house after lunch, although if there was a rush job he'd continue through the day and into the early hours if necessary. Dividing the day between sedentary and physical work appealed to him greatly, enabling him to 'use a different set of muscles' a much quoted phrase, although not quoted as frequently as 'it's better to travel hopefully than to arrive' the significance of which, although we didn't know it at the time would accompany us through our years at Tironnen.

The postal service from London and the south coast from where this requested work was coming was excellent, always arriving the following day, unlike the London to Basingstoke post which a friend complained took three or four days. Some years later, having written a letter to The American Arab Horse Society magazine, I received a letter from an Arab Horse breeder in Germany commenting on my letter in said magazine, the envelope being simply addressed to 'Jenifer Green, Breconshire, Wales, and this was delivered four days from the postmark. Take a bow postmen of Wales in the 1970's. So, much to our relief we had this wonderful postal service, for at the time we believed our future would largely depend on it.

The first construction work to be attended to was the installation of a septic tank and to this end we contacted a large building firm (highly recommended) and yes, they'd install a tank for us and their Mr Jones would call on us in two days to advise on the best place to site it. Gordon phoned the River Authority to check that we were far enough away from the stream below and confirmed permission with our neighbour on whose land the filter beds would lie. Mr Jones arrived and almost immediately pointed out the most suitable spot for the tank and a date was set for the work to commence a fortnight hence.

Early on the appointed day we heard the sound of a J.C.B. roaring up the track. Then a pause as it reached the gate into the yard, the engine ticking over while some unseen person opened the gate followed a couple of seconds later by a loud crash. We rushed outside to find one of the monumental ten-inch square wooden gateposts angled drunkenly.

How anyone could drive an eight foot wide machine through a ten foot wide gateway in such a ham-fisted way stopped me in my tracks. I went back into the house leaving Gordon to make sure the damage would be repaired. Four days and a seemingly endless parade of tea and coffee mugs later, our septic tank was installed and the gatepost thundered back deep into the ground. Of course, the septic tank wasn't connected to anything. It was there as a reminder that things would get better. It was a beginning.

A beginning meant optimism.

Optimism meant intended progress.

Progress, for me, meant planning the vegetable garden and thinking about animals.

Progress for Gordon however took on a different meaning.

We had no quarrel with the excellent work the builders had done installing the septic tank but we both found that having people around outside was bad enough and the idea of them being inside didn't bear thinking about. This meant that Gordon would have much more to do on the house than had been intended and although it would take a very long time to get things done I had to agree it would be a great deal nicer not to have people underfoot although it wasn't something I'd have suggested myself.

What should be the priority?

We had a shower so we were clean. We had an Elsan loo. We had a septic tank that wasn't connected to anything.

The floors in the two larger bedrooms still sloped and had furniture propped up on books but I had come to regard their eccentricity as something quite charming and although their rehabilitation was periodically spoken of their levelling no longer seemed so important. One thing however, stood way above all others in urgency. A working

67

kitchen would benefit everybody and because food preparation was to be such a major part of our life-style it became the priority.

The previous Christmas we'd received a card from a friend in Malmesbury, containing the cryptic note, exciting things happening – will write soon, and sure enough in the middle of February a letter arrived from Jane in which she enthused about the glorious and no doubt horrendously expensive kitchen she was having installed. I was furious with myself for not having contacted her earlier when I could have asked what she was going to do with the old units. After all this time I didn't for one moment think they'd still be around, but as my thoughts had turned to Jane I decided to drop her a chatty note that evening.

Two days later the phone rang. It was Jane, full of exuberance, always seeing the funny side of even the most mundane events and when questioned, glossing over the many activities in which she involved herself for the benefit of others. We chatted about general family doings for a while and I told her how I wished I'd been able to avail myself of a few of her old kitchen units when they were taken out, and was cut short.

'But you're not too late' she said. 'They've only just been removed. The men are here now putting in the new lot. We made all the plans, decided on everything down to the last door hinge and were about to give the go-ahead when I went with my cousin Marie, you remember Marie, to visit her friend Janie who bred whippets? Such sweet animals. Well Marie wanted a whippet, so we drove down to Wells to the most beautiful, beautiful house you ever saw.......' my mind was on neither sweet whippets nor beautiful houses but fixed on the one sentence 'you're not too late', and I was mentally rushing Jane through all this stuff in which I had no immediate interest. Get on with it. Get on with it.   What about your old kitchen?.........'the kitchen just blew my mind. American oak. Do you know it?' and without waiting for an answer 'Of course using different wood meant that several other things had to be changed to harmonize so that evening......Oh, lovey I'm so sorry, you want to know about the old units don't you? Of course you can have them, as many as you want. When I changed our mind, ha ha, the kitchen people had to alter so much, order new wood and different handles and things, so I knew we wouldn't get it done for months. Now it's underway. I'm absolutely

68

thrilled. Can't wait for it to be finished of course. When do you want to collect? They're quite old fashioned you know, does that matter? Goodness, I was going to advertise them and if they didn't go they'd have ended up on a bonfire.'

So we acquired our kitchen units, declining the stainless-steel sink because I'd set my heart on a two-full-bowl-double-drainer job. I reckoned that with all the vegetables and goodness knows what else I was going to be dealing with I'd need nothing less. We bought quarry tiles to lay on the working part of the big room and it all looked very smart, old-fashioned units withstanding. Anyway, they didn't look very old-fashioned to us.

The living part would later have all the large flagstones lifted, scraped, scrubbed and re-laid upside down. Gordon then connected drainage pipes from the sink to the septic tank, and although we still had to fetch water to the house it was quite thrilling to see it going out without manual labour involved.

Then things improved even further, for within a couple of months a very long piece of stout black piping was laid down the sloping field behind us, connecting the taps, which had up to that time been purely ornamental, up to a spring some 200 hundred metres above the house. Later, much later, the pipe would be sunk well below ground level but there was a lot to be said for leaving it where it was because even the smallest amount of sun heated the water in the pipe and in fine weather it was very hot indeed. We were well ahead in the environmental stakes.

An advertisement in the local paper produced a second-hand solid fuel Rayburn which our neighbour collected in his horsebox. He and Gordon manoeuvred it up the two steps from the yard and up the further two steps into the house on a series of rollers and placed it in position in the kitchen. By this time we were referring to the whole of the room as the big kitchen, and the working part with the sinks, units etc. as the kitchen.

'Has anyone seen the scissors?'

'They're in the kitchen.'

This automatically eliminated two-thirds of the searching area. It was very convenient.

The garden was producing its first crops and I took great pride in growing, making and preserving things. We ate vegetables that had

69

been growing only minutes before and tasted as only really fresh produce can and I immersed myself in the joys of horticulture.

So the first years continued with a steady stream of orders for graphics keeping Gordon busy, and working on the house let him use a 'different set of muscles'. At week-ends and during the school holidays we explored the surrounding countryside, driving further a-field to glorious sandy beaches, visiting great fortresses, some in ruins, some breathtakingly magnificent. Cardiff Castle amazed us with its fantastic wall paintings and decorations covering every inch of space. In complete contrast we wandered round St. Fagan's museum of Welsh life, where amongst other buildings we marvelled at the smallest, most humble cottages and wondered how on earth large families had managed to live in them.

Friends came; the girl's friends came. We sauntered up the hill behind Tironnen for leisurely picnics and occasionally drove to Cardiff to enjoy a shopping spree in what was, along with Chester, the most covered shopping experience one could have. This, of course, preceded the ubiquitous 'malls' of later years, things not to be compared with the natural growth of elegant cities. Malls......Ugh!

Sometime in midsummer I decided that things horticultural were pretty much under control and that we should consider taking the next step in our rural existence; the producing of our own milk, and that meant becoming acquainted with one of the most beguiling species one could ever wish to meet.

A FOOT IN THE BUCKET

I can't say that uncontrollable hysteria took possession of me when I realized it was quite useless to think I could place a neat row of milk bottles outside our lonely door at night expecting to find them replaced by full ones in the morning. This was just one of the things we had to get used to, having moved from the town where so many things are taken for granted. So I began to think about milk.

I suppose a lot of people think about milk. The long since defunct Milk Marketing Board having been established for that very purpose and possibly disbanded because they didn't do it very well. But I couldn't see that any organization, functioning however efficiently could solve my milk problem, which was quite simply that we were on our hill, the milk was in the village and two and a half miles of country lane and farm track separated us. A world without milk was not a lovesome thing and the consequences of allowing my children to set off for school, return, and retire to bed without it was unthinkable to a mother who had been at the receiving end of the high-powered publicity which proclaimed that without its benefits they would be weak in mind and body.

Yet time passed and the following summer found us still collecting bottles from the village store, supplementing it when I'd forgotten to buy enough by dried (ugh) or evaporated (ugh,ugh). The vegetable garden was taking up most of my time and the renovation of the house was occupying most of Gordon's, so although acquiring a milking animal was a very tempting idea, we thought it better to wait awhile until the projects already under way had reached a less daunting stage. But none the less we talked constantly about getting a milk producer.

At that time we thought that cows were pleasant enough creatures although to our eyes singularly stupid, and a good milking cow would cost between £200 and £250 and that was the sort of money we couldn't spare. Also we were surrounded by beef cattle, which at that time was not subjected to tubercular testing. This would have meant double fencing the whole of our five acre paddock to ensure that the milk from our house cow could not become contaminated. All far too complicated. I later realised that I owed the cow an apology for they can become most responsive creatures. Indeed I made the acquaintance of a Jersey heifer that believed herself to be a Welsh pony, running with the mares and leaping over obstacles in a most sprightly manner. But we were a long way from wishing to become emotionally entangled with a cow.

So we talked about goats and if we knew what it was that didn't make us crazy about cows we were now totally in the dark, as neither of us had ever met a goat face to face.

When we asked our farming neighbours if they knew of any goat-keepers in the area they shook their heads with horror, and informative books were almost impossible to find. The local library produced a twenty-year-old copy of the British Goat Society yearbook, and with that as sole guide, our education of the species Capra began.

As the yearbook was quite well endowed with photographs, one thing immediately became clear; some goats are different from other goats. This was at least a beginning. It seemed that a variety of breeds existed in Britain. The heaviest milkers being the pure white British Saanen, the chocolate coloured British Toggenburg and the striking black and white British Alpine, all of which, judging by their photographs, viewed the world with an air of quizzical amusement. There were also several other breeds, amongst them Swiss Saanens and Swiss Toggenburgs, smaller than their British cousins, and an engaging floppy-eared creature, the Anglo-Nubian. But it was a good milker we were after and it seemed that any of the first three would suit us. Records of milk production, glowing descriptions of stud goats and the knowledge that Mrs Blank's Rosy Lea of Dinmore was supreme champion of the Great Mudding show was information which meant nothing to us, so for our purpose the yearbook had exhausted itself as had the library, since this was its sole contribution. We were back to square one, or almost, for while visiting relatives in Salisbury, a browse around a second-hand bookshop brought forth a very practical work by a smallholder. This I bore in triumph back to Tironnen. We both read the book, discussing its contents ad nauseum and having acquainted ourselves with the basics of management decided that I, as general manager of the dairy department, would get on very well with a goat.

For several weeks I looked through the 'livestock' columns in our local paper without success and then one morning a friend who lived just outside Hereford phoned. Without any preamble she asked, 'Have you found your goats yet?'

72

'No, nothing's turned up' I replied.

'You don't get the Hereford Times then?'

'Not regularly.

'Well it's as well I do because this might be your lucky day. Listen. 'British Saanan goatlings for sale, excellent milking stock'.'

'Oooh, you could be right. Does it say anything else?' I wanted to know.

'Only a phone number. If there was anything else would it mean anything to you?'

'Probably not' I confessed, 'So tell me the number. Is it anywhere near you?'

'It's a Worcester code so it's somewhere north. Have you a pen at the ready?'

With a feeling that this was the beginning of great things I rang the number.

***

Driving through wide white gates we entered an immaculate yard, but I was far too excited to notice anything else about it because through a gap between two buildings at the far end I could see some goats in a field. Anyway, before Gordon had even switched off the engine a young woman was walking towards us.

'Hello, I'm Frances Wickham.'

We exchanged the usual pleasantries and then Frances led us through the gap in the buildings to meet our first goats. Light-footed and elegant, they careered gaily round the field, a far cry from the unfortunate picture so frequently held of them. I was enchanted. At a call from Frances they came leaping towards us, pressing round, eager for introductions. There were twenty or so, all British Saanens except for three exotic creatures whose floppy ears, Roman noses and brilliantly coloured coats in all shades of brown, orange and cream marked them out. In order to prove that my association with the Goat Society yearbook had not been in vain I proudly announced 'Ah, Anglo-Nubians.'

A fine three-month-old British Saanen was singled out. Then, because Frances was anxious that one goatling would be lonely and because she had assessed us as people who were going to be caring

73

with her animals, she put the welfare of the goats before her pocket and offered us another at a greatly reduced price. We could hardly believe such kindness and we left with two adorable little sisters, but with no idea of the delightful part they were going to play in our lives. The goatlings accepted the journey in the back of the Land Rover with equanimity, giving motorists who found themselves behind us a good view of one end or the other, providing hilarity or distaste, depending on the person concerned and what was happening at the time.

So Snowdrop and Bluebell came to Tironnen and immediately endeared themselves to us all. They confidently jumped down from the Land Rover, and after wandering about the yard for a few minutes delighted us by giving a display of truly balletic virtuosity. It wasn't long before we realized the potential danger of this, for such nimbleness could move them in the direction of the garden and I can vouch for the truthfulness of stories about goats and lines of washing. But they were creatures of gentle disposition, great humour and the ability to give the flattering impression that their pleasure in human company superseded all other activities.

Not that all went swimmingly from the start. They were maiden milkers. That means that unlike a cow, or I believe any other animal, they will produce a small amount of milk even before an eager billy-goat has clapped eyes on them. So after several weeks, when Snowdrop's milk glands began functioning, I picked up my stainless steel milking pail in one hand and my newly acquired three-legged milking stool in the other and marched purposefully forth to the goat-house. Some bailing twine slipped through her collar and fastened to a ring in the wall secured one end of her but what of the other? It looked disconcertingly mobile. However, she appeared quite content and in my innocence I imagined that when settled on my little stool, the pressure from my knee against her side would hold her secure.

'Now Snowdrop' I said lowering myself onto the stool beneath me and reaching for the bucket, 'This is a great day for both of us.' I pushed the bucket under her udders, but she moved backwards so that her head was alongside my chest. The book hadn't mentioned this sort of behaviour. As the bucket was now under the wrong end I gently pulled her forward and pushed her slightly against the wall, at the same time moving inwards to get a better hold on her.

'Steady girlie' I murmured soothingly.

74

Patience was everything when dealing with animals and especially at a time such as this. She looked at me balefully and then moved backwards again. Once more I pushed her forward, this time pushing my knee more firmly into her side while my hands felt for the milk bar beneath. At this intrusion on her privacy she lifted both back legs, thrust them forward knocking over the pail, and with her rear end twisting round in mid air swung herself over my knees with the ease of a gymnast, and with a bland expression looked at me from the opposite direction to which I'd originally placed her.

I studied her for a few moments. Her anatomy was the same as when viewed from the other side so I retrieved the bucket and in a series of small jerks moved the stool and myself along her length until I was once more in a position to think about how to continue. I glanced down to check that my inexperienced hands were moving in the right direction. I leaned over, pushed my head against her flank, and grabbing the teat, squeezed. This gave me some hope for she didn't leap skywards. I held my breath for a few seconds while an air of complacency crept over me until I realized that her body was slowly sinking onto the bucket below. I clung on, trying to heave her determined white mass upwards, but the more I tried to lift the more she sagged, and her udder with my hand tenaciously clinging to it disappeared inside the bucket as she rested her weighty carcass on the top. Somehow I managed to heave her stomach up enough to extricate my hand, scraping it painfully along the top of the bucket. I sat back to consider.

Part of the trouble I decided, was that her neck was too long. She could move backwards or forwards a distance of about twelve inches because the collar had that much leeway to move up or down between her head and shoulders. As a neck is an integral part of a goat my ability to do anything about altering it was nil. However, I thought that a hand on her collar might help, so I reached out and grasped it, pulling slightly downwards while I manoeuvred myself once more into position.

'Now keep still' I commanded, and was shocked to hear a faint note of impatience in my voice. Steady, steady, I warned myself, remember, patience with animals is everything.

I reached for the teat with my left hand, grabbed it, and squeezed. Something wonderful happened. A spurt of white liquid shot out at an

75

angle which could hardly have been anticipated by a seer. At the same time Snowdrop's hind leg blasted upwards with the force of a lift-off at Cape Kennedy then shot down kicking over the bucket.

'What on earth do you think you're playing at?' I shouted.

But it was too late. The words ricocheted accusingly off the stonewalls of the goat-house.

This won't do, I remonstrated guiltily with myself. You're supposed to be more intelligent than she is so behave as though you are. Remember, patience with animals is everything.

Snowdrop looked ahead wearing the air of one who was completely disinterested in what was happening but fully confident of her ability to handle whatever might arise. I considered the situation. If I held the bucket, I could pull it away should she decide to make contact with it, and were I able to hold one leg off the ground she'd be helpless. If however, I was holding her collar and a hind leg or the pail, with what did I milk?

Perhaps a compromise was possible. I pulled the stool closer to her and took hold of her collar, placing my right foot alongside the bucket with the vague notion that if disaster loomed I could hurl it to safety.

Leaning towards her, hardly daring to breathe I watched for any slight movement but she stood quietly chewing, a picture of contentment. I reached for the teat and twisted my arm at the wrist so that it rested against the top of her leg, thinking that if she raised her leg I'd be able to move my arm up with it, and by forcing the arm to remain in mid-air prevent the offending leg from coming down, at least until I'd got the bucket out of the way.

I clasped the teat, and milk squirted out but I was too preoccupied to see where it went. She kept on chewing and I squeezed again and a well-aimed shot clattered into the pail. More squeezes, more milk, oh such wonderful milk, and my beautiful goat was being so good. Squeeze, milk, squeeze, milk. This was the beginning of a great partnership. In a very short time the udder was empty. But of course, the work was only half done, and because the teats on a goat are side by side it followed that a different pattern of operation had to be adopted.

Instead of using my left hand I would now have to use my right, which meant that I'd have no hold on her collar, but I thought that as she was now standing quietly everything would be just fine.

76

Snowdrop had the hang of it; I was getting the hang of it; what could possibly go wrong? Her body juddered slightly as she realized that the milking wasn't just a one-sided affair but apart from the odd shuffle she behaved like a veteran. I stripped the last drops from her and congratulated myself. At last I had the knack. It just goes to show, patience with animals is everything.

Success was mine and its heady smell intoxicated me. I sat back on the stool and gazed with pride at my beautiful co-operative goat. Visions of the happy times to come, sealed by such intimate beginnings illuminated my mind. In the dark winter, when my goats and I would share the milking, the soft light of the oil lamp playing on the mellow stone and the golden straw; the atmosphere cosy and serene. Or in high summer when the thick walls ensured that however intense the heat outside, the interior would always be cool and restful.

I stirred myself from this reverie and raised my hand to fondly pat her. She turned her huge amber eyes towards me, stayed motionless for a second, then just as I was about to tell her that she was the most wonderful goat in the whole world she leapt up and forward, the tether stopping her from travelling further, whereupon she speedily descended to the floor.

'You idiot' I yelled. 'You absolute idiot. You've put your bloody foot in the bucket.'

KNIGHT OF THE ROAD

I'd been in a pensive mood all morning. This led to a frame of mind guaranteed to slow whatever activities required my attention, from scattering handfuls of corn (prolonged thinking twixt each scattering) to sowing seeds of beetroot and beans (gazing at each completed row as though mesmerised). When later I found myself chopping down swathes of nettles whilst all I'd meant to do was nip off the tender tops for some soup (I didn't even remember picking up the shears) I realised I had to take myself in hand.

I wandered down to the house. When we'd first moved in I'd fixed a piece of green painted wood over the cellar door with red letters proclaiming, Prevarication is the Thief of Time. I didn't have to look at it to know what the proverb was, for I'd painted it myself and it was that all too true statement which had galvanised me into decision making. Well, not exactly 'galvanised' perhaps but certainly 'jollied'.

There is no problem here I said to myself. You can't go on like this forever, relying on Gordon every time you want to go out. You're just a wet-nellie. If Truly Scrumptious can do it wearing her frilly frocks you certainly can, and before I'd given myself a chance to think further I shouted 'Gordon. Gordon......where are you? I'm going to book driving lessons.'

Phew! First step accomplished. A voice from upstairs called 'Good......I'm just fixing some panelling. Is there a small screw-driver down there? Possibly on the window-sill?'

How could he be so indifferent.

'I've been thinking about this for simply ages' I yelled as I rummaged through an assortment of tools, 'and not doing anything about it is ruining my life and when I eventually pluck up the courage to do something about it all you can say is look for a bloody screw-driver.' A head appeared round the bend in the staircase.

'What do you mean, pluck up courage?'

I knew I was going to be all wimpish. 'Well, I think I might not be able to, to drive you know, not be any good, not able to pass the test and then you'd be having to ferry us everywhere and you'd wish you'd never come here.' I could feel the drama taking over, 'and I'd be such a burden.'

He bounded down the stairs saying 'Oh you are such a silly sausage' and hugged me tightly. 'Of course you'll pass a test. Is that what's been bothering you? You had lessons when you were seventeen didn't you?'

'Yes' I replied, 'a few. It was a terrible winter with so much black ice everywhere that I stopped them. I wish I hadn't'

'But you enjoyed them?'

'Yes. Until I encountered the black ice.'

'So what makes you think you'll fail?'

'I don't know.'

This elicited a shaking of the head and some tut-tut-tuting. 'Now, say after me' he began. I eased myself from the hug and took a step backwards, wondering what on earth was coming. 'Say after me, 'this is not a problem''

'This is not a problem.'

'I will learn how to drive and I am going to be a very good driver.'

'I will learn how to drive and I am going to be a very good driver.'

'Because I am a very confident person.'

'But I'm not' I protested. 'That's the problem. Everybody thinks I'm so sure about everything I do but I'm not, I'm not. I'm not confident at all, it's all show.'

'Don't be ridiculous, of course you are. Now repeat after me, I am a very confident person.'

I pulled a protesting face but acquiesced. 'I am a very confident person.'

'So. What's the next move?'

I hesitated, then, 'I book lessons.'

'Good.......by the way did you find the screw-driver?'

***

The lessons I had with my instructor were in a small Ford and I was enjoying them very much, but when I enthusiastically climbed into the driving seat of the Land Rover and was ready to drive off I couldn't release the handbrake. I felt as though I was dealing with an iron girder set in concrete. No matter how I tried I seemed completely unable to lift it a fraction in order to release it and I wondered, assuming that I eventually conquered its resistance, how on earth I

79

was ever going to get it back on! Visions of high drama on the hilly lanes swam before me with the Land Rover sliding forwards, slipping backwards, zigzagging from side to side because of my inability to control this inflexible lever.

This will not become a problem, this is something to be overcome, I kept repeating. So with persistence I eventually managed, the Land Rover started forward and we were off, with Gordon giving praise and encouragement. Although my lessons seemed to be progressing quite well, because of the steep hills, the recalcitrant handbrake and my horror of some imaginary event which could bring disgrace upon me, I was in no hurry to go far afield. But boldness and ability grew so it was with fewer anticipated fears that one day I drove in the direction of the village.

I was confidently driving up the incline towards the main road when I saw the rotund figure of Mr Isaac Watkins slowly crossing the junction. On hearing something approach he looked up, then recognising the vehicle paused where he was in the centre of the road. Presumably this was to pass the time of day, and after a goodly time imbibing in the Farmer's Arms it would not have occurred to Mr Watkins that standing in the centre of a busy junction in order to bid a friendly greeting to a neighbour was in any way odd or dangerous. However, as I drove closer something seemed to strike him as wrong for his face folded into a perplexed frown and he lifted his left hand as if to shade his eyes in order to see better, craning his neck as he did so, then waving both arms wildly in the air, gesticulated to me to stop. This I did, several yards from the junction.

'What on earth's he doing? D'you think he wants a lift?' I asked.

'I've no idea' said Gordon, 'anyway, we're about to find out."

The pink roundness that was Mr Isaac Watkins walked sedately towards us, and as always when we saw him after an hour or so bar-propping were amazed at the dignity of his slightly staggering gait. Six sheets to the wind but always the gentleman, controlled and decorous, the delivery of his words purposeful and the conversation never more than slightly unusual.

'Hello' we said as he stopped alongside. The rosy face framed itself in the open window. The words, some of which had great stress laid upon them for no obvious reason, were enunciated with the utmost care, and the cherubic features beamed with pleasure.

'I didn't know you were driving Mrs Green, and when I saw you in the driver's seat I thought, it can't be and when I looked and saw you I said to myself, yes, it is, it's Mrs Green driving. But Mrs Green doesn't drive I said to myself and then I saw that it definitely was you driving. Well, well.' After a few seconds silence the beam vanished, and in a voice falling almost to a whisper he said, 'I'm so sorry.'

I couldn't imagine what he was sorry about and didn't like to ask in case for some reason I might hurt his feelings, so I just looked at him hoping an explanation might be forthcoming, but he was now gazing as though unseeing through the window and beyond us at some distant point, every breath bathing us in alcoholic fumes. While we sat in silence waiting for further developments several cars drove up behind, then, the occupants sensing that the matey congestion in front was not disposed to hurry, passed us by with a nod or a wave. Such is the tolerance of human foibles in the land of song and this day I was grateful for it. I doubt it would have happened in Hampshire. Then without warning, Mr Watkins broke from his reverie, as though no significant time had passed since he last spoke.

'Yes, I'm so sorry about that. Had I realised sooner that it was you driving Mrs Green, I would have done something about it when I first saw you coming.'

Still wondering what this was all about I was even more puzzled when he said 'Wait here,' and holding up a forefinger and indicating by a couple of shakes of it within six inches of my face that I was to take note of his words, he turned and walked with purposeful step out to the centre of the A40. Peering for quite some time towards the village, he carefully positioned himself so as to see clearly in both directions, although as the road to the east bent sharply after fifty yards his vision was somewhat limited. However, in his own mind he obviously knew what he was doing, and having satisfied himself that all was now safe for a novice driver he looked towards me wearing an expression of paternal fondness, and with an expansive gesture of his left arm beckoned me forward.

'Oh crumbs, what shall I do?'

'Move up to the line and stop there.' As Gordon said this the hand movements from the main road changed to a frantic 'stop' signal accompanied by several jogging movements of the feet, evidently meant to indicate a dangerous situation developing which indeed it

81

was, for at that moment a large hay lorry shot past missing him by inches, but the little man remained quite indifferent as he concentrated on ensuring that I should have peace of mind as I ventured onto the highway.

I revved the engine and edged slowly forward. 'Just go' said Gordon, 'get across as soon as you can. We'll say something nice to him when we're in the village. Just go. Be positive.'

It was a bit difficult to be positive. My wrist was hurting from holding the handbrake, my left foot was protesting at being glued to the clutch, my heart was in my mouth and my stomach about to join it. My mind didn't seem to be anywhere at all. I looked quickly along the length of road and moved out positively, when to my horror Mr Watkins took several hasty steps to his left, placing himself firmly in my direct line of progress. I slammed on the brakes and he came towards my window.

'You're doing very well' he breathed beerily at me. 'Mr Green, don't you think Mrs Green is doing very well? You must be very proud of how she is doing Mr Green' and with all sense of his instructions apparently forgotten, he continued, 'Now, I wonder if you would be so kind as to give me a lift to the village.' I nodded weakly, and watched as with much fumbling with the door handle he successfully climbed in to seat himself in a posture which would have done credit to a Victorian governess, and without further ado continued his monologue praising my outstanding ability.

'Mrs Green, I said to myself when I saw you driving my goodness that's Mrs Green driving and then I thought, it's a very dangerous road for anyone not used to all this traffic. Some of these drivers go too fast you know and that made me quite worried when I saw you driving Mrs Green, it made me quite worried.'

We stopped outside the general store where our passenger opened the door, and turning to face the interior, ponderously reversed his person down onto the pavement. He then moved along to my open window and spoke in the same the same clear, measured manner as before.

'Thank you. I am now going home to partake of my beautiful Sunday dinner. Goodbye to you both,' and he gently inclined his head towards us, smiling benevolently before turning to move off down the street, hesitating just fractionally to concentrate on the business of

82

placing one foot before the other as he made the last lap of his journey. What a trip that had been! How had I survived it?

Two and a half miles of uneventful driving and then the last half-mile packed with enough activity to keep my poor nerves tingling for the rest of the day. I'd held traffic up at a junction and had nearly knocked down Mr Watkins. My left wrist felt as though it was about to fall off, and my ankle after its prolonged union with the clutch felt much the same. Yet as I drove home the thoughts in my head were very comforting, for I knew without doubt that chivalry was not yet dead.

CURDLED HOPES

Even the smallest village in Wales has its annual show, and Pontbrynach's is a very grand affair with a wide variety of competitions to suit all tastes and abilities, from the sedentary embroiderer to the limb-breaking enthusiasm of the rodeo-rider, and its reputation is justifiably spread far and wide.

It was shortly after Easter when I became aware of talk about the show. Just the odd comment at first but as the year progressed it seemed that any casual conversion would soon be steered round to the delights of that first Saturday in September.

'Oh, the horticulture tent is fantastic, fantastic it is. So many entries, not that I'd ever buy great vegetables like that, they can't be very tasty that big but you've got to marvel at anybody growing them to that size.'

'Wait till you see the handicrafts. Such beautiful things, even the Royal Welsh has nothing to compare.'

'Such gorgeous things, I don't know how some people find the time. Ooooh, it's so   lovely to see.' 'And the animals......the sheep......all shampooed and brushed, like great woolly cushions.'

It seemed that local children were born with the words 'Pontbrynach Show' engraved on their hearts. Each of them, having been carried round the showground during the course of their first year and subsequently taken as a matter of course to this annual highlight, soon reached an age when they could enter numerous competitions with a full comprehension of what was expected of them. Their Welsh cakes, ornaments, carvings and paintings were arrayed for all to see, the winners triumphant in having reached the standard set, the losers, after initial disappointment undaunted, and determined that next year things would be different. So each generation vigorously flew the flag of super-excellence and the future of The Show was assured in the hands of such youthful zeal.

It had not occurred to me to exhibit anything. I was going to gaze and admire and generally enjoy myself. Then one summer afternoon when I was in the village store Mrs Thomas walked in. At the time I didn't know Mrs Thomas from Adam but she knew who I was.

'Do you like living up at Tironnen?' she enquired as she closed the shop door and without waiting for an answer said she hoped I was aware that The Show was imminent, and continued with a list of reasons which would be unacceptable as an excuse for not exhibiting an entry of some sort, death it seemed being the only valid reason.

'Oh, I don't know' I hedged, 'I......'

'That's no excuse' she interrupted in a tone that left no room for protest. 'Mrs Matthews at Bryncellyn House has been living in these parts less than two months and she's exhibiting several things.'

I was on the point of saying that Mrs Matthews, driving around in her expensive car looking as though the most onerous task in her life was keeping her hairdressing appointments, was hardly leading a life of toil on the land as was I. But I had heard how hard Mrs Thomas and so many others worked to make the current show an even greater success than the previous one so it seemed churlish to refuse, if not impossible.

What do you suggest I do?'

'What to do?'

Her astonishment at my question caused her words to issue forth at a pitch so high as to make the two other customers in the shop pause in their deliberations.

'What to do? Well, what are you good at? We all have talents of some sort don't we?' I thought I detected a note of doubt as the words were being framed and indeed, talent was not a word which easily sprang to mind when recalling all the mismanaged endeavours of my life, but this small wiry woman whose soulful expression belied an energy and determination which brooked no opposition had to be appeased.

I decided there and then to make lemon curd. Now there are two types of lemon curd: the edible and the inedible. The latter is manufactured in great vats from a recipe which somehow manages to impart a horrible greasiness on the tongue, although how this is accomplished I cannot imagine. It's only lemons, sugar and butter so how can it possibly taste so awful? My recipe had been handed down from mother to daughter through at least four generations and was always a great favourite with family and friends. Its sharp sweet flavour and smooth texture had been much commented on through the many years I'd made it and I reckoned it would be as good as anything else entered. Also, with an unexpected touch of the romantic creeping

85

in on my thoughts, it would be a nice little dedication to the memory of great-grandmother.

The day before The Show I assembled my ingredients. Some of the buzzing enthusiasm must have rubbed off onto me as with a wooden spoon I stirred my curd in a bowl set over a pan of simmering water and I had no qualms that my entry, when placed alongside all the others would do nothing to disgrace the standard of local domesticity. After a while the mixture responded to the gentle bubbling in the pan beneath and I watched with satisfaction as it thickened, then, with great deliberation I poured it into a warm jar, no drips being allowed to despoil the rim as the hot liquid rose gently to the top, and I left it to cool.

I peered at both sides of one of those little rounds of paper, unable to tell which side was waxed. Nobody else I know has any confusion with this but my brain refuses to acknowledge that one side of these disks is different from the other, so to be on the safe side I always covered the disk with melted wax. But there was no question of doing that now. Any judge about to sample my lemon curd and finding her mouth awash with bits of some unknown object would discard my entry immediately, so I made a guess at which side of the paper was waxed and placed it carefully on the top. The cellophane lid secured by an elastic band came next, the fitting of which caused some apprehension lest I should judder the precious jar, tilting its contents to blemish the shining glass band between curd and rim. A label was then chosen with as much regard to it's size as that taken by a designer fitting out the public rooms of a luxury hotel; neither too small to look out of proportion nor too large to distract from the glorious colour within. I carefully printed the words 'Lemon Curd' and with great precision stuck it at a pre-determined level on the jar.

Next morning we drove onto the show field, I clutching the precious pot. Each entrant had been given a number by which they were able to identify their allotted spot on the display table and I thought I'd find out what the form was before collecting my exhibit from the Land Rover.

Two enormous marquees dominated the far end of the field with smaller ones pitched at intervals between them.

'DOGS' said a large notice outside one of the smaller ones.

86

'POULTRY' announced another and so on, each identifying itself as Mecca to those whose interests it embraced.

'DOMESTIC AND HANDICRAFTS' was writ large above one of the big marquees. I set course in its direction and on entering found a scene that was both busy yet subdued. There was a lot of seriousness here. Many of the entries were in place and I walked between the rows of long tables, avoiding the occasional groups of men and women engaged in quiet conversation, showing no hint of the rivalry which existed between them on this one day of the year. Each table was covered from end to end in a white cloth and I enjoyed stopping to admire the numerous exhibits so carefully placed. Large dark fruit cakes, sugar-coated apple pies, various fruits arranged in intricate kaleidoscopic patterns glistening inside Kilner jars and eggs in many shades of brown nesting in small hay-lined baskets or cosseted by linen napkins in flowered china bowls. The variety was endless. Fine embroidery, complicated crochet, gaily-coloured patchwork, fashionable garments knitted and sewn. All arranged by their makers so as to be shown at their best. I was amazed at the sheer volume of articles on display; paintings and woodwork, flower arrangements of all shapes and sizes......there seemed to be no end to the talents displayed in the large tent.

Down the furthest aisle were the preserves I sought. Jams and jellies of bright ruby red or dark purple sparkling under the lustre of highly polished glass. Honey, both pale and dark, glisteningly transparent, the succulent taste and tantalizing smell seeming to hover over the squat shining pots. Next to the honey was the lemon curd. Half a dozen jars were already in place and there was my number, 28, awaiting my entry. All the curds looked fairly similar.... variations on a sharpish yellow, and I was sure the judge would have a difficult time if the flavour of all was as good as their outward appearance.

'Gosh, it's good,' I reported to Gordon, passing him near the tent as I made my way back to the Land Rover to collect my entry. I picked up the jar, slammed the door then realized I'd left my shoulder bag inside. Feeling the ground with my hand for a spot that was perfectly level I put down the curd, opened the door, grabbed my bag then noticed the show schedule on top of the dashboard behind the steering wheel. I climbed into the vehicle and leaned over to get it, then lowered myself down, but before my left foot reached terra firma

87

it had knocked over my precious pot of curd. Panic stricken I picked it up hoping for one fleeting moment that my reaction had been swift enough to avert disaster but one look sent my hopes tumbling. The curd had oozed over the waxed paper. This in turn had been sucked back into the coagulated mass which was already attaching itself to the pristine cellophane cover.

My heart sank.

What on earth could I do?

There was no magic remedy to put right the sorry-looking object in my hand, my carefully prepared entry, my one bright hope, the banner of the townie turned countrywoman with which I was going to astonish my rural neighbours.

It seemed that only two choices were open to me. I could put it back in the Land Rover or set it between its fellows on the table.

How everyone would laugh. I could just picture the scene; dozens of people feverishly thumbing through the schedule to find the page at which alongside the number of the entry my name and address would be disclosed. Word would get around and hundreds would push their way to the table to point and jeer, splitting their sides with laughter at the sight. Nothing like this had ever happened at The Show. No one would have the slightest interest in what was going on elsewhere. The livestock showing, the show jumping, the dogs and the poultry would pale in novelty beside the spectacle of my lemon curd and the organizers would slap on a hefty fee to look at it and implore me to enter next year.

The fantasy faded.

I made a decision.

I don't mind giving people something to chuckle about I thought. I can always hold my head high another time, and tucking the jar inside my jacket I strode towards the marquee.

Louise was simply thrilled when she won first prize with her oil painting and the local schoolmaster bought it for three pounds, and equally pleased when a farmer's wife bought the sausage rolls she'd made even though they hadn't won a prize.

Jessica tore out of the 'DOGS' tent with two first prizes and a second, for Dylan, with his great brown eyes and thumping tail had persuaded the judge that, amongst other things, he was 'the dog the judge would most like to take home'.

No one made any comment about my lemon curd.

It was only after it was all over that I wondered what great-grandmother would have thought.

FOR LACK OF SUPPORT

I was washing towels in the sink, the television was on and Princess Anne was walking down the aisle in Westminster Abbey. Having a day's holiday to celebrate the wedding was an excuse for the girls to do a bit of partying so Louise and Angela had stayed the previous night with two friends who also happened to be sisters, and their parents were taking them all to spend the day in Cardiff with the intention of doing some Christmas shopping. Gordon had taken Jessica to spend the day with a school friend in the next valley and hadn't yet returned.

I was alone; in a foul humour dwelling on the injustices of life.

He arrived back at Tironnen to an atmosphere that was positively caustic, and while I pummelled away he studiously avoided more communication than was strictly necessary, for it bothered him a lot that I did the washing by hand although it didn't normally bother me. But on this particular day there I was, stubbornly refusing to say whether or not it was the laundering aspect of my life which was causing such obviously deep felt feelings. He was becoming more perplexed and whilst sympathizing with me was fast losing patience with my silence. My washtub bashing had grown more aggressive with the passing of every second, and by the time the wedding service was well under way my simmering had turned into a furious boil.

'I know it's tough not having enough water pressure to run the washing machine but you did say you weren't bothered and I'm always offering to do it for you. If you like I'll make improving the pressure top priority.'

'It's got nothing to do with the washing.' I fumed.

'What then? Tell me what's bothering you.'

After a considered pause I said 'Alright' and swept a sud-encased hand in the direction of the television, bestowing a smattering of lather on everything in range while I glared at the screen in the corner of the room where the camera was relaying a scene of elegance and serenity.

'Can you see any of those women doing the family wash by hand?' I demanded.

Gordon studied the screen for a few moments, obviously bemused.

'No, I can't, but perhaps they've left their laundry outside in their Rolls Royces and after the Queen's gone home they'll bring it into the

Abbey and start then. What are you on about? You've just said it's not doing the washing that's upsetting you.'

'It isn't. It's not that.'

'Then what is it?'

I found it difficult to put into words what was bothering me. Gordon was working so hard doing graphics and improving the fabric of the house. I knew he felt a great responsibility for our welfare and it did seem awful to impose another task on him which was far from being a necessity. But I took the bull by the horns.

'That' I said, dramatically indicating once again with my wet hand the television set, 'That is where it's all happening. Nothing is happening here, nothing at all.'

My husband passed a hand slowly across his brow.

'But we moved out here to get away from places where everything is going on. I thought that was what we wanted.'

'Oh, I don't mean that sort of happening,' I moaned, 'I mean getting things done here. We're not doing anything here.'

'Not doing anything?' Gordon obviously couldn't believe what he'd just heard. 'Not doing anything? We've been here just over a year and during that time we've levelled floors, replaced flag stones, straightened doors, mended chimneys, demolished and re-built walls, sorted out two of the bedrooms, installed a kitchen, involved ourselves with animals and produced vegetables by the hundredweight. And that's just what I can think of off the cuff. Besides that I've been trying to earn money, not to mention our involvement with the children and their interests. Goodness, there are only twenty-four hours in a day so how can you possibly say we're not getting anything done?'

I was already beginning to feel a bit guilty. Well very guilty, but I plodded on. 'Yes I know, but all the things we are doing don't make the place look different.' Gordon was about to say something and I hurried on. 'They all improve the building and benefit us and make life easier and pleasanter but so far we've not done very much to restore its character.'

'I am simply longing to begin cosmetic restoration as you well know.' Gordon sounded a trifle hurt and I could hardly blame him. 'Maybe this is a good time to talk about it because obviously you've got something in mind. What is it?'

91

Pulling up a waterlogged sleeve and pushing its sogginess up around my arm, I considered for a moment. My feelings of antagonism towards the hideous kitchen range on the wall opposite had been growing for quite some while and now they erupted. After glancing once more in the direction of Westminster Abbey, I muttered 'Nobody there would tolerate a thing like that......nobody would' and I glared sulkily at the object of my hatred.

We had occasionally talked about taking out the blotched horror but Gordon was a bit apprehensive. It was something to be done when he had plenty of time to think about any problems that might occur. 'What problems could there possibly be?' I'd say. 'Surely it's just a question of getting it out and cleaning up what's behind?' But he always stuck to his guns. He didn't know what problems there might be. Maybe there wouldn't be any but if there were they could be difficult to put right and could well be dangerous. It was something to be done when there weren't too many other pressing commitments.

I was very impatient with all this caution. It was quite clear to me that behind this monstrous edifice just waiting to be unmasked and show itself to the world once more was a fine inglenook fireplace. Someone had put the oven in; surely it was an even simpler task to remove it. I pulled a towel out of the water and ferociously squeezed it, trying to decide whether Mata Hari's cajoling or something reminiscent of Henry V's resounding call to arms would meet with most success. Unable to make up my mind, I heard a silly 'little girl' voice whine 'All we need is a crow-bar.'

I knew I deserved the look I got.

'All you need is a crow-bar? You think it's that simple?'

'Well......' I mumbled, 'I suppose there's a bit more to it than that.'

***

I finished the washing in fine spirits, and we moved the table and chairs out into the garden. Gordon went to the barn to collect a crowbar. Princess Anne and Captain Phillips emerged from the Abbey and I began to pull several layers of ancient flowered wallpaper off the chimney breast.

'Now I'll just prize this side out a little,' Gordon pushed the long end of the crowbar behind the metal structure of the range at one side of the grate 'That's alright.'

Of course it was. What did he expect?

He moved the iron bar up a foot or so. Evidently satisfied again, he inserted it a few inches from the top, pulled the grate fractionally out from the wall and shining the torch in through the narrow cavity put his head first on one side then on the other, peering in, trying to see more clearly. This took some while then he straightened up.

'There's nothing there.'

'Of course there's nothing there.' Ye Gods, I needed patience. 'Well, there'll be a hole there I suppose but surely that's what you expected to see; a hole.'

'Oh, for goodness sake,' I noticed he was looking rather white. 'There's nothing holding up the wall. Just the grate. I'll check the other side but as sure as eggs is eggs there's no beam at this end.' He repeated the exploratory process with the crowbar and torch and confirmed that apart from a short length of oak at one end, there was nothing supporting the tons of stone which made our huge chimney.

We held a meeting there and then, and while downing coffee and large slabs of sticky ginger cake decided to throw caution to the wind and get on with the job. We rummaged around in the barn and found a variety of iron bars and numerous balks of timber and dragged them into the house. Gordon worked out the probable thrust-load of the chimney and drew chalk marks in a rough triangle along the lines of the stones to an apex at the top depicting where the chimneybreast was supported by the side pillars.

'We must support everything below here.' He indicated the chalk line. Then he made a big timber and iron frame support and put iron rods between the relevant stones. We removed those beneath, then inch by inch began to force out the tiled grate hoping that the wall above would hold. It was very tricky removing it as we had to reach between the uprights of the temporary support frame before wiggling it loose and hacking at all the bits and pieces that had to come away. It took hours but by late afternoon we'd got it out.

Behind the grate was our first glimpse of the inglenook fireplace...... completely filled from top to bottom with large stones. Gordon had been right. At one end, some eighteen inches of charred

93

wood was all that remained of the great beam of oak that had presided over the seven foot wide hearth since the house was built in early Georgian times, and I wondered at the sort of fire that could burn through such timber.

We began lugging the stones outside. There seemed to be hundreds of them, and we were about a third of the way through when the phone rang. It was Louise. She and Angela had been invited to stay a second night with their friends and go straight to school with them the following day. Was that alright? Was it just! I'd been getting anxious about the dreadful mess they were going to come back to so this idea was most welcome.

'Did you have a good time in Cardiff?'

'Oh, great. I got most of my shopping done and we went to Cardiff Castle which is just like Castel Coch that fairy-tale place we visited on the hill. It was built for the same man and decorated the same but much bigger. Amazing. You'll have to go there Mum. I'll tell you about it tomorrow, bye.'

'Well, they seem to have had a good time' I remarked, then I was struck by a thought. 'I wonder if I could ask Mrs Williams if Jessica could stay the night. We could get on so much quicker and get an early start in the morning. I'll phone and see.'

I began to explain the situation but before I'd finished Mrs Williams interrupted. 'I was just thinking about what a good time they're having and what a shame it is that you'll be coming so soon to collect her. Megan would love her to stay, I know. They're in the middle of a game just now. Wait a minute and I'll ask Jessica if she'd like to stay.' She put down the phone and I heard her footsteps retreat down the hall, then faint squeals of delight. The footsteps became louder. 'Did you hear that?'

'You're very kind. I'll bring her nightclothes and things over.'

'Oh, don't do that. She can wear some of Megan's pyjamas. You've a lot of work ahead of you by the sound of it. I'll see her safely to school in the morning. Do you want to speak to her?'

'Well if she wants to have a word I'll hang on.' The phone was put down again but I didn't hear any receding footsteps. Instead Mrs Williams raised her voice. 'Jessica?' A faint noise emitted from some distant part of the house. 'Do you want to speak to your Mam?' Again a faint noise. 'No, it seems she doesn't' translated Mrs Williams.

94

'They're completely immersed in their game' adding 'it's so nice for Megan to have a friend to stay.'

Now there was no rush to do a quick clear up. In fact there was no need to clear up at all until the job was done, although looking at the mess surrounding us I couldn't envisage the room ever looking clean and tidy again. So we plodded on for an hour or so, carrying out the larger stones but suddenly it was all too much. I went outside, took off the old shirt I'd worn over my clothes, shook it and returned to the kitchen. We brushed the dust from a couple of chairs, flopped down and I felt as though I'd never get up again. But I did, and fairly soon, because with all activity having ceased, my mind focused on the fact that I was jolly hungry.

'Ooooh, I'm hungry. Are you? We've hardly eaten anything all day' I said to Gordon.

The light had long gone when I took a dried-out casserole from the oven and we sat amongst the debris and dust, our feet perilously near the scaffolding, to relax over our supper. Gordon switched on the television and we watched the news showing some of the day's ceremony. The happy couple on the palace balcony acknowledging the good wishes of the multitude below. The camera panned to the crowd and zoomed in on a banner held aloft by some wag bearing the unforgettable words 'it's too late to say neigh', a reference to the bridal pair's association with horses but just as applicable at this moment I thought, to us. I looked at Gordon. His hair was completely white and I assumed mine was too. My throat felt like sandpaper, my arms ached, the skin of my hands seemed to have disappeared and the burning sensation in my back made me wonder if I'd ever stand upright again. We were both desperately tired. I looked at the chaos around me then at the nearly empty inglenook gaping from the shadows and the jumble of wood and iron shoring up the great chimney piece above.

It was most definitely too late to say nay!

***

Five o'clock the following morning saw us clearing the remaining rubble and stones from the cavity and after a substantial breakfast I began phoning friends and anyone I could think of who might know where we would be able to get an eight foot oak beam. Just when it looked as though we were going to have to spend the rest of our days with a pile of scaffolding decorating one wall, a glimmer of hope came our way. The village shopkeeper remembered someone saying that they were pulling down an old cottage. It hadn't been of any interest to her at the time but maybe we should get in touch with them. This sounded fine. Unfortunately she couldn't remember who it was. Not a problem though in a village where everyone knows who's doing what, when, and not infrequently, with whom.

Excited to be on the track of our wanted beam we drove to the village to make further enquiries, convinced that it wouldn't take long to find out who was knocking down a cottage, and sure enough when Gordon climbed back into the Land Rover after paying for petrol he said, 'Right. Out on the Merthyr road and then we turn left just beyond where the old road has become a lay-by. Bryn Williams is the name.'

No-one was about when we reached the farm, just a couple of sheep dogs chained at opposite ends of the yard and seemingly indifferent to our approach, so we poked around in the ruins of what must have been the original farmhouse, noting that several beams were lying about. We sized them up for suitability and one was just made for our purpose apart from being a few inches too long. I went back to the house to try to attract attention but knocking on the door and shouting 'anybody at home?' through the open door produced no result other than to make the dogs break into frantic activity barking excitedly. But as I wandered back to the cottage I saw Gordon raise an arm to point in the direction of the hill above and I detected the faint sound of a tractor in the distance. We walked through a couple of steeply sloping fields, then passed into a third which evened out to more level ground where ploughing was in progress. A tractor was coming towards us and slowed to a halt though the noise of its engine lessened but little, and the driver eyed us curiously.

'We're looking for a beam and have been told you might have one for sale' shouted Gordon trying to make himself heard. He always found it very difficult to shout and this was a real effort.

Cupping his hand to his ear in an effort to catch the words above the roaring engine the driver bellowed 'What's that then?'

Gordon tried again. 'There's a beam in the cottage we'd like to buy. Is it you we should see about it?'

This time his voice carried sufficiently and the words proved of enough interest to cause the man to switch off the engine, which fact he immediately forgot as he shouted 'By golly yes.' The words hit us with the power of an artillery shell and evidently surprised the man as well, for he looked rather sheepish and lowered his voice. 'Yes, it's me. It's me you see.'

He climbed down from the cab and rested against it in silence for a few seconds as though recovering from the shock effect of his force ten vocal chords.

'A beam you want is it?'

We felt bad about interrupting the farmer at his work and offered to come back later but he said he was pleased to have a break. We introduced ourselves and explained our dusty appearance and while we walked down to the cottage gave him a brief resumé of what we were doing at Tironnen. Gordon pointed to the beam.

'Is that right for you then?'

'Just fine.'

'You taking it in that?' He nodded towards the Land Rover.

'Yes.'

'By golly.'

The farmer and Gordon agreed a price with surprising speed and with equally surprising agility heaved and pushed it up onto the Land Rover and we drove off in a somewhat down-on-the-springs vehicle.

Back home we manipulated it out of the Land Rover by using a sort of seesaw motion and it finally landed on the ground. I was amazed at how quickly Gordon sawed through the beam to the required length and we then manoeuvred it onto a sort of conveyor belt of logs and up the steps onto the forecourt. With much manipulating and frequent pauses for breath and gulps of coffee we brought it into the house setting it on the floor before the chimney. Gosh, it was exhausting. Gordon removed what was left of the original beam without much difficulty and again I mused on how long a beam like that could have been smouldering before it actually burned through and what had happened when finally it had. There was no sign of burning on the stones on the front of the chimneybreast so probably a major fire had somehow been averted.

97

We put a breezeblock in front of the inglenook and lifted one end of the beam onto it. We put a breezeblock at the other end and placed the beam on that, then added another breezeblock and continued adding and lifting until the beam was four feet six inches from the hearth, at which point we manoeuvred it into the cleaned out cavities that had held the original beam. Apart from the fact that we had to be careful not to knock the scaffolding in case the whole lot came down, it hadn't been a difficult job, just a rather tiring one, for the beam was eight feet long and measured ten inches square. Anyway, we were well pleased with the way we had got on.

We cemented in the stones above the beam and cleaned up as best we could although dust continued to settle over everything. But I knew that when the cement had hardened and the scaffolding came down we would be looking at the restoration of the big fireplace and how wonderful it would be to see it in all its glory.

Then the great day dawned. We cleared everything away, swept out the inglenook and scrubbed the hearth, stopping frequently to exclaim over its grandness. I thought about the noisy shooting parties that in days gone by had returned from their exhilarating sport and about the women and girls who had been preparing dishes for them in this great fireplace. I doubted that they would have viewed the inglenook in quite the same way as we did.

We cleaned up the rest of the room and finally ourselves, and I hoped that Princess Anne had enjoyed these first days of her married life as much as I had.

SERVICE WITH A SMILE

'She's doing it, she's doing it' I yelled as I raced up the steps into the house. 'She really is and we must be off as soon as the girls have gone to school else she might stop and I must phone Mrs Roseland to tell her we're coming and will you put plenty of straw in the Land Rover because it'll be a long journey and I want her to be comfortable.'

My family looked at me over their porridge and eggy bread. At 7.15a.m., my excitement was something they weren't enthusiastic about, although I heard Gordon mutter 'Thank goodness' as he downed his coffee, adding without apparent interest, 'Which one?'

This had been the day I'd been waiting for. The day one of our lovely goats was to visit her mate; a day I might have missed if it hadn't been for the billy-rag. A female goat will usually come into season about September and generally make quite a song and dance about the matter. I knew that because I had read it in my goat book. It stated quite clearly that when a goat is in season she would call loudly, wag her tail constantly and go bright pink under the tail. So I watched for the tail wagging, listened for the loud bleating and peered at their rear ends but to no avail. No animals were ever observed more carefully for indications of their sexual maturity, yet September had turned into October and then November and December and still I had detected nothing. I couldn't make it out. Why would they not co-operate?

So a couple of weeks before Christmas I had gone into the goat-house, picked up the milking stool and opening the gate of their stall went in, plonked down the stool and sat on it. There was nothing unusual in this. I enjoyed their company and often lingered in the goat-house.

'Hello my darlings' I patted each snow white head in order to gain their undivided attention and they affectionately pushed their faces into mine breathing waves of regurgitated grass odours over me. 'Now, what I have to say is very serious and I want you to listen to every word. You are now eighteen months old yet you don't seem to realize that certain things are expected of you. You're well fed, warmly housed and much loved, and in return I ask for one thing only, that you produce offspring. You see, I need all the lovely milk you will give so that I can make butter and cheese.'

They regarded me without registering any emotion, silently chewing but otherwise not moving a muscle. Then Bluebell moved slightly. I wondered if she was going to throw any light on this sorry state of affairs, but no; instead, she leaned her hundred and thirty-five pounds against me at an angle of about sixty-five degrees and rubbed her body slowly and luxuriously along my back, turning when she'd finished to repeat the exercise in the opposite direction. I pressed my feet hard down on the floor to avoid being pushed off my little three-legged stool and put out a hand to stroke Snowdrop under her chin. She was not given to the exhibitionism of her twin, as though aware that breeding such as theirs demanded a more refined attitude, so she stood quietly as Bluebell continued her exercises. I knew from experience that Bluebell could entertain herself in this way indefinitely so I pushed her off and looked at these superb products of breeding, anatomically correct and in every way structured to produce as much milk as any cottager could wish for. I rested my chin in the palm of my hand. 'I don't know what to do' I moaned, 'I don't know what to do.'

They regarded me balefully but obviously this wasn't going to get me anywhere, so I picked up my wooden stool and went out closing the gate behind me. They stood up on their hind legs and draped themselves elegantly over the wooden walls of their pen, surveying me with wide-eyed seriousness, no doubt hoping that perhaps an early supper was on the way. 'Don't you worry.' I patted each white head in turn and they lowered their lids demurely, 'We'll think of something.' Two pairs of large round amber coloured eyes followed me as I moved away, ducking my head to avoid a low beam. I looked at them before shutting the top half of the outer door. They remained festooned over the wall; their interest in my departure equalling that of my arrival and it was obvious that the content of my soliloquy was of no significance at all. Worry, they would not.

I closed the door and walked thoughtfully to the house. They should be coming into season every three weeks and they weren't. I pondered this fact for some while. It's your opinion that they're not coming into season but for goodness sakes, what's your opinion worth? Think laterally. Maybe they are and you just don't realize it. Maybe they don't all wag their tails and bleat. You're just a novice at this game, you really don't know much at all.

100

Before any more time passed I had to get advice and the best person, indeed the only 'goat' person I knew, was Frances from whom we'd bought them. I phoned her and told her of my problem.

'Don't worry' she said soothingly, 'It's not always easy, especially when you're new to goats. I'll send you a billy-rag."

'A what?' I queried.

'A billy-rag. It's been in close contact with a male goat. Just hang it in their stall and your problem will be over. I'll put it in the post tomorrow.'

Two days later a small package arrived. Being slightly wary I opened it outside which was just as well, for as I did I was almost overcome by the odorous object it contained. 'Phew' I gasped, quickly folding the wrapping paper over it and holding it at arms length. Then I hurried to present it to my lovely girls. With my head turned as far as possible from the pungent rag I hung the thing on a nail. They were not impressed. After a few days the rag seemed to simmer down or perhaps I just got used to it, but anyway like me it appeared to be waiting for something to happen.

And then it did. Six days into the New Year I opened the goat house door to the loud strains of Bluebell's strident soprano and the sight of a tail which, if not wagging wildly was definitely twitching.

We piled straw onto a sheet of plastic in the Land Rover and went to fetch Bluebell. Being unaware that the real thing was about to loom in her life she had reservations about leaving the billy-rag. We had to lift her protesting into the Land Rover, and minutes later after bumping down our stony track, we were speeding in the direction of the stud farm.

Just over an hour later we drove into a small yard around which stood several stone and wooden buildings of various sizes and conditions and a picturesque cottage which appeared to be held together by a web of Virginia creeper. Goats were everywhere; strolling leisurely in paddocks, watching us curiously from several pens, and to my horror peering through glazed windows. Glazed windows? Was I really seeing glazed windows? I couldn't believe it but had to because sure enough panes of glass separated several of these energetic and fun-loving animals from the outside world. I nudged Gordon's arm. 'Look over there. Have you seen? There's glass in those frames. Crumbs, I'm glad we didn't book Bluebell in to stay overnight.'

A small incredibly thin woman emerged from the cottage and walked towards us. Everything about her was wispy, from her hair which was obviously a law unto itself to her anorak on which quilted threads stuck out in all directions, down to her shoes that seemed inordinately long and narrow for a person of such little height.

'Oh, my goodness, you've come.' Her voice was as thin as her appearance and high. After introducing ourselves we encouraged Bluebell from the Land Rover and Mrs Roseland studied her for a few moments.

'I think Romano Champagne will be the most suitable. Yes, Romano Champagne.'

Champagne, eh? Nothing but the best for our girl.

'He's young' continued Mrs Roseland 'But he's already sired some very promising kids. Come along, my dears, bring her in' and she moved towards a stone barn calling 'Come along dears, bring her in.'

Inside were three quite large pens one of which was occupied by a fine young Sanaan male goat standing in deep straw. Having already sensed Bluebell's presence in the yard her arrival in the barn precipitated a rush towards the gate and Mrs Roseland took hold of her collar. 'I'll take her now.' She opened the gate of the pen. 'Now get back you silly boy, get back. This nice young lady has come to see you and won't be impressed by a display of bad manners.'

Bluebell was ushered in and promptly bolted to the far side with Romano Champagne in hot pursuit. She turned and made a triple circuit round the pen before Mrs Roseland caught her collar, and fending off the amorous swain with an outstretched leg, pushed her through the gate. 'She's not ready, not quite ready. Probably this evening or tomorrow morning. It's not always easy to tell but at this time of year they're only in season for a short time so you have to get it right. I can't offer to keep her here as I have no room.' She waved her hand encompassing in its orbit the various buildings and once more I glimpsed the goats playing behind the glazed windows.

'No, quite' we said, speedily bundling Bluebell into the Land Rover in case Mrs Roseland found that after all, she did have room for another boarder in this melee of potential disaster. 'We'll come back tomorrow then.'

The following morning Bluebell was still serenading the Billy-rag at full volume and we repeated the trip of the previous day. This time she was as delighted to see the young billy as he was to see her and two seconds after hurling himself at her Mrs Roseland said 'That's fine, now we'll leave her here for a few minutes while I sign the certificate.'

'Surely you don't sign the certificate before they've mated?' I asked.

'Oh, but it's all over dear, didn't you see? That's it. That's all there is to it. It just happened now. Everything's fine. Follow me dear. Have you got her papers?' I handed her the precious pedigree papers and a cheque.

We stayed in the yard while she went in search of the form that would be proof that Bluebell's potential kids were the offspring of Romano Champagne. We looked around us. Through a window I could see bales of straw, over which several young goats were hurling themselves with great delight as they chased each other. Kids are a joy to watch and can consume far too much of a goat-keeper's time but we had nothing else to do so we watched the nursery school antics with amusement, when suddenly a white shape shot through the window, scattering glass in all directions. The goatling landed at our feet, her snowy head fast becoming stained by a spreading mass of blood. I grabbed her and knelt down, the better to keep a hold on her while Gordon hurried towards the open door of the cottage, at which point Mrs Roseland appeared.

'There's been an accident.'

'What? Oh my goodness.' Her shrill voice echoed round the yard and she launched into a sprint, her large feet flapping in front of her as she hurried down the path. 'Oh, my goodness, they have such fun playing on the straw. This happened once years ago.' She leaned over the goatling and began to part the bloody hair. 'This one is a visitor; she doesn't know about these things.'

I couldn't believe what I was hearing. Gordon and I sometimes discussed whether we were too cautious in our animal husbandry but here was this woman, a goat-keeper of renown, housing animals in these extraordinary conditions and considering it the goat's business to know that they could be dangerous!

The goatling didn't mind all this attention and Mrs Roseland pronounced a small cut on the jaw and another on its head to be only superficial wounds and released her hold on it. The adorable creature affectionately rubbed its head against me as blood still oozed from the cuts. Its landlady sponged the cuts, searched for any fragments of glass that might be lodged in the fine hair and then sprayed on a purple antiseptic. After completing the search I let go of the kid which scampered off.

'Oh, my goodness, just look at your coat dear.'

We all looked at the patch of blood on the front of my jacket and I marvelled that the goatling, having transferred a good part of the contents of its veins to me had found the strength to move away. Mrs Roseland disappeared but within seconds hove into view carrying a bucket of water and a not too clean looking cloth. Before I realized what was in her mind she'd grabbed my jacket and was sponging it down with the dripping rag, liberally spreading the stain to hitherto uncharted regions.

'Don't bother' I pleaded 'It's only an old one.'

'Oh my goodness, I can't let you go with your coat like this.'

'It doesn't matter really, I only use it in the yard' I insisted but she held the garment out from my person and once more flung the sopping rag in the direction of my stomach, watching with evident satisfaction as some of the loosened surface stain mingled with the icy water and cascaded like Niagara Falls into my wellingtons.

'It won't show much when it dries' she said encouragingly, then as though unconvinced by her optimism, added 'Oh my goodness, I feel very bad about this.'

I was beginning to feel a bit bad about it myself as the saturated jacket rested on my middle. The wetness had seeped through the jersey beneath to my skin, while in my wellies the water sloshed about as a great swell, unrelenting against my cold protesting feet. All the while the goatling pottered about and I couldn't understand why Mrs Roseland was giving more attention to my jacket than she was to it. She should really have been teaching it about the foolhardiness of playing on bales of straw in the proximity of a glazed window.

By this time I was beginning to shiver. Goodness, I thought, we only came to get Bluebell mated and I end up wet through, covered in blood, my feet swimming inside my boots and very, very cold. A heart-rending epitaph on my tombstone loomed large before me. 'She died of pneumonia that her goat might become a mother.' Perhaps some animal loving philanthropist would set up an animal sanctuary in my memory. It was an emotional moment which soon faded. 'I think we'd better go' I said puddling towards the pen where Bluebell was still ensconced with Romano Champagne but Mrs Roseland was ahead of me. 'I'll get her dear'

She walked Bluebell towards the Land Rover and the goatling moved closer to get a better look at the stranger. I'd just lifted Bluebell's front legs and Gordon had bent down to pick up her hind ones when she noticed the young goat hovering nearby and swung round with such force that we had no choice but to let her go. Immediately she lunged at the goatling and the hard sound of crashing skulls showed that the youngster was good for a game, which is all it was. Mrs Roseland grabbed the goatling, we secured Bluebell and I bent down to once again lift her legs up into the Land Rover, when with a gesture of great affection she rubbed her head against my shoulder, depositing on my jacket several streaks of the purple spray transferred from the goatling during their brief encounter.

A voice close by trilled 'Oh my goodness.'

'Hurry' Gordon commanded, and with one mind we heaved up, slammed the door on Bluebell's rear end leapt into our seats and moved off.

'You haven't got your certificate dear' The voice was pitched high to reach us over the sound of the engine as she waved the piece of paper frantically to attract our attention. I stuck my head out of the window and waved. 'I'll send for it' I yelled 'Goodbye and thank you.'

I poured the water from my wellies out of the window as we drove along and found a couple of plastic bags under my seat which I stuffed under my jumper to alleviate the unpleasant feeling of wetness against my skin, although plastic wasn't that cosy either. 'I'm longing to get home' I cried.

'We won't be long' said Gordon and then remarked 'I'm sure this sort of thing doesn't happen to other people.'

'Oh, I don't know.' I squeezed a sock tightly, watching the water stream past the window. 'I think it probably does. Other people just

105

don't talk about it that's all; they think it makes them appear foolish. Anyway, who's going to know about this?'

ENGRAVED ON OUR MINDS

The miner's strike of early 1974 and the defeat of the Heath Government which followed occupied most of the news, and the pundits had a great time endlessly dissecting the whys and wherefores, how it had happened and what should or should not be done. They argued with politicians and each other and no doubt enjoyed themselves immensely. Inflation had been a cause for concern for some years but in spite of this Gordon still had plenty of work coming in although as the year wore on a couple of clients fell by the wayside and certainly no new ones appeared on the horizon, but we were not unduly worried. However, by late autumn continued inflation was causing people to really tighten their belts. No one was thinking about new designs for anything. What they were already using would have to suffice until things took an upturn and that could be a long way off.

No work – no income.

Fortunately the vegetable garden was producing a good variety of things and the hens were laying well but a diet of vegetables and eggs, even prepared with all the inventiveness I could muster, which wasn't much, was going to be very boring indeed. I could hear myself saying when the mob arrived home from school 'Guess what darlings, we're having lovely fresh vegetables and omelettes for dinner. 'Guess what darlings, we're having lovely fresh vegetables and boiled eggs for dinner.' 'Guess what my loves......' I was mentally vomiting just thinking about it.

Our savings from the sale of the Southampton house had long since disappeared and the only money in the bank was what was left from the last cheque. I knew it wasn't much. All we had coming in was the child allowance of £1-80pence, which didn't go very far. In those days nothing was given for the first child, 80pence for the second and £1 each for any subsequent children. With winter approaching the girls would need new clothes and every few weeks we required a delivery of logs for the sitting room fire and coal for the Rayburn. We had hens, goats and a pony to feed. To say we were sinking into despair was putting it mildly. I tentatively suggested to Gordon that he seek some form of unemployment benefit just to tide us over but he wouldn't hear of it. 'We'll manage' he said with more confidence than I expected. 'We will, you know. The answer is in finding a different market and producing something of quality that is inexpensive, something that people would like for themselves as well as buying for presents. It's just finding the right thing.'

The word 'finding' jolted a thought into my head. A couple of tea chests full of stuff we either didn't consider suitable for use at Tironnen or simply didn't like, had been put somewhere when we'd moved in. Apart from a silver plated tea service, a wedding present that I'd never have used in a million years, I hadn't a clue what else was packed in them.

'Do you remember where we put those two tea chests?'

'Er; yes they're in the workshop.'

'There are things there we could sell. Could tide us on a bit. Let's go and see what we've got.' In the workshop Gordon cleared a variety of tools from an old door that lay across the top of the tea chests then we lifted off the door. We prized off the top of one of the chests and the first thing I unwrapped was a hideously patterned dinner plate, with green medallions circling its edge, bringing back the moment of disappointment when I'd first seen it. It also had been a wedding gift, from a very dear friend of my parents and I could remember the jolly letter of appreciation I'd written to him. He'd died shortly afterwards, so he never knew that it had been re-packed almost immediately.

'I wish I didn't hate this' I said, grimacing as I looked at the plate, 'but it is Royal Doulton and there's a lot of it; it's got to be worth something.'

But Gordon's mind was elsewhere. 'I've seen pieces of slate in several shops with animals and scenes either engraved or painted on them.'

'Oh yes, very amateurish all the ones I've seen.'

'Exactly.' He paused and thought a bit, while I brought forth more of the Doulton muttering at it in a sneery sort of way.

'The screen printed ones haven't got much going for them' he continued 'and the hand done ones are pretty awful. I'll work on some ideas.'

'Would you paint them?'

'No, I'll engrave them. But I need to think about it' Then, after a pause 'You don't need any help with this do you?'

Already things were looking a little brighter. If his idea was feasible, and I had every reason to believe Gordon would come up with something very attractive, it could save our bacon. Although not knowing what was involved my mind was racing ahead, with the possibility of getting some engraved slates in a few shops in time to catch the Christmas trade and then we'd have an indication of their viability. In the meantime I was sure we could raise some worthwhile cash on the dinner service, and the silver tea service was bound to appeal to someone with greater pretensions than ours. We were living in exciting times! Well, maybe more worrying than exciting but isn't necessity the mother of invention? Of course it is.

I emptied the tea chests, carefully putting the pieces of the now precious dinner service on whatever available spaces I could find. Apart from a couple of unidentifiable but pretty candlesticks which I thought might fetch a bob or two, nothing else of value was revealed, so I re-wrapped the remaining stuff in the newspaper and plastic bags and shoving it back into one of the chests placed the lid on top. When I returned to the house to fetch the jam pan that was going to serve as a carrier for the dinner service, I poked my head round the sitting room door.

'How's it going?' Gordon was pouring over several books that were open on his workbench and I noticed several sheets of paper scattered about with various shapes pencilled on them. 'I think I've got something. Have a look at this.' He leaned across the books to reach for one of the paper sheets. 'I think four inches would be about the right size to cut the slate.' On the paper he'd drawn a square. Inside this was an oval within which was the rough sketch of an owl. 'I've made a list of subjects which we can go through later but I've yet to find out where we get the slate. First however, I'll see how these ideas work out in reality. There are enough pieces of slate lying around to practice on, so, here goes.' He followed me across the yard and we went our separate ways, Gordon to the barn to rummage for slate while I returned to the workshop thinking about his idea. I was impressed. I could imagine the fine engraving within the oval and couldn't wait to see the slates in the shops in time for Christmas. That however, was something I had to keep quiet about.

It took several trips to transport the china and the silver tea set to the house where I stacked it by the sink. Two kettles were already hissing away on the Rayburn and over the next hour I washed and dried twenty-eight pieces of the unloved dinner service, the two candlesticks, and the silver which I then polished. Having spent most of its life wrapped in tissue inside Sainsbury's plastic bags and over the last few years left in an outhouse, it responded to this treatment very well. It looked brand new, which in a sense it was. I found a couple of stout boxes and packed up what I could but I needed several more. I'd get some the following day in the village.

I thought that sending the dinner service to auction would secure the best price but I'd never sold anything through an auction before. In the late '50's a neighbour had asked if I'd like to attend a house auction close to where we were living at the time, so I did and was jolly glad because I bought an oval Victorian dining table of burr walnut for £1.15shillings. (£1.75p) We dine off it still. Now I needed advice and I knew where to get it.

Stephanie was somewhat older than I and an auction addict. In the early 1950's she had persuaded her husband that buying a large Victorian house would be a good idea. At that time a mammoth new housing programme was under way and after years of austerity people were fed up with the old and wanted new......and new furniture too. So she reasoned that if big old houses were being vacated, there must be a lot of big, old furniture being sold because the only place for big, old furniture is in a large Victorian house. She and her husband went to auctions and had a glorious time taking their pick of furniture, carpets, lamps, ornaments and bric-a-brac with which they furnished their latest home for a song.

Both Stephanie and I had lived in a variety of places over the years but had kept in touch regularly by letter. Occasionally something of particular interest would instigate a phone call, as when a 'new address' card arrived followed a few days later by an ecstatic Stephanie telling me what a wonderful time she was having buying elegant pieces to compliment her Georgian house – at the auction rooms of course. Now was the time to phone her.

'Well, as you can imagine, the more people at an auction means the competition could be more intense so the more chance of a better price' she said, 'and what you're selling sounds quite respectable, so go to the big boys. I don't know about Cardiff but we've got a good firm here. Always choc-a-bloc with people. Sales every fortnight. Just had one. It's not as though you've got furniture to get rid of or masses of boxes, so why don't you both come for lunch, bring the stuff over and I'll do the rest. If you'd like me to, that is.'

Some offers are too good to miss and whilst it fleetingly crossed my mind that in such dire circumstances we couldn't afford to drive to Cheltenham I gratefully accepted and a visit was arranged for the following Thursday. I became quite excited, already thinking that a stroll round Montpelier before we arrived at Stephanie's would be pleasant, soaking up some of its elegance. I poked my head round the sitting room door. 'Gordon, if you'd like a change from your labours next week, we've been invited to Cheltenham for lunch on Thursday.'

'Who do we know in Cheltenham?' he asked absent-mindedly as he worked away on a piece of slate, then as memory disturbed his concentration, 'Oh yes, that'll be nice. I should have got these things worked out by then. By the way, I thought of calling them Slate Cameos. How does that sound?'

Slate Cameos......Yes. The words tripped off the tongue nicely.

'Steph said Guy won't need any persuading to take a long lunch break' I said as I walked over to the work-bench, and anticipating that I wanted to see what his now named Slate Cameo was like, he stopped working and held up a four inch square of slate within which he'd drawn a double-lined three inch high oval. Within the oval was a beautifully engraved owl. 'The slate will have a deckled edge. What do you think?'

Gordon had said he had to come up with something that was of quality and inexpensive. Something people would give as gifts but would also like for themselves and I knew I was looking at it. They'd sell in droves.

'It's absolutely lovely and you're onto a winner. What d'you think they'll sell for?'

'Well, obviously this one is experimental so I'll be able to get the timing down. I don't know what the slate will cost but I should think we could sell them for well under two pounds. Oh, and I phoned the quarries at Blaenau Ffestiniog. We can go up anytime so I'd like to make a trip soon' he said.

'Fine. Time for some tea I think' and as I reached the door added 'I knew you'd come up with something good.'

I left the sitting room and was halfway across the kitchen when a thought struck me. We would be taking the dinner service and the silver to Stephanie's the following week and she had said that the auctions were held every fortnight. Would our things be in time for the next one or would they have to wait until the one after that? I had no idea how these things worked. She'd also said that one had just been held, so it could be nearly a month before they were sold. Then another thought even more alarming than the first entered my head. How quickly did auction houses send out their cheques? Not very quickly, I guessed.

Ye gods, it could be eight weeks before any money materialised!

Even if Gordon's slates were in the shops and selling we'd not receive payment until four weeks after delivery, and we were a long way from having any to deliver. We had yet to get the raw material. Christmas would be upon us! I wanted to scream and throw things, and it was in a state of deep gloom that I put the kettle on the hob.

On the wall in the sitting room were two large Imari plates. I first saw them in my grandfather's house and the orange, dark blue and gold pattern had enchanted me from a very young age. Then they had hung in my parent's house and for some years now they'd hung in ours. I knew they were worth something. I looked at them for some time but left them where they were.

I opened the drawer in the top of the bureau and saw the chequebook lying there, trying to pluck up the courage to open it. Actually, I was trying to gain the courage to pick it up ...... looking inside was going to take far greater willpower. Pick it up and open it. Slowly I stretched out my hand. In the space on the chequebook stub where organised people regularly keep a note of how much is left in their account and we seldom did, Gordon had actually made a note. £33 - 64.

£33 – 64pence! In those days a very modest week's wage. I contemplated this as I poured the tea, the hand holding the teapot shaking and the butterflies in my stomach having a high old time.

***

That afternoon we drove to Brecon. Gordon wanted to look at some books in the library, for although we had plenty of references at home he needed to be sure he would be using the most suitable photographs. I took with me a plastic bag containing the silver tea service and the candlesticks. I thought that if I could sell the tea service immediately we'd at least have something to supplement the thirty-three pounds, sixty-four pence in the bank, and a bird in the hand was worth two in the bush.

The man in the antique shop held up the milk jug and studied it briefly before turning his attention to the teapot and sugar basin on the tray.

'It's never been used. I've always hated it' I said, with such over emphasised dismissiveness that I knew he'd realise my real reason for selling. What a mistake. I tried to rectify this by studiously ignoring him and looking with interest around the shop. Almost the first thing I saw was an Imari plate. I walked over to get a closer look. It was smaller than ours and wasn't as attractive either. I noticed a chip on the edge and a sort of pale grey blemish on part of the pattern, as though some chemical had been wiped across it.

A price tag dangled. £13.00.

£13.00! We had two at home...... nicer...... larger.......perfect condition.

Maybe these would be our lifesavers. But I did so hope it wouldn't come to that.

A voice caught my attention. 'Eight pounds.'

'Eight pounds?' I thought for a second. It didn't seem very much.

'Can you not improve on that?'

'Eight pounds, no more. I've got to make a profit you know. I can't just hand out pound notes for something nobody wants and money's tight right now."

I wondered why he was offering me eight pounds for something he was so sure nobody would want, but I was too low in spirit and too ignorant to challenge. I could see his point; it could be in the shop for ages tying up his money. Maybe silver-plated tea services were the most unpopular things on the planet. I didn't know. But eight pounds wasn't going to do much to get us out of our predicament, so declining his offer I packed the things back in the bag and left, to make my way through the town to another shop.

A pleasant woman whose over large teeth rather detracted from her wonderfully high cheekbones, looked at the things on the tray.

113

'I sold one very similar a few weeks ago then a lady came in a few days later and was most disappointed that she'd not snapped it up when she first saw it. She left her phone number so I think I can sell this straight away.' She carefully examined each piece, wiped a smear which I'd missed from the sugar bowl, replaced it on the tray and was silent as she studied the complete set, presumably working out what she could ask Mrs Disappointed for it.

'It doesn't seem to have had much use' she said.

'It's never been used. I don't like it.' Then suddenly becoming expansive in the presence of this nice woman who wasn't averse to letting me know that she actually had a customer ready and waiting, I blurted out 'I need to sell it.'

Having actually said the words the enormity of our situation really hit home, and I felt hot tears behind my eyes but managed to keep them there. I don't think she noticed.

'I'll give you fourteen pounds.'

'That's fine. Thank you.'

'I don't get these very often' she said as she opened the till and began counting out the money. 'People like to have them to use on special occasions.' Or leave them in tea chests in outhouses I thought, but I nodded my head as she handed me two five-pound and four one-pound notes. We chatted for a minute or so and then picking up the plastic bag I remembered the candlesticks. 'Oh, I've got these. Are they of any interest.'

Removing the wrapping I handed one to her. 'There's another one the same.'

'This is very pretty. And another to match?'

Determined to hold my own in the honesty stakes, I offered, 'They're nothing special; no mark on them' as I unwrapped the second one and held it out.

'No, but things like this are little gems in their own right aren't they? So delicately patterned and the lacy effect round the top takes it out of the run of the mill. I'll give you a pound.'

Several minutes later I found Gordon with a couple of books approaching the desk in the library, then as we walked to the car park I reported what had happened. We now had £48-64pence, which was a lot better than £33-64 but was still a long way off the comfort figure. Even so, I was quite elated. It didn't last.

114

'Don't forget' counselled Gordon, 'we've got slates to pay for.'

'How much will they be?'

'Depends how many we get. I didn't ask the price. If we need slates we need slates, but it'll be quite a lot.'

Ye gods!...... Still, as the man said, if we need slates we need slates. Well, there were always the Imari plates.

***

The following Monday we crossed the River Wye at Builth Wells and headed north up the Wye valley through Ryader, the river always close to the road as it wound its way south along the foothills of the Cambrian Mountains, until we reached Llangurig. There we left the river turning towards Llanidloes, where a 16th century half-timbered market hall creates an unusual traffic hazard in the centre of the cross roads. It's not really a hazard though, because who's hurrying? We decided to cut across country, thinking it would be a quicker route rather than continuing on the main road but this proved to be false, for the road was hilly and very winding.

But it was also beautiful for the countryside through which we climbed was wild with a few isolated farms set in the hills, the occasional wind-tortured tree relieving the skyline. Hardy little Welsh Mountain sheep grazed these highlands, their whiteness becoming smaller until they became distant unidentifiable dots. Beyond lay the peaks of Snowdonia.

Re-joining the main road we were approaching what used to be called the county of Merioneth, now sadly re-named Gwynedd after the ancient kingdom it had once been. But who was I, an Englishwoman, to complain? Maybe all the inhabitants were quite happy with the change, but for me, in this country of wildness, soaring peaks and lakes of un-fathomed depth; of brave deeds, faithful hounds and noble princes; of wizards, magic and fantasy; this particular county held a special place in my heart. Merioneth...... just to say the word conjured up a mystical past. It was a county much loved by my father who had imbued in me the same affection. His spirit is in these hills......this would never be Gwynedd to me.

With Cader Idris ahead of us we stopped for coffee in a lay-by then continued to Dolgellau, a town frequently visited in my childhood, where at the age of six, when staying with my parents at the Golden Lion, I sleep-walked from my bedroom to another, climbed into what was fortunately an unoccupied bed and continued my slumbers. (I've since looked up The Golden Lion but it's not mentioned. How strange. It can't have disappeared as it was a large hotel in the centre of the town, so I think I've got the wrong name).

'I'd like to stop here for a few minutes' I said as we drove into the town. 'I want to look for something. I won't be long, and leaving Gordon I wandered off in search of a narrow lane of tiny cottages where a long time ago an old lady, well, she seemed old to the child I was, although she was probably nothing of the kind, used to sit in the window of her front room making needle cases out of coloured felt in the shape of a Welsh hat. Two pieces of cream flannel for securing needles were sandwiched between two circles of felt which formed the brim, and the crown was decorated with flowers made of minute pieces of felt. Inside the crown was a thimble.

Whenever we had visited the town I'd made a beeline for her cottage, and as I studied the rows of little hats set neatly on the windowsill to attract passers-by, I thought long and hard as I considered the merits of this colour or that. After I'd made my purchase I'd spend time peering and poking, uninvited of course, into the numerous boxes of felt, ribbons and cottons that almost covered the surface of the table on which she worked. This was guaranteed to keep me occupied for quite some time, after which I'd turn my attention to the china plates hanging on the wall, all of which had a narrow ribbon of blue or pink threaded through slots round the edge, and in the middle a picture of Welsh ladies deep in conversation. I thought they were beautiful.

The mantelpiece also held artefacts of much interest, where an enormous meat dish decorated with pale blue flowers dominated the centre. This was prevented from falling by two large nails hammered into the mantelpiece. I knew this because I had once asked her why the dish didn't fall and she had told me to climb onto a chair to find out. I had felt very privileged to share this secret.

At one side of the meat dish was a pretty pink vase with two handles, a picture of a ruined building on the front, and a top that was divided into several points rather like a star. On the other side was a large white jug, embellished with the sepia photograph of a man with a bushy white beard. Beneath the photograph was a cartouche within which his name had been inscribed for posterity but posterity had not been kind, for both the name and the elegant swirls surrounding it had suffered over time and little remained. I'd once asked the lady who the man was but she didn't know, other than that it was somebody very important. Between the jug and the meat dish a wooden love-spoon intricately carved from one piece of oak, hung from a hook, the handle of the spoon fashioned to form a complicated maze of twisted wood before swelling out into a bowl. I wondered if it had been given to her by a young man when she was young, but didn't like to ask.

Apart from the table at which the lady worked, the chair on which she sat, and the rickety chair on which I had climbed to find out why the huge meat plate didn't fall, a grandfather clock had been the only piece of furniture in the room but it was very plain and had held no attraction for me. Perhaps it should have had, for throughout these visits I'd prattle away, happy and at ease, and the poor woman must have been desperate for me to leave, which I did only when the thought of my mother's disapproval surfaced in my mind. The 'lady of the hats' probably spent part of her Sunday devotions in chapel praying that I'd find another interest when I visited Dolgellau but it would be several years before God took pity on her. How I'd loved my visits to her cottage where I'd found paradise in one tiny room.

That November day in Dolgellau I found the row of cottages and fancied I remembered which one had belonged to the lady of the hats. I think it was the fourth in the row......but maybe not.

***

We were now only twenty miles or so from our destination and our route took us through forest and highland to where the huge grey bulk of the Trawsfynydd nuclear power station hideously transformed the scenery, and maybe it was my imagination but I fancied that the lake below it looked ominously black and sinister even on this bright winter's day.

Eventually we reached Blaenau Ffestiniog, a scar of grey amid much beauty, which held in its drabness our hopes of salvation. I knew nothing of slate, other than that in the 19th century welsh slate

117

was in colossal demand all over the world for roofing and that whole families worked in the mines. I was about to find out more.

Climbing higher we left the main street to reach our destination where we sought out the foreman who told us how hundreds of thousands of tons of welsh slate used to be transported via the Ffestiniog railway, built specially for that purpose in 1832, down to Portmadoc from where it was shipped to distant shores. Portmadoc must have been a bustling place then, with hundreds of ships coming and going, but I remember it for days of endless summer when my parents would rent a house in the area. A trip into the town meant a delicious ice-cream cornet from Mr Paganuzzi's ice-cream shop, and an occasional visit to the chemist which always had me wondering if the gentleman who from time to time emerged from the dispensary was the person whose intriguing name was proclaimed in bold letters above the shop window ...CHRISTMAS WILLIAMS ......CHEMIST

***

The foreman at the slate mine enlightened us with much pride as to the various processes in the art of slate mining and cutting. He nodded in the direction of a large shed. 'Over here.'

We followed him to where several men were splitting large pieces of slate by hand with astonishing dexterity. Most sat with the slate leaning against one leg while they tapped methodically with a hammer at two chisels placed strategically along the bedding planes until the sheet split, the layer was put aside, and the chisels inserted once more between the next natural layers. The sheets of slate must have been quite a weight for they were two and a half to three feet square. One man was standing, leaning over an enormous piece. Surely I thought, that must be about five feet in length. This was held firmly between his knees as he gave several taps, first on one chisel then on the other, moving each beyond the previous one along the length of the slate. They all seemed very relaxed about their work but it looked a bit nerve-wracking to me. Other men placed these sheets on a bench pushing them towards fast-spinning steel wheels that cut them to the required size, after which the cut pieces were taken outside the shed where they were stacked in rows.

We watched for a while, occasionally being enlightened on some point by the foreman and as we turned away from this activity towards the rows of cut slates outside remarking on the skill we'd observed, he said, 'Ah, well, only Welshmen can do it' adding sagely, 'There is a saying that slate doesn't like Englishmen.' We nodded our heads but he was quite wrong of course for there had in the past been many slate mines in England, and a few were still working.

Gordon began his search for 'perfect' slates along one row and I started on another. As they were intended for roofing, smoothness of surface to the extent required for Gordon's purpose was not a prime consideration in the slicing, and it took a couple of hours for us to find enough slates which were entirely without ridges. Finally with aching backs, broken fingernails and roughened hands we paid our bill of thirty-four pounds and hastened home, only stopping on the way to buy a new pair of slate cutters at a builders merchants.

That evening Gordon cut ten of the slates into 4"x 4" squares, damaging only one in the process. The girls and I had a go but had to admit defeat. I picked up one of the little squares and slowly rubbed it with my hand. Was this humble piece of slate from deep in the ground of Snowdonia really going to see us through the hard times?

***

Tuesday morning and the milking had been done and the animals fed. The girls had set off for school, the breakfast things were cleared away and a perfunctory tidying in the house attended to. I turned the goats into the meadow and spent the next twenty-minutes making everywhere outside ship-shape, all the while wondering how Gordon was getting on. He had long since settled down at the drawing board, mug of coffee to hand. I was just swilling out the last of the buckets in the iron tub in the yard when he appeared at the door.

'Jenny.' I looked up. 'Have you got a minute?' Wiping my hands on my trousers I hurried indoors in a state of great excitement. On the drawing board were four engraved slates; one each of a badger, owl, squirrel and hedgehog. My excitement was not misplaced.

'Gosh, these are good.'

'I think twelve subjects will make a reasonable range, don't you? A seal, a mouse and a fox. I've a list here if you want to look at it. You

119

might think of some alternatives.' But I was quite happy to leave the choice to Gordon.

'They'll go like hot cakes' I enthused. 'You said they'd probably wholesale at under two pounds; does that still stand?   Have you included petrol costs?'

'Absolutely. I've allowed for everything. There'll be a limit to the number I can do each day because it's quite arm aching; I'll just have to see how it goes. I think they'll sell, don't you?' There was absolutely no doubt in my mind.

By the time I'd put the kettle on for our mid-morning coffee five more subjects had been added and by lunchtime twelve slates were completed, among them a fox, mouse, seal, peregrine falcon and the head of a welsh pony. On the back Gordon had written his signature and instructions for cleaning: to clean, simply rinse under running water and leave to dry.

I went into efficiency mode and strode over to the bureau where I sought out a form for address labels.

'Gold or white?'

'Gold I think, don't you?'

The form completed, a cheque was written and placed in an envelope. I then phoned an acquaintance who made greeting cards of pressed flowers, to ask about her source of plastic bags. Having acquired it I contacted the suppliers, wrote out another cheque and put stamps on both envelopes. We were moving on.

The following morning I wrapped each Cameo in a small freezer bag and having placed them in a box, each separated by a square of corrugated paper, I set off for Brecon.

There were several gift shops from which I could choose but I knew which would be my first choice. I'd bought things there on several occasions and felt it to be the right one for Gordon's work. I was very confident as I made my way through the town, making a detour on the way to buy an order book from Smith's but as I approached the gift-shop I suddenly felt quite wimpish. I'd never been a saleswoman before and I'd given no thought as to how to approach a potential buyer. It was however, a bit late to start thinking about a strategy so all I could do was go in and see what happened. If I did something wrong, I'd soon find out.

The proprietor was a middle-aged woman with a Birmingham accent and a mass of shoulder length frizzy brown-going-grey hair. She had a penchant for much personal adornment in the form of enormous drop earrings, weighty bracelets, large stone rings of various colours and several gold chains round her neck, the background to all this being a garment of bright hue, giving her a decidedly exotic appearance. Her shop was set out with great flair, which wasn't surprising, and exquisite taste, which was. Two women were browsing among some scarves when I entered so I went straight to the counter.

'I've got something new and I wonder if you'd be interested' I blurted out.

'Well I've done all my Christmas buying' she replied pleasantly enough 'and I can't possibly consider anything else. You're rather late in the year Christmas being only six weeks away, so I'm sorry, but I'm not interested. Come back some time in the New Year and if I like what you've got I'll buy for Easter.'

Easter! My heart sank.

What do I do now I thought. I glanced over to where the two women were still examining the scarves, one holding a scarf in each hand while they seemed to debate their relative merits. I thought it might be a while before they'd require any help from the shopkeeper who had turned her attention to some paperwork, so I took out a slate from the box, saying as I held it before her. 'Would you just tell me what you think?' She gave a slight sigh of annoyance but nevertheless looked up from what she was doing. Immediately I noticed a shift in her attitude and after a moment's pause she reached out and took the slate from me. I slowly brought out another. She took that also, then briefly looked at me then back at the slates.

She took them out of the bags. 'These are very nice. Beautifully done. Do you do them?'

'No; my husband does them.' She turned one over, examined the writing on the reverse then placed them both on the counter. I had her attention now.

'There are twelve subjects. We call them Slate Cameos,' and becoming quite bold I brought out two more, which I placed beside the others. 'You're the first person to see them.'

'How much are they?

121

'One pound sixty.' I hardly dared breathe.

'May I see the others?'

I placed the remaining Cameos on the counter and was just explaining that I had ordered proper bags and labels when the door opened and a woman walked straight to the counter. I moved away while she made an enquiry about something, then, obviously on friendly terms they chatted for a few moments until catching sight of the slates she angled her head slightly the better to see. She picked one up.

'Marion, these are lovely. How much are they?' I moved further away so that the shopkeeper would know I was not eavesdropping and after a short while the woman left the shop, smiling at me as she did so.

I returned to the counter.

'Is there a minimum order?'

'No.'

'Right. I'll take two hedgehogs'...... I delved into my bag for the pristine order book, 'two mice, two owls, and one of all the others and we'll see how they go.'

I could have hugged her!

As soon as I left the shop I hurried to the nearest phone box eager to give the news to Gordon.

The phone rang, and rang. Come on, come on, come on I willed, but there was no reply.

***

'I tried to phone you' I said as soon as I got home.

'Oh, I went to stretch my legs a couple of times. Had a long chat with Bessie.'

Gordon was delighted but guarded as I reported the reaction of the shopkeeper and the customer. I said nothing about the fact that if she had all her Christmas stock ordered the same would most likely apply elsewhere, because I was so confident that the slates would be seen as a very saleable item. It wasn't as though a huge outlay was needed; a set of twelve would cost a mere nineteen pounds twenty, plus postage. Surely most people would see there was little risk in that.

122

Having been engraving for most of the morning Gordon was ready for a break, so I rustled up an early lunch while he spread the road map out on the table for in a few days we planned to go on the road selling. We studied it while we ate, choosing a circular route which encompassed several country towns where I hoped there were enough shops to entice the local population to do their Christmas shopping on the doorstep, but small enough for it to be obvious to me if no suitable gift-shop existed. We didn't want to waste time. Our journey would go east through Hay, then north to Leominster, Tenbury Wells and Ludlow, from where we'd cut across country to Knighton then head for home via Kington.

The following morning Gordon engraved slates.

The day after that we put the Royal Doulton dinner service in the Land Rover, (unknown to Gordon I'd put in a sample box of slates) and set off for Cheltenham, stopping off at Brecon to deliver our first order. While I was doing this however, he noticed the sample box and was decidedly crotchety when I returned.

'You're not taking those to show Stephanie are you?

'No, although she'd probably like to see them. I just thought we might see a likely shop somewhere. Ledbury perhaps.' I sensed I was on a losing battle.

'No........ Definitely not. We've had a stressful time lately and we don't know what will happen tomorrow. We may get orders, we may not. I don't want to think about slates today. I'm looking forward to enjoying a few hours in great company. Maybe you're looking forward to tomorrow and maybe you'll turn out to be the greatest saleswoman in the world but right now I don't want to know.'

Gosh!

***

We arrived home from our selling spree in high spirits. We had orders. One hundred and fifty-three pounds, sixty pence worth of orders.

Without exception, the response from all the shops had been the same as I'd had in Brecon. 'Too close to Christmas' but I knew now how to react and the shopkeepers knew a good thing when they saw it. Some became quite chatty and talked about the tourist season the

123

following year. One very flamboyant lady even going so far as to prophesy exceptional sales of the hedgehog engraving once the tourist season started, proclaiming airily 'These townies know about hedgehogs……..they see them squashed on the road.' When I reported this observation to Gordon, his reply was that perhaps that's how he should engrave them.

It didn't matter that only two of the orders were of any size for twenty and twenty-four slates. People wanted Gordon's engravings and I knew they'd want more. By the end of the following week six parcels were carefully packed and posted. The shopkeeper in Brecon phoned with another order. Within a week others were phoning. Could we let them have some more for Christmas?

Gordon worked on the engravings from eight until one every day. By the end of that time his arm was aching and he needed a break and a change of activity. The bank account was looking better and on the strength of our order book we took out a small loan. The dinner service fetched twenty-two pounds at auction, although we didn't get the cheque until February. We needed to go carefully though, for there wouldn't be any call for engravings until the shops began to stock up for Easter when the tourist season began. Before then of course, we'd have been on the road calling on new shops. We'd travel west. Pembrokeshire beckoned and that was a very pleasant thought to carry us through the inhospitable weeks to come.

What was it Gordon had said? 'The answer is in finding a different market, producing something of quality, that is inexpensive, and that people would like for themselves as well as buying for presents.' He'd found it, and snug on our hillside we celebrated Christmas in high spirits.

KID'S STUFF

Five months had passed since our horrendous visit with Bluebell to the Billy. It was now the end of May and she was on the point of kidding. Snowdrop also was in kid and due a week after her sister. They were both in excellent health and benefiting from the multitude of herbs in our meadow, although they were both rather weary and spent a great deal of their time lying down. Snowdrop particularly seemed to be carrying an enormous burden, and would by way of a change sit on her rear end, looking rather like a wobbly man as the greatness of her tummy swelled out around her. A goat lies down by settling on its forelegs, then lowering its hind legs, getting up in the reverse order and to see one sitting on its haunches was very novel. So while Snowdrop and Bluebell were contemplating imminent maternity and wondering why they couldn't reach up to their favourite branches, I too was preoccupied.

Malo, our elderly tortoiseshell cat had been spayed at an early age. Bouncer our blue-merle sheltie had produced one litter, while Grot, Claude and Tigger, Louise's newly acquired ginger kitten, and Dylan, Jessica's cross-bred Labrador being male and neutered had never been in the line-up for motherhood.

With such limited experience my knowledge was almost nil, and while I knew that animals generally just got on with the job of giving birth knowing instinctively what to do, I was very much aware that things could and did go wrong. By this time I had acquired a good all-round book on goat keeping, McKenzie's Goat Husbandry, and I poured over this daily, studying the diagrams illustrating how a kid should be lying as it began its journey to the outside world and those showing how it could be lying with a foreleg bent back, a head twisted sideways and several more unorthodox presentations.

I read over and over again what I would have to do if faced with anything other than the norm, hoping that only the norm would happen. Could I trust myself to remember what I should do if my intervention was needed? Would I remember where I'd put the book? Clearly, panic had set in.

Don't be so stupid, I remonstrated with myself, Of course you'll know where you've put the book. You look at the thing every day......of course you'll know where you'll have put it. Anyway, you'll manage perfectly well if you need to. Just stop getting in a spin about it and if you really find yourself in difficulty all you have to do is phone the vet.

That was it! At last I'd had a sensible thought. How silly I'd been. All this worrying when all I had to do was dial a number and help would materialize. The diagrams I'd been studying didn't seem quite so scary now that I knew I'd not be alone during this drama. Then just as suddenly panic returned. Spring is a particularly busy time for vets. Maybe by the time I knew about any difficulties of Bluebell's labour the various members of our veterinary practice would be scattered all over Breconshire......Unreachable.

For a moment I froze, then grabbed my book, feverishly scrambling through it until I arrived at the 'kidding' chapter. But Mr McKenzie was a man of vision and ahead of me. *The veterinary surgeon is not always readily available at short notice but a middle aged shepherd of good repute is unlikely to refuse assistance.*

That was it! My neighbours, even though I suspected them of regarding our goats with some suspicion would not refuse help. They whose living depended on their livestock producing healthy offspring would come to my aid. So if the vet was not available I'd call on one of my neighbours. I left the book open upside down on the table. Some vegetables were awaiting my attention so I began preparing our evening meal and was just about to slice a second carrot when my mind began to whirl again.

Supposing these hypothetically ill-positioned kids arrived on market day. That would be terrible. I pictured myself scanning the faces ranged along the metal rails in the market for the familiar features of one of my neighbouring middle aged shepherds of good repute, and wondered if I'd have the nerve to venture into this masculine stronghold with my pleas for help, or searching the numerous pubs to prize one away from his pint. This had even less appeal than the market and I dropped the knife I was holding and stared helplessly into the sink.

With the vet and my neighbours inaccessible one fact stared me in the face. It could be that I would have no option other than to deal with the problem myself, and by this time I'd convinced myself that there would be a problem so I began to appraise the situation again.

You've got Mr McKenzie's book and hopefully enough common sense. Of course you'll manage. People everywhere are facing hurdles like this constantly. You're becoming paranoid. Nothing untoward is going to happen. Just shut up and get on with the vegetables stupid!

I picked up a potato and absently began to peel it. Scenes of great drama flooded my mind and I saw myself scrubbing up, bathed in Dettol, reassuring my goat that help was at hand, observing her gratifying reaction of calmness at my encouraging and confident voice. Gently I eased the tiny leg forward so that it lay alongside the other one under its head and Bluebell gave another push, which this time was rewarded by the movement of the kid within her. All was going well and my lovely goat was able to manage without further help. I saw myself looking at her fondly, wondering if she associated my calm intervention with the cessation of her distress. Yes, I decided, she's thinking, let the vets gallivant around Wales and the neighbours live it up at the market......I've got Mother, and I smiled at her.... Move over Dr Kildare, you ain't seen nothing yet, and I plunged my hands into the nearby bucket of soapy water to find that it had turned into a bowl of potato peelings.

The following morning Bluebell stood outside the goat house door and refused to go into the meadow with Snowdrop. She appeared a little bewildered but seemed content to stand in the yard looking about her and calling loudly whenever I appeared. By midday she was getting restless, going into the goat house, wandering round her stall, then coming out to stand and bleat before repeating the exercise

I was making beer when I heard it. A loud bellow followed by another, then another.

I hurried outside. Halfway across the cobbles I pulled myself up to walk quickly and quietly the remaining few feet. Inside the goathouse I peered into her stall. In the straw lay a little kid, a panting mass of wetness with Bluebell standing a foot or so away looking at it.`

'Oh, Bluebell' I cried 'You are clever.'

I waited for her to make the next move. She didn't, but instead looked at me as though I should do something.

I stood there for a minute or so but still she didn't move. I took a towel from a shelf and quickly wiped the mucus from the kid's eyes, mouth and nostrils, then, with some sacking, rubbed the thick slime from its body, finishing off with the towel. I put the little thing which

I'd by now identified as male down beside its mother, who looked at it and moved away. The kid tried to rise and flopped down again but after a few attempts was on its feet, veering in all directions before balance came to its aid. Bluebell watched without any sign of interest so I went out, thinking that if left to her own devices the idea of motherhood would kick in.

Ten minutes later the bellowing came again. I made for the goat house and entered the stall. Another kid lay in the straw, and Bluebell who had already positioned herself well away from it, was looking at this newcomer with as much enthusiasm as she had at her firstborn. I fetched another towel and another sack. Clearing it up as before I saw that this kid was female and considerably smaller that its brother, who was now tottering about looking for its mother and the milk bar. As before I placed the newborn kid beside Bluebell and again she backed away from it. Soon this one was on its feet and now both were calling for her, wanting their first feed of the thick creamy colostrum without which they would not easily survive, but she continued to ignore them moving away at their approach.

I couldn't believe what I was witnessing. I'd spent no more than a few minutes in the goathouse and couldn't see that my presence could have upset her. I had cleaned both kids quickly and quietly because she hadn't been inclined to do the job herself, yet even with this menial task done for her she appeared to want nothing to do with them. I was beginning to have grave doubts about Bluebell's mothering ability, yet still believed that in a short time she'd see where her vocation lay and do the right thing. I went back to the kitchen and opened my goat book. It didn't mention anything about non-maternal goats.

I returned, hoping that things might have improved, wondering if I should make a box of hay bales to put the kids in, reasoning that if she was able to look at them for a while without them bothering her she would get used to the idea that they were here to stay, but as soon as I entered the goat house I realised something was wrong. The male kid was lying in the straw, its head at a slightly odd angle. I picked up the limp body. It was obvious it was dying. The damp fur on its neck had a flattened appearance, and it didn't require much deduction to work out that a hefty mother had trodden on it, probably whilst trying to flee the attentions of the interlopers. I laid it in some soft hay and covered

128

it up to keep it warm in its last moments then went back to the stall to rescue the surviving kid from its incompetent parent. It would, I reckoned, be better off with a foster mother......me.

As I was about to open the stall gate doubts crept into my mind. Was this really the right thing to do? Wouldn't it be better to leave the kid with her for a while before making a decision? But if so for how long? Ten minutes? Half an hour?

If I removed the kid I'd be denying Bluebell the chance to succour her should her natural instincts come into play, although looking over the wall to where the little thing was wandering round bleating pitifully as she tried in vain to make contact with her mother, I thought I was being very optimistic.

I phoned Frances. She would know but there was no reply.

'Gordon' I called 'I have a decision to make but I can't make up my mind. I'll put the kettle on for some tea but I'm just going back to the goat house. Be back in a minute.'

A quick look confirmed the situation as unaltered yet still I dithered.

When I returned to the house Gordon had put two steaming mugs on the table and I told him about the dead kid and how Bluebell wouldn't let the remaining kid feed.

'If I leave it' I explained 'she may inadvertently hurt it. If I remove it ....'

'I don't think you should leave it' interrupted Gordon, cutting through the red tape in my indecisive mind. Maybe she's not going to feed it. Have you any idea how long you'd have to wait to find out about that?' I shook my head. 'If you leave it, it could get damaged, if it's hand-reared it'll be O.K. I'd settle for the latter.' I decided to compromise. 'I'll leave it for ten minutes. If nothing's changed I'll bring her in.'

I didn't really expect to find any change when ten minutes later I entered the goat house, except that it was clear the little kid was extremely anxious and hungry, so without further ado I scooped her up in my arms, gave Bluebell a withering look and......was it pure imagination that in those great amber eyes I saw an expression of relief? Could she really be thinking, you wanted it....you have it?

I put the kid in a hay-lined box near the Rayburn where it remained until I could attend to its needs which were still in its mother's udders.

I made a warm bran mash for my undeserving goat, collected a Pyrex jug from the cupboard in which to milk some colostrum, marched out again and on reaching her stall was confronted by the sight of Bluebell munching her way through the thick membranous afterbirth. I swallowed hard, flung down the bran bucket, clamped my hand to my mouth in an effort to hold back my stomach that had risen to my throat and raced out to the yard.

I'd heard about this. Some goat owners remove the afterbirth, burying it deep in their gardens away from marauding dogs and foxes. Some leave the goat to devour it as nature dictates. I'd opted for the latter as many people swore that this prevented constipation and ensured the righting of the system after parturition. I'd once met a gynaecologist who used to take the human variety home to dig into her strawberry bed, assuring me she that it really did produce the most wonderful fruit. Having foster-motherhood thrust upon me with such unexpected suddenness had quite driven the afterbirth thing from my mind and I stood in the yard trying to compose myself hoping that the intervening hours between now and dinner would erase the unlovely vision. I decided to give lunch a miss.

After counting to ten, composure returned to something like normal and I re-joined Bluebell but kept my eyes averted from the head end of the still gorging animal. I could avert my eyes but couldn't do anything about the crunching sound that went on rhythmically as a seemingly never-ending length of afterbirth slowly found its way to the first of her three stomachs. By clenching my mouth tightly shut I somehow managed to retain my breakfast and as soon as I'd got enough colostrum I grabbed the jug and ran out of the goathouse. I poured the colostrum into a baby's bottle, fixed on a teat and knelt down offering it to the bleating kid. For a few seconds the little thing struggled with the soft teat, seeming not to know what to do but soon found the rich liquid to be worth the taking. Back in her box, sated with that first meal and sleeping soundly as only the young of any species sleep, she was a picture. How beautiful a young goat is I thought, with her snow-white hair, tiny pink nose, prissy mouth, neat ears and dainty feet which belied the rock-hard little hooves. Dogs and cats examined the newcomer at various times during the course of the afternoon but found it of little interest.

130

After few days we exchanged her small box for a slightly larger one, which, after another couple of days was discarded for a larger one still. The girls adored her and after much discussion settled on the name Blossom, which was very apt, for blossom she most certainly did, growing bigger by the day.

It didn't take her long to associate the first sounds of movement from upstairs with the arrival of her breakfast shortly afterwards, although the intervening time while we scurried round attending to our dressing and ablutions, was accompanied by her strident demanding voice. By the time she was five weeks old she was house-trained and bleating at the door when nature called. Who said goats were stupid?

Of course she still slept a great deal, growing all the while so her boxes grew bigger, and I wondered if we might end up with something the size of a packing case in the kitchen. However, I was never going to find out, not because Blossom stopped growing, but because she had ideas about her sleeping arrangements, which in no way included anything as lowly as a cardboard box.

Dylan and Bouncer slept on an old sofa. It was small as sofas go, but there was adequate room for them to lie stretched out if they wished. They had their own pillows as well so all in all it was quite a dog heaven.

One night after we'd gone to bed a scuffle broke out downstairs, punctuated by grunts and snarls. What on earth was going on? I pulled the blankets over my head but the noises continued, taking on a nasty tone and reluctantly I got up to investigate. I found Blossom on the settee, pawing at Dylan's hind-quarters and the fact that I'd arrived on the scene disturbed her not one jot. She didn't even look up. The poor dog was cowering into his pillow, determined even in the face of such persistence not to give up his rightful place but Blossom was equally determined that he should. Bouncer was sitting bolt upright at her end of the bed, obviously not happy but probably glad not to be a part of the onslaught.

'You naughty girl'. On hearing my words Dylan sat up and Blossom leapt nimbly into the vacant space on his pillow and butted him smartly as he tried to regain his territory, then as he moved disconsolately to the other end of the sofa to join Bouncer, she settled down, gazing wide-eyed at the defeated pair as they circled several times in typical dog like manner searching for a comfortable spot.

131

The poor dogs lay together, buddies against a common foe, so I placated them with a biscuit each, hauled Blossom off the pillow and plonked her firmly back in her box. But it was no use; she'd tasted luxury and luxury she was going to have. In a twinkling she was up again. Realising that I was on a hiding to nowhere I collected a spare pillow and put it in the middle of the sofa, and plonked Blossom down on it. Dylan moved cautiously past her back to his spot at the other end. I patted each dog's head, shook my finger at Blossom in admonition, which was a pretty useless thing to do but the dogs understood its meaning and knew I was on their side, so hoping there would be no further disturbance I went back to bed.

Snowdrop had, of course, kidded a couple of weeks ago and was delighted with her triplets, giving them every care and attention, and on Blossom's periodic sorties into the meadow all four kids played together, racing up the bank or leaping onto a fallen tree trunk, playing a very obvious version of 'I'm the king of the castle'. Frequently one of them would break away to come over to me for a pat or a cuddle before rushing off to re-join the others, leaping and twisting in mid air, as goats love to do. They were endless fun to watch, consuming far more of my time than I should have allowed. Yet in spite of the fact that borrowed time had somehow to be recouped later in the day, watching the antics of such joyful creatures was something not to be missed, and the immense pleasure they gave far outweighed the disciplines connected with their welfare.

Strangely enough the episode of the pillow snatching became a turning point in the relationship between the dogs and Blossom. As though realising for the first time that this animal wasn't just something that wandered about making a noisy nuisance of itself, they sensed that here was another playmate. She epitomised gaiety and her exuberance was insatiable. They'd frolic about until exhaustion set in, rest for a while then begin all over again. I imagine it was with some surprise that our various postmen, who worked a six-weekly rota, came through our lower gate to find not just dogs ready to give them a barking escort to the house but also a small white goat, bleating, leaping and twisting in mid-air.

Indoors nothing was sacred. The top of the dresser became the home of the fruit bowl, pot plants, magazines, stray books or a pile of mending, and when that was choc-a-bloc, things were banished from

132

the kitchen. Dealing with food changed dramatically with Blossom standing on tiptoe, eyes fixed on whatever it was I was doing, neck and hind legs straining as she fought for a better view of the goodies being prepared and calling loudly and often for samples. Her appetite for fun and food was insatiable.

Then one day, driving up the track from the village, we noticed a few newly acquired bantams in our vegetable garden having a fine time among the sweet young crops. This was not allowed. They were out of order. They had to learn the rules.

Gordon collected the 'catcher', a net for recalcitrant poultry made from a piece of netting fixed onto a long pole, from his workshop and I raced into the house, flung my shopping basket onto the table and rushed out again, aware of the dogs and Blossom playing on the lawn as I passed. Gordon was already up amongst the rows of peas, wafting the catcher in the wake of several screaming, flying birds, which hopefully were taking note of the fact that some places were sacrosanct. After having sent them scurrying we took the opportunity to stroll leisurely among the rows of plants. It was a pleasant thing to walk along the lines of so many growing things. Sowing a seed and a few weeks later seeing something recognisable always spelled magic to me and this particular day we lingered, admiring and commenting on things doing well or not so well. I pulled a lettuce and some beetroot thinnings for our evening meal before ambling back down the field.

That's funny' I mused as we approached the yard 'I'm sure I closed the door when I came out,' and after considering a moment said 'I did close it' but as the door was open added, 'Well, I'm pretty sure I did.'

'You can't have done' replied Gordon, 'Or it wouldn't be open now. Anyway what does it matter?'

'It doesn't' I agreed, then after a pause muttered to myself 'but I know I closed it.'

By now we were in the yard and there was no sound of the usual scuffling and playful snarling which accompanied the dogs and Blossom at play which was strange, and at that moment a small white figure appeared in the open doorway of the house with a banana skin hanging from its mouth. It then disappeared inside.

133

Simultaneously we broke into a run laughing at the wickedness of the vision we'd just seen. My shopping basket lay upturned on the flagstones, its contents strewn, mangled and chewed. Tea, sugar, fresh fruit and dried, were all jumbled in an unappetising mess. We stood on the step reviewing the chaos, lost for words, and the dogs flinching slightly at our arrival but taking our laughter as permission to continue the feast, carried on enjoying the goodies. Blossom, unconcerned about our presence and not being the flinching kind didn't even look up.

'Well, we'd better get this lot cleared up.' Gordon, ever practical.

'Oh gosh' I moaned looking at our precious supplies, 'It's all my fault. I couldn't have shut the door' yet even as I spoke I could hear the latch clicking. I knew I had shut it.

I then found voice. 'Out......Out.' The dogs shot off and I prized an orange from Blossom, my hand getting covered as I did so in the mixture of tea leaves and sugar which adhered to her mouth. I pushed her unceremoniously outside, shut the door and picked up two oranges and two bananas that appeared to have escaped the onslaught. The rest of the fruit I put in a pudding basin. It would be a treat for Bluebell, Snowdrop and the horses. Nothing else was salvageable. The rest I swept up with a pan and brush and dumped it on a sheet of newspaper, which I put on one side. I'd take it out to the yard later where the hens would appreciate the sultanas, possibly the sugar and for all I knew maybe the tea as well. Gordon handed me a mug of tea and was about to say something when a familiar shrill bleat issued from the other side of the door.

'Go away,' I yelled, but another, more piercing than the first, followed.

'Push off'. I was just about to add a further expletive when after a short rattle, the iron latch shot up, the door flew open and Blossom walked in looking decidedly pleased with herself.

'What on......'

'Ye gods, we have a goat that can open doors.' How we laughed. I gave her a cuddle but she struggled free, turned to where the debris of food had been, then pottered over to the window sill where she stood elegantly on her hind legs intent on seeking out anything edible that might have been put there since she'd last looked. I reached into the pudding bowl and picked out a couple of grapes. Seeing the tit-bit in my hand she trotted over to devour it with a strange mixture of delicacy and gluttony, reaching her head out for more well before the previous one had been finished. With the last grape gone she sniffed my hand, the air, the table edge and the floor in case any bits might be lurking but her luck was out. I knelt on the hard floor and put my arms tightly round her.

'Little goaty' I whispered 'The time has come for your life style to change. You're not a dog who understands what it may or may not do. Even in an ill-run household such as ours there are limits and a goat as versatile as you is beyond that limit.' Oh dear; I felt quite emotional and pulled myself together adding sternly, 'You see, you are not to be trusted' then I took hold of her collar and led her from the house towards the meadow.

Snowdrop's kids, Lettuce and Bramble, were busy hurling themselves off the edge of a steep bank, while their mother and aunt dozed in the warm sunshine. Their play stopped as we approached, Blossom ran to join them and with a mixture of sadness and relief I closed the field gate behind me.

Now we could put the fruit bowl and plants back on the windowsill, the mending back on the trolley where I just might notice it occasionally, and return a multitude of other items to their original homes. All this led to a good deal of confusion as we'd got into the habit over the last three months of finding things in unusual places and it seemed strange to be bending down or stretching out after so long reaching up.

Blossom had no difficulty in adapting to life in the goat house but whenever we had visitors she put on a great welcoming act which invariably required some form of explanation from us, resulting in pleas for her to be allowed in to the house 'just this once.'

'Be it on your own head' we'd warn, but our visitors always thought we were exaggerating Blossom's idea of correct social behaviour. 'She can't be that bad' they'd say as they looked at the beautiful innocent-looking creature, but as sure as night follows day, the second she got through the door she'd demonstrate her lightening reversal to the domestic life......well, the domestic life as she saw it. If we weren't thinking quickly enough she'd begin to demolish the contents of the fruit bowl before setting off on a circuit of discovery.

Most of our visitors were in holiday mood and happy to take the rough with the smooth, but as our guests viewed their belongings being ransacked they realized the rough could be pretty rough indeed. Eventually she'd find a knee to settle on and all would be forgiven as the silky white kid settled down, tired after her exertions, to gaze around at her audience, her great round eyes and prim little mouth a picture of innocence and charm. It was strange just how many people enquired whether Blossom was still with us before announcing their wish to visit.

I think she made quite an impression!

A FRANK LOOK AT OUR LOT

In 1973 we bought Self-Sufficiency, a newly published book by John and Sally Seymour. Today its grubby dust jacket and well thumbed pages bear witness to its constant use as mentor and guide during our years at Tironnen, so we were not surprised when many years after its first publication a gloriously produced coffee table version appeared on the market.

Its profusely illustrated presentation must have had immediate appeal. Many of its devotees, probably having to confine their back-to-nature desires to growing a few vegetables, are never the less fascinated by the breadth of economy in which others appear fortunate enough to indulge, while those who previously thought self-sufficiency meant putting home grown mint on bought potatoes have a whole new world opened to them.

And so some of our friends, and a greater number of acquaintances, having spent the winter snug in their centrally heated houses, indulging in fantasies of the good life between the covers of this admirable tome, would feel the first stirrings of spring and rush to grasp pen and paper, or phone.

Were we free? Could we put them up for a couple of days?

The onset of more clement weather had its socializing effect on us also, so old friends were welcomed with the anticipation of a few pleasant days in their company and acquaintances told that they would be most welcome to call if they were in the area. Yet in spite of the compliments which came our way in respect of our industry we soon realised that not a few of our visitors viewed our first couple of years at Tironnen as something they could have managed far more efficiently and successfully than we did.

Oddly, it was people with whom we were not on the closest terms who challenged our methods and incentives, possibly because they were not familiar with how we had managed our lives before we decided on such a radical change. For whilst Gordon was of an orderly nature, taking one step at a time and always working things out before 'doing', I bowled along in a hit and miss way, hopefully learning from my mistakes, not becoming disheartened by failure and generally tackling too many tasks at once. So on the smallholding, with a vast

137

variety of jobs to be done......at nearly all of which I was a novice......the mismanagement of some was pretty obvious.

We were constantly bombarded with questions beginning, 'Why don't you.....?' and at first found ourselves permanently on the defensive, justifying our reasons for doing such and such the way we did. The subject in question would be changed almost immediately to another and the inevitable 'Why don't you.....?' sometimes varied to 'Don't you think it might be better to.....?' would recur again and again. These folk all seemed to have competence at their fingertips and whilst the challenges were most politely put, the implication that they could have organised themselves better and a great deal sooner than we appeared to be doing was quite clear.

It was very irritating.

Initially we would tell them about our first six months here spent making frequent round trips to the hospital in Merthyr Tydfil where our asthmatic youngest daughter had spent so much time. We would explain how, even with our own land the outgoings connected with getting to grips with our new life-style were considerable, and coupled with a very modest income there was less cash around to get on with other things. Politely the suggestion would be put across either by direct statement or innuendo, that our top priority should have been a bathroom and a lavatory. Nothing else should have been considered until such aids to gracious living were installed.

But they didn't know of the joy of the early morning chats with our sweet smelling pony mare nuzzling up to us over the gate, or the pleasure on entering the goat house of seeing our lovely goats artlessly draped over the wooden partition of their stall or the delight of watching them as they danced their way across the yard and into the meadow. Yes, it all took time, but you cannot equate that sort of thing with a plumbed-in lavatory...... impossible.

We weren't complaining just explaining, and only that because we were so frequently put in the position where we felt we had to. And our visitors would nod and say they expected we'd soon get the bathroom in, the outside walls painted, the patched up fencing replaced by something more aesthetically pleasing etc, etc, They knew in their own minds how they would have coped.

We were just not doing it the right way.

We were disorganised.

138

What we needed was a good book.

But one way and another we did cope and no one who felt able to advise us had put into practice the theories and practicalities which abounded in their heads with such certainty. It was all very odd.

Were so many of these folk really known to us at all? They remained in jobs, which they insisted were mentally unbearable, appallingly underpaid and bad for their health. Jobs which forced them to live in areas where the rates were crippling, the drinking water foul and exhaust fumes rotted their lungs. They would tell us how fortunate we were to be here. How wonderful to breathe the clean air, drink sparkling spring water and smell a dozen delicious fragrances on the breeze. And we wondered why, if their environment was so frightful and our incompetence so glaring, they didn't pack it all in and set up as an example to us. But no one talked about that, and after their visits they would go back to their living hell which they apparently made no effort to leave.

So we stopped explaining anything to anyone. There was no point. It was a wearisome and boring occupation, so people could think what they liked about our attempts at being self-sufficient, and anyway, that is a label which had been pinned onto us. We did our best and if our life-style meant suburbia could dine out on how we lived then at least we'd achieved something.

The irritations we suffered at the hands of the theoretically successful all seemed to be bound up and magnified in Frank, who arrived at Tironnen by chance one lovely summer day in 1975. He was accompanied by his wife Enid, a thin mouse-like woman who appeared to bow to her husband's superior knowledge in all things by remaining totally mute during the whole encounter.

We first met Frank and Enid when, having parked their car for a picnic on the common a couple of miles away they decided to walk up to the hill above. After strolling some fair distance they descended across the fields behind Tironnen, and as I was in the yard at the time on impulse I invited them in for a cup of tea before they returned to the common. They seemed to enjoy their respite, Frank doubling up with mirth at almost everything he said and Enid smiling politely when we told a couple of stories about the animals, which we thought quite funny but which Frank pointedly ignored.

Settling himself comfortably as though for an indeterminate stay, we heard that they were on a touring holiday and loving every minute of it. We listened to a detailed account of each day they'd travelled, culminating with their arrival on our doorstep on the sixth day, which brought the saga up to date and ended that particular tale. But Frank was a man who lived in a world where the most stimulating sound was that of his own voice relating the daily activities of Frank. Totally oblivious to the relatively unusual surroundings in which he now found himself, he regaled us with a blow by blow account of his fascinating job as manager of a branch of a large chain of supermarkets, the activities of the local tennis club of which he was number one seed, the amateur theatre group which without his invigorating presence and multiple talents would long ago have ground itself into oblivion, the local Conservative association of which he was quite the most active member and recipient of his frequent benevolence, and a general rendition of the life of a solid citizen of the suburban north as led between the hours of rising and retiring. His wife, who I imagine must have heard this monologue many times, hung on every word.

Frank and his doings were amazing......to Frank. Clearly he saw us as a captive audience and seemed slightly surprised when after twenty minutes Gordon announced that he had work to do and would they excuse him. Pouncing on this disruption I leapt to my feet saying that I too must get on and ushered our loquacious visitor and his doting wife towards the door, the forecourt gate, the yard gate, down the track......as far away as possible.

'What on earth did I invite them in for?' I shouted as I returned to the house. Gordon was sitting at the drawing board fighting for inspiration that was evidently slow in coming and gave me a rueful look.

'Have a drink.' I poured a glass of elderflower wine 'At least we'll never see them again.'

But I was wrong.

Three years after their first visit, Frank and Enid once more came to Tironnen. Unannounced they appeared while I was potting up cabbage seedlings on my bench in the yard and I had no difficulty recalling at once who our visitors were.

Frank emerged from his car, flung out his elbows and stretched luxuriantly in what I thought to be an irritatingly proprietorial way, while surveying the view. I put down the pot I'd just filled with compost and hoping that what I was thinking wasn't too obvious walked across to greet them. We exchanged pleasantries and I deliberately kept them lingering beside the pond while I muttered banalities, wishing without much conviction that they might remember some important engagement and curtail their visit. I hoped in vain of course, and I don't know how it happened but I heard myself offering them refreshment! This was accepted as though it was expected and I ushered them towards the house and into the kitchen. But I was determined not to be alone in this unwelcome situation and called to Gordon in a voice designed to give entirely the wrong impression, 'Come and see who's here.'

Reaching the kitchen he stopped in his tracks, his natural expression of greeting swiftly changing to horror and then to one of forced pleasure. A soft voice said 'We were so hoping we'd find you in,' and as though startled at having said so much, Enid quickly put a hand up to her mouth as if to make sure no more sounds emerged and lapsed back into silence.

I stared, barely able to give credit for such boldness. Gordon smiled at her and Frank looked at her in a kindly way but with overtones of dismissal. Enough of trivia his expression said, there are important things I wish to discuss.

Fool that I was I made coffee.

Frank took a mug, regarding it with deep concentration for several seconds while Enid helped herself to milk. Gordon took some sugar and when the stirring was done and Frank was sure of our uninterrupted attention he made his announcement.

'We are self-sufficient.'

This was followed by a pause while he looked at us in turn giving us time to digest this piece of information. 'Self-sufficiency you know.'

Another pause, then, 'You do a bit of that don't you.' It was a statement rather than a question.

'A bit.' I remembered the tales of the competent store manager, the number one tennis seed, the impresario par excellence and the supremo of the Conservative club.

141

'I've bought a book on it, on self-sufficiency. Not that I'm going to try half the things in it but it's a grand book and I've followed it all, adding a few ideas of my own here and there you understand and things are coming on just lovely aren't they Enid?'

Enid smiled. 'Frank's very clever' and again clapped a hand over her mouth.

'All winter I've had my nose in that book. Filled with illustrations it is. I know it off by heart, every word and picture I don't mind telling you.'

He sank back into the cushions, silent for once while he gazed into space, the rosy glow of success enveloping his whole being. Then he cleared his throat importantly.

'So this spring I got down to it, putting all this knowledge into practice you know, then I had this notion to see how you people who set yourselves up do with your growing, so I said to Enid, let's go away for a few days and we can call on those people who were trying to grow all their own stuff and see how they're doing. And here we are.'

'And here we are' echoed Enid in a near inaudible voice, followed by a slightly lop-sided smile and nervous giggle.

'So,' said Frank, crashing his fist down on the arm of the chair, and heaving himself up he moved to the centre of the room to strike an authoritative pose. 'Let's see what you're about.'

We were lost for words but after a few seconds Gordon recovered himself. 'I've got to get on......' but I nudged his arm and whispered 'I can't manage this on my own.'

'Come now. You're the experts aren't you? You want to show us townies what it's all about don't you?'

Of course we should have said 'no', but a much quoted family phrase subconsciously raised it's head, for 'it's not a problem, it's life' can turn most things into a challenge, so did we view this ghastly man as a challenge? Someone to do battle with?

His request was made without jest. He'd seen it all profusely illustrated in 'the book' and indeed faithfully portrayed by his efforts in his own patch, and it was no doubt with great faith in our ability that he set out from the house towards the vegetable garden anticipating a replica of the pictures imprinted so vividly on his memory.

142

The first thing they saw as we processed through the yard was our muck-heap, of considerable size in spring and summer as we only borrow our neighbours tractor in October to cart the stuff up to the meadow. Our muckheap was not the right shape. We knew it was not the right shape. Angela frequently forked and prodded the thing into a glorious steaming rectangle and I'd have liked to keep it that way but apart from not being dedicated enough, when twenty or so chickens use it as a larder, its outer regions would become not so much a heap as a carpet over which we had no control. We learned to live with it without too much heart-searching, and on a smallholding where something always needs to be done, making a dung–heap look respectable was not a priority.

'Getting a bit out of hand isn't it?' Frank's jocular remark with its underlying reprimand was received in stony silence and Gordon and I continued up the yard to wait under the ash tree until he'd finished staring at the hens and the muck.

'You won't get any heat in it like that. What you've got to do is fork it up into a good heap. Goodness, you've got enough there. Wonderful, wonderful but it's not doing any good the way you've got it spread all around like that. If I had the time I'd show you how it's done. It's all there in the book you know. I use all our garden refuse and kitchen waste and because I keep it all of a shape it has a lot of heat in it, a lot of heat. I manage mine very well but it's obviously a bit of a problem for you.' I caught hold of Gordon's arm and whispered in his ear, 'Wait till we get to the veggies' and Gordon rolled his eyes heavenwards.

Instead of viewing something like two hundred plants of cabbages, sprouts, calabrese and kale with awe, I imagined Frank reflecting on the diminutive rows of brassicas growing as specified in his garden at home.

'Some didn't do so well then?'

There was no point in saying that the burning sensation in my back caused by long hours of bending is not just a memory, and that sometimes the piffling little job of replacing a few seedlings may well get done, but if it doesn't we do not consider our life here a failure.

Frank had moved along to where beans and peas were growing vigorously, studying the rows of peas with an expert eye and judging by the prolonged silence couldn't detect anything amiss. Then he

143

moved onto the French beans. He looked long and hard, then bending down he placed a bean across the palm of his hand and observed, 'These are much smaller than mine,' and straightening up, smacking his lips in satisfaction added 'I've been picking mine for some time but it doesn't look like you'll be getting many from this lot.'

My thin smile which I suspect was more of a grimace was probably translated as embarrassment but I wasn't going to tell him that most of our fantastic crop was in the freezer.

Our potatoes we were told were way behind Frank's. Were we planting the right sort? It was, we were told, very important to plant the right sort. Did we dung well enough? He impressed upon us the necessity of lots of dung. Of course, with a dung-heap like ours there was no telling if it was doing any good anyway...... We were reprimanded for not thinning our carrots far enough apart and for spacing our onions too close together, although for years we had cropped both with success, and uncontrollable guffaws greeted a bed of beetroot which for some reason was not doing too well.

By this time we'd had enough. Why on earth should we be polite to this appalling man who had inflicted himself upon us and done nothing but criticise? Why should we tell him that with so many calls upon our time it was only through sheer will power that any weeding was done at all? Ye gods, our plot was almost the size of a tennis court, his probably that of a pocket-handkerchief.

Stifling my anger I ushered them towards the gate and just as he was about to pass through it Frank suddenly stopped. 'I didn't notice an asparagus bed.'

'You wouldn't' replied Gordon coldly, 'We don't have one.'

'You've not got an asparagus bed?' The words were enunciated with disbelieving precision. 'Do you hear that Enid? They've not got an asparagus bed!'

Within seconds however, he had recovered from the shock and one-upmanship came into play yet again.

'A lot of people are very frightened of growing asparagus and I suppose it does take a bit of expertise but if they followed the instructions in my book they'd soon get the idea. It's such a lovely vegetable and I'm surprised you're not growing any.' Then, encompassing the vegetable garden with a final heartbroken look and evidently having second thoughts about his last oration sighed, 'But it

144

looks as though you've got problems enough without involving yourselves with anything else.'

We walked back down the yard, Frank deep in thought, Enid her usual invisible self. The difference between the vegetable plot at 'Chez Nous' or whatever it was, some small degree above sea level, feeding two people during the growing season and that at Tironnen, nearly a thousand feet above sea level, feeding five people for twelve months of the year plus numerous visitors plus extra roots and greens for animals, did not permeate the hard crust of Frank's mind, and it was quite clear that he was in no doubt regarding our failure.

We were a disappointment.

We did not measure up.

Gordon and I went back into the house, but Frank, followed by the admiring Enid, wandered up to the patch where the soft fruit bushes grew. I watched through the window as he examined at length the leaves and budding fruits of blackcurrants, redcurrants and gooseberries, then coming face to face with some blueberry bushes, and presumably not having studied 'the book' thoroughly enough to know a blueberry bush when he met one, turned quickly and sauntered down the path. The herb garden also was passed by without comment and it struck me that of the fifteen herbs planted there Frank would not wish his knowledge to be confined to the mint and parsley.

Against a wall, inviting to a pair of willing hands leaned an array of tools, the usual ones quite ancient, having been bought at auctions and far superior in our eyes to anything new, and a superb collection of custom-made ones for specific tasks. Custom-made by Gordon of course, but after a disinterested glance at these strange looking objects Frank passed them by and joined us in the big kitchen where he adopted an authoritative pose by the hearth.

He was however, still silent. Enid never said a word other than in admiration of her spouse and as Gordon declined to make conversation I grasped at this unexpected respite to gather my thoughts. Frank must be removed as soon as possible. Any minute now he would make observations on our goat keeping, quoting of course, from 'the book'. He would ridicule our unprofessional dairy equipment, tell us how to get more eggs from our hens and scorn us for not putting Bessie in front of a plough. The idea of asking him for a demonstration of this was not unattractive. One sure way to get rid of him was to produce a harness, put Bessie at one end and Frank at the other and watch his substantial figure rapidly diminishing as the ensemble fled west towards the coast.

'We have to get on with our work now.'

Frank remained silent, his brow furrowed in concentration.

Was this hint not enough? How much more blunt can I be, I wondered. Was I really going to have to say 'Go', and propel him through the door? Maybe it was the expression on my face that jogged him into life, but whatever it was Frank evidently decided that he was in a now or never situation and that the bull must be taken by the horns. After a slow intake of breath, which was expelled in a long and noisy 'Aaaaaaah' sound, he pronounced on his findings, speaking in a voice that was heavy with kindness and concern.

'Now, I think you ought to know about this book I've got.' His words were emphasised by several firm taps with the palm of his hand on the table. 'This book on self-sufficiency I was telling you about. You see, it's got everything in it that people doing what you're trying to do should know. Vegetables, fruit, animals, beer-making, just everything, and'......he paused in order to emphasise the importance of what was to follow......'every page is illustrated.' The last four words were slowly and patiently delivered implying that with pictures to guide us even idiots such as we could just about digest it. He droned on. I became aware of the sound of hammering and noticed that Gordon was no longer with us. I felt myself getting hot under the collar again while Enid gazed in wonder at this son of the soil who was hers, all hers.

'You should......' was varied only by 'It'll only take you a few minutes a day' and of course, the compulsive 'Why don't you......?'

'Now you make a note of this book,' his speech was gaining speed in the excitement of the moment, 'What's that man's name Enid? What's the man's name?'

Enid smiled, oblivious to the rising temperature about her and was about to reply but was not quick enough to keep up with Frank's enthusiasm. 'John' he burst out 'er, 'er......John, John Seymour, that's it......Seymour, John Seymour. Now, your local bookshop is bound to have it and I've no doubt at all you'll improve no end once you've read and digested it......thoroughly.'

146

I held his gaze for a few moments, reflecting on the irony of the fact that our well-thumbed first edition of the subject in question (minus illustrations) lay on a shelf barely three feet from where he stood, then I snapped.

'I don't give a damn about your bloody book.'

There was a stunned silence then Frank leapt to the defence of the absent author.

'Hold on now, hold on. That's not a very nice thing to say. I'm only trying to be helpful.'

But I'd had enough.

I felt great about the fierceness of my response and I stood unsmiling and severe-looking, waiting for his next move.

It was rather a surprise when it came for he apparently decided to make the best of this feminine outburst. In mock admonition he nodded his head slowly in my direction and chided, 'I've suspected all along that you've got a hasty temperament and it's reflected in the way you go about things,' and with the sound of my recent expletive still offending his sense of justice changed his tone to one of hurt reproach adding, 'That man went to a lot of trouble to pass his expertise on to people like us.'

.

A MIDSUMMER NIGHT'S DREAM

Scattered about in the middle of the seemingly never ending wetness that was the summer of 1974 were a few lovely days, warm with blue skies and buzzing business. The sort of days to lean on a gate and gaze, letting the senses grow drowsy, the vision blur and sounds drift a million miles away until the happy idea floats into one's head that if this moment could go on for ever all would be well with the world.

It was in the evening of just such a day when the gnats were proclaiming the dawn would break with as much welcome brightness, that we set off to attend a barbeque at the home of a recent acquaintance.

We had guessed from our scant knowledge of Arnold that his retreat would be snuggled away somewhere far from the beaten track and how right we were. Turning off the road into a narrow lane we drove gradually upwards with much twisting and turning until suddenly it ended. The lane to Tironnen turns into a track someway before it reaches the house but this one just ended with fields all round and no indication of anything except a farm gate opening onto a field.

So we left the Land Rover with several other cars abandoned by those who had arrived before us and tramped across the field. After about five hundred yards we came to an avenue of trees bordering what would normally have been a rough track but was now turned into a veritable mud bath by the constant rain of the previous few days. On one side the trees extended to form a small wood which looked as saturated as the path and standing under the trees was a little girl of about eight years clad in a long sleeved tunic belted at the waist, and a gay print skirt that reached down to cover the top of a pair of wellington boots. Long dark hair floated round her shoulders and she looked as though she'd stepped out of a Thomas Hardy novel.

'Are we at Tir-y-Dial?' we asked.

The child scrutinized us for a few seconds saying nothing, then indicated a crudely written notice attached to a long pole which was set in a cairn of stones and half hidden by bushes and overhanging branches.

'Yes,' she said, 'This is Tir-y-dial.'

The notice to which she had drawn our attention bore the words 'TO THE BARBEQUE' painted in black on a piece of hardboard shaped to a point at one end but as the pointed end faced the direction from where we'd just come we were really no wiser so we just kept going.

Fifty yards further on another notice was pinned to a tree. This announced 'MUD BY-PASS', but as there didn't appear to be an alternative to the uninviting stretch of sludge before us we sloshed and sidestepped our way through, each seeking for a tiny island of dryness on which to balance before plunging once again into the mire.

After about forty yards we emerged at the far end to meet our host who expressed amazement at our choice of route greeting us with 'Oh, you've come through the mud. That was the wrong way. I put the notice there so everyone would go round the other side of the trees. Still you're here, that's fine.' Whereupon off he strode, leaving us to introduce ourselves to his other guests and I felt rather foolish having misunderstood what must have been crystal clear to everyone else until I noticed that all and sundry were wearing mud encrusted shoes with a liberal smattering of brown mud on trousers or legs.

Now that we had made our entrance, albeit a rather messy one, I looked about me. The scene we had come upon was one of sheer delight. A tiny stone cottage, its stones set firmly into the hillside, was surrounded by towering trees closing round it as though shielding it from intruders, leaving only a small lawn in front where a footpath led to the door. Dusk was already upon us and through the windows a blazing fire tossed magical patterns at the trees outside and lit up the little house as though it was part of a unique firework display. The smallness of the cottage and its patch of grass gave me a more than usual sense of intimacy, particularly as the protecting woods prevented any glimpse of the southern hills or of anything at all beyond the confines of the garden. The effect was of a haven of enchanted whimsy, tranquilly harbouring the whispered secrets of generations long since gone.

In this picturesque setting lived Arnold, a melancholy and reticent man, who somehow managed to fold his six foot six inches into the little house whenever the frequent need to retire from the tortuous city world overtook him. We first encountered him when he loped down the hill behind Tironnen to find out who were its new occupants. He had introduced himself in a vague sort of way and gave us an elusive sketch of his life, talking to my left ear, whilst nervously wrapping one never-ending leg round the other. Gordon was equally intrigued by this strange habit. He had re-appeared twice more, climbing over every gate when each would have opened in the conventional manner, and had departed after his visits a good deal wiser about the Greens and their doings than we were about him and his. We got the idea that he was something in publishing. Maybe it was something he said but we never enquired which was rather odd. We enjoyed his company, that was enough.

On his fourth visit however Arnold arrived in some degree of style, chuntering up the track in an old Riley, the green of which had faded in parts to a greyish turquoise, but my study of his car ended abruptly when I realized he was not alone. Arnold had a passenger, and his companion was a very beautiful and elegant woman.

'This' he said 'is Rachael'.

Now stylishness is spread fairly thin in these parts and if I ever possessed any it certainly was lost during the time of our removal from the city, in fact my only serious fling into the realms of fashion during the past years was when shopping for a second pair of wellies I'd opted for green rather than black. So when Rachael appeared, her tall slender figure encased in a cream cashmere sweater atop an Irish tweed skirt in muted tones of heather and beige, beige suede boots encasing her elegant legs, her face superbly made up and pale blonde hair swept into an elegant French pleat, I was quite overawed..

Thank goodness I was wearing my best green wellies.

I put bread and cheese on a tray, poured some home brew into glasses and took it up to the ash tree where Rachael, Arnold and Gordon had ensconced themselves. It transpired that Rachael was having a few days away from the hurly-burly of city life but was happy to chat about what she did with herself and it all sounded very sophisticated and exciting and a thousand miles away from our neo-peasant existence.

Her life appeared to consist of visits to theatres, concerts, invitations to the latest exhibitions, dining in the most fashionable restaurants where she could observe the great and the good. For all I knew she might have been one of them. It seemed her days were one long cultural adventure and her life-blood. For a few minutes I was quite envious then I thought, we're not so impoverished. In the last few months we'd attended Jessica's school play. A couple of jolly

150

good exhibitions in Brecon library had been well worth a visit, and a trip to the village fish and chip-shop where mine host, known to us as Callmebertie presided over the best eaterie of its kind in Wales, meant we were not outdone in the cultural stakes. And a fleeting glimpse of the Bishop of Llandaff on his way to attend a service at Brecon Cathedral could surely count as observing the great and the good.

So passed a most enjoyable hour, and Rachael's company obviously had a socializing effect on Arnold for he proposed the idea of a barbeque three weeks hence. A few days later a card arriving duly inviting us to 'vino, cider and beer, sausages and anything else we can get in the fields and waters of Tir-y-Dial.' This sounded delightfully rustic, conjuring up visions of a warm balmy evening, agreeable talk and the tantalizing aroma of bacon and sausages sizzling over the charcoal. I was so looking forward to it. So three weeks later, on that glorious summer evening I grabbed a bag of sausages from the fridge and a couple of bottles of blackberry wine and off we set duly arriving at Arnold's retreat via the mud path.

A dozen or so people were there, but apart from a couple of neighbours we recognized no-one. Most of these people looked more like bank managers and their wives, well dressed and respectable and apart from their muddy shoes strangely out of keeping with the whole scene and I wondered where they all came from.

Arnold appeared and announced that Rachael had gone out to dinner with friends which seemed rather odd as she had obviously put some input into this venture, but without further explanation he continued 'Now, with what can I tempt you. Cider, wine or beer?' We made our requests known and he moved towards another group, then disappeared round the back of the cottage. Chatting with others in the deepening shadows was a pleasant way of passing the time but there was no sign of any drinks, and I didn't know whether Gordon or the girls were more fortunate in the refreshment stakes. Perhaps they'd also gone round to the back but as I was now in conversation with a couple who told me they had a holiday cottage close by I was happy to stay and hear whatever they wanted to talk about. The bewitching place was relaxing enough, even so, a drink would have been welcome. My throat was really dry and I suspect I wasn't the only one wondering where our host and the promised liquor had got to, for as the evening wore on and I wandered about chatting with all and sundry, I was aware that we did after all have something in common with several of those present for whilst I observed two people with a glass in their hands (actually a plastic throwaway) everyone else was empty-handed.

Having stood for well over an hour battling with thirst, it was evident that one had to fight for survival and I was determined that the eating would not be as elusive as the drinking. But even as I made my resolve I was rather puzzled, for there was no sign of anything even remotely connected with the usual equipment required to produce barbequed food, and conversation flagged and became somewhat stilted as the evening finally passed into chilly night.

Then suddenly things began to happen. Mine host emerged from within and suggested to a group by the door that they might like to partake of refreshment. Like dying men clutching at straws they eagerly offered help with any preparations but all suggestions were brushed aside. Anyhow I thought, things were under way. I could see the company perking up and whispering things like 'Not long now,' and smiling and nodding to each other. Not long now I told my stomach which was protesting that it hadn't had anything sent down since lunchtime.

Several minutes passed then Arnold reappeared holding an enormous black iron frying pan, which contained some, mismanaged looking lava bread which is a sort of scone made from seaweed, very popular in parts of Wales.

This he broke into several portions by stabbing at it with a fork, then wrapping each piece in a square of kitchen paper handed them to the folk in the immediate vicinity. Having assuaged the hunger of those by the door he retreated into the cottage reappearing almost immediately minus the frying pan.

It seemed that not only had I lost out on the liquid, the barbeque had eluded me too.

Whilst these Alice in Wonderland scenes were being enacted outside, the little girl in the print skirt and wellingtons had taken herself into the tiny living room and was playing a recorder. The glow of the fire and candlelight, the sweet sound on the night air, the dancing shadows, and the smells of all the growing things enhanced as a light dew settled on this unreal world caught at my heart, and I felt

152

as when a child I was enthralled by the magic of the pantomime, being part of it yet outside it.

Time passed and still we lingered, the empty feeling in my stomach kept at bay by the pleasant chatter and constant delight at the enchantment of the place, and occasionally Arnold would put in an appearance and have a few words with some of his guests before vanishing again. Presumably he was quite satisfied at having carried out his duties of host in a competent manner and waved farewell to his guests as they began to drift away. We, however were more privileged as he whispered to us that he would like us to visit him again when the more conventional of his friends would not be around, and to make the invitation more enticing added that the invitation would be for dinner.

We were mouthing our enthusiasm for this experience to come, when Rachael arrived, emerging from the wood in a dazzling white trouser suit, the embodiment of grace and polish. It was a sickening sight to one who somehow manages to get messy sewing on a button.

Arnold welcomed her. 'Have you had a good time?'

'Wonderful' replied the vision. 'The food was glorious. Oh, the syllabub was out of this world. The wine was a bit disappointing though. With every sip I tried to imagine it was your glorious elderflower champagne. I've been too spoilt,' and turning to the few remaining guests enthused, 'It really does something to you doesn't it. Still, as I said the food was first class so I didn't lose out altogether.' Somebody muttered something inaudible and I fancy I caught a faint 'lucky you' from behind me. Gordon nudged me in the ribs, the girls dissolved into hysterical giggles and I had an urge to throw something at this glamorous creature who had achieved what none of us had managed, by arriving without a spot on her expensive clothing, and in the dark too, then having the audacity to go into raptures about the glorious meal she'd had..

'Can we go home now Mummy?' A plaintive voice at my side interrupted my spiteful thoughts. 'I'm tired and,' the voice dropped to a whisper 'ever so hungry. I've only eaten one sausage all evening.'

So we said goodnight, and with the remaining guests began to make our way through the wood and down the hill, stepping warily, guided by the light of a torch that someone had brought with them, maybe knowing or anticipating the terrain. Apart from one or two

153

exclamations as a misplaced step made contact with the squelchy path it was a fairly silent little party that eventually reached the cars in the field and I wondered if the other people had the same thoughts as those occupying my mind.

'Goodnight,' we called to each other as we climbed into our various vehicles and began to pull away …….. 'Goodnight.'

The girls were chattering and giggling amongst themselves, interrupting their chat every so often to complain about their hunger, but after a while they lapsed into silence and as we drove through the moon-lit lanes I reflected on the evening.

'You know, that really was a lovely experience.'

'What?' exploded Louise, 'You……are…...joking.'

'I don't call being starved a lovely experience,' added Angela.

'Neither do I' piped youngest, 'I had a cup of watery orange juice and one sausage and I'm hungry, really hungry.'

'No, no…… I do mean it. I'm aware that the food thing was rather odd and that you're hungry and thirsty, but there was such beauty there.' Sounds of derision issued from the back seat. 'You may scoff, but there may come a time many years hence when something will jog your memory of this night, and whilst you'll chuckle at the singularity of it what you'll really remember and see in your mind's eye is the firelight glowing through the open door and windows, that child playing such melancholy tunes, the moon shining through the trees. That's enchantment. Many people could live a whole lifetime and never experience it. It's as near to fairyland as we'll ever get. As it is……'

'As it is, we're jolly hungry. Gosh, I'm going to eat like a horse when I get home.'

So we tucked into grilled sausages, tomatoes, fried eggs and baked beans, and I closed my eyes while I ate and remembered only the sights and sounds of the enchanted evening spent at Tir-y-Dial.

GORDON GETS THE WIND UP

Having bought a new television with the new 606 lines some months before we had decided to move, we found that Wales, well, our part of Wales, had not yet caught up with the new system. The picture we received was a blurred one and the only signal we could get was from a Welsh language station. Something had to be done, so at a cost of thirty-two pounds a new aerial was installed. This gave us an excellent picture. In Southampton the local news kept us abreast of what was going on in our area, but nine hundred feet up on our hillside what we were receiving was hardly local for our signal came from Plymouth.

We listened to the weather forecasts with more attention than we did when we lived in the city because our animals had to be safely installed in their shelters before any onslaught from the elements caught us unaware. Also, of all the houses scattered about the hills, ours was without doubt, the target of every gentle breeze which left the Azores, gathering strength as it raced across the Atlantic until it became a gale and hit us fair and square on our hillside.

So hearing the warning 'Lundy – severe gale 9' was enough to send me into a panic. I'd rush around filling water buckets and hay-nets, put the goats in their stalls and Bessie and the other equines which had become part of our family in their stables, and warn the ducks that within half an hour their pond would be the scene of twenty foot high waves. It wasn't really necessary to put Bess inside, as being a native pony she was as tough as old boots, but I liked to think of all of them being snug and warm out of the driving wind and rain. During this activity I'd regret having planted peas which grew to thirty inches rather than those which only made eighteen, and remember I'd forgotten to tell Gordon about the corner of the hen-house roof that was flapping. But by that time it was too late to have second thoughts about such things and as we eventually settled down in warmth and comfort I'd tell myself that all was well.

Was it though?

The trouble was the roof. A gale battering the house, screaming round corners, pitching off slates, would keep us rigid all night, dozing momentarily, to wake with a jerk as the next blast lifted another slate and sent it rattling down the high pitched roof. In the gloom we could just see a piece of wallpaper keel over when it gave up the fight to stay attached to the damp wall and we'd listen to the plonk of water as it dropped into a strategically placed bucket while the dark outline of the enormous oak beam, which normally confirmed the strength of the house, took on a frightening aspect. Common sense told us that there was nothing to fear but one couldn't help wondering if we'd become casualties of the hysterical buffeting outside as it landed on top of us. How stupid!

Contact with several builders had produced the same reply......a wait of twelve months at least before an order for work could be attended to, and rumour had it that one local craftsman on receiving a complaint that after eight months he still hadn't appeared to do a job, replied, 'Well, if you want it done in a hurry, you'd better find someone else.' Oh dear.

So I began to search further afield, something about which we weren't terribly happy. Paying for one and a half or two hours journey time every day would add considerably to our bill but it seemed we had no choice. However, casting our net wider produced no better results. I either received 'fully booked for months' in reply or no return of my message. Then a couple of days later I'd just cleared the table after our evening meal when the phone rang.

'I'll get it.'

'David Rollins here. You left a message with my wife. Got a problem with your roof then?'

A builder! Oh joy! Our troubles over at last! 'Yes, Mr Rollins, just one moment, I'll call my husband.' Gordon briefly explained our needs and was then silent for a while before saying 'That's fine,' and followed this with instructions of how to find us.

My spirits soared. A builder phoning and Gordon saying 'that's fine' could only mean one thing. But as he replaced the receiver and saw my look of expectation he held up a finger and paused before saying 'Don't hold your hopes too high; he's passing through the village tomorrow afternoon and he'll come to have a look but......' I knew what he was going to say, so I said it. 'He's booked up for months.'

The following afternoon, Mr Rollins arrived and the grovelling welcome we gave him was quite disgraceful. He looked at the roof from the west, the north and the east and then walked down our

156

neighbour's field to view it from the south but as the field fell steeply away he was unable to see above the eaves.

'A high roof,' he announced, craning his neck back as he stated the obvious, 'A very high roof.'

We smiled nervously and nodded. This sounded akin to criticism and could possibly be a foretaste of a massive financial prognosis.

'A high roof. No gutters.'

'No, except on the front.' Gordon said in a repenting sort of voice and I shook my head from side to side so that Mr Rollins would know that we were both guilty of this heinous crime against our building.

'On the front. I expect you get a fair bit of rattling around in the loft on a bad day.'

We nodded again.

'On a bad day. Scaffolding. It's going to take a lot of scaffolding. High walls you see, high walls. High walls put the price of the scaffolding up.'

'Well, can you give us some idea of what it will cost to put it right?'

'Put it right? Well you see, you've got the roof......', at this point he made a clucking sound followed by a noisily sucked in 'Oooooooooh,' and rubbed his chin with his forefinger as though drawing inspiration. 'There's a very high pitch on that roof. Then you've got the gutters: they're not there. You've got these high walls......well......' More clucking followed as we waited with baited breath. 'Scaffolding is going to cost five hundred pounds.'

'And?' More baited breath waiting.

'Five hundred pounds and'......he wandered off and we followed him, watching as he cast his expert eye over our high-pitched, gutterless, scaffolding-hungry roof, and after more considered rubbing of the inspirational chin pronounced judgement. 'The whole lot'll have to be done. You can't do a job like this piecemeal. The whole lot will have to be done. Re-slated.'

'Re-slated' said Gordon, 'I thought as much.' I looked at him wondering if this bizarre form of speech was catching.

'Thought as much. Well, it'll cost over two thousand pounds. About two thousand two hundred pounds. I can send you an estimate if you want me to go ahead.'

We looked at one another and made doubtful faces.

157

'To go ahead. It's the scaffolding, you see. About two thousand two hundred'

'Mmmmmmm, well; it's very good of you to come and of course we'll discuss it. We hadn't the foggiest idea how much it might cost and I think it might be out of our range at the moment but we'll certainly let you know one way or the other.' said Gordon.

'Or the other. But you'll need to get something done about it. It'll only get worse. Too many slates missing already. You must have leaks galore when it rains,' and then as neither of us said anything he could pick up on added, 'When it rains.'

His peculiar way of beginning every sentence affected me far greater than the disheartening news about the cost of the roof and it was difficult to hide my hilarity. I headed for the kitchen where a short time later Gordon joined me.

'Well it seems a reasonable price for the work involved' he said. 'It's a big job and I can quite see why the scaffolding would be so much but it's still a lot of money,' then after a short pause, 'I'll think about this roof business and see if I can come up with something.'

'I don't want you working on that roof,' I said, my knees weakening at the thought.

'No, I'm not considering working from the outside. There's got to be some way of doing it from inside. I'm going to think.'

'Going to think' I added.

'What......Oh yes. An extraordinary habit, repeating the end of every sentence.'

'Every sentence.'

'All right all right, have your bit of fun but don't become addicted to it.' Then giving me a funny look he went off to return a few seconds later with a pad and pencil.

Sitting down at the table he deliberated for some while before beginning to draw various diagrams.

'Jenny, is there any home brew about?'

Ah, that was what was needed to give an extra fillip to the mighty mind.

With glass to hand and brain in top gear, the solution became apparent, for in short order he stood up and in a purposeful manner crossed the yard to the workshop. Filled with curiosity I peered through the window to see him emerge carrying a bucket that seemed

158

to have tools in it. He then headed for the barn where the store of things which might one day come in handy for something increased with amazing rapidity. From there much noise ensued. Looking for something was always a major exercise as there was no order whatsoever. If ever there had been good intentions regarding tidiness they were not apparent and when hunting for one item several others would invariably spark off inspiration for another idea so a barn search could take some time.

But not this day. A one-track mind was at work dedicated to the job in hand. No treasures found would deflect from the purpose of this search. Something was definitely afoot. 'Necessity is the mother of invention' is such a truism, and combined with the 'something out of nothing' mentality we had the pioneer spirit was alive and well and working diligently in my spouse's brain.

'I'll be able to secure the whole roof,' he announced on returning to the kitchen, 'But first I've got to replace the missing slates,' and off he went again. Forty minutes saw the inventor emerge from his workshop, smiling broadly whilst holding aloft 'Green's Unique Exterior Slate Re-placer', an ingenious device employing string, wire, old roller skates and an extending handle which had at one time been part of an upstairs window cleaning gadget. Armed with this he spent the following two days at the top of the long ladders replacing fallen slates without having to climb onto the roof. Brilliant.

The roof space had originally housed two rooms, the walls of which were lath and plaster, and while these were now more or less non-existent, enough remained to make the clearing of them quite a major task.

'Will you be able to give a hand clearing all the debris over the next few days because it's going to be a hefty demolition job' said Gordon. I could understand that it would be, and quicker by far with two pairs of hands.

The next three days were not enjoyable ones. They began well enough, for spirits were always high at the onset of a new task but I knew it wasn't going to last. With scarves tied over our mouths and noses we began to demolish the walls, filling plastic sacks with the dusty rubble and slats and taking them down to the yard. It was back-breaking work but by the end of day the floor was clear enough for Gordon to begin making the roof secure with his second invention;

'Green's Unique Interior Slate-Securer.' I therefore became the chief, well, the only sack carrier. It took me seven minutes to fill a sack, cart it down two flights of stairs, the ones to the attic requiring careful negotiating, empty the sack and return to the dust filled attic. It was a horrible atmosphere to work in but at least I was able to enjoy a good intake of fresh air in the middle of my seven minute excursions. Gordon took regular breaks in order to give his arms a rest as much as anything else.

Working at a slow, steady pace (I was instructed to do this. It was not my normal way of working) I reckoned that after seven trips I'd take a break of ten minutes and after three hours I'd have emptied twenty-one sacks. This would be my lot for the day as animals, garden and food required attention but it took three mornings before the loft was cleared although more sacks were emptied at intervals by Gordon, who said his arms were aching so much from stretching upwards it was lovely to have them reaching down instead. Nor did it include the many sacks we filled with old dresses, cardigans, overcoats, and goodness know what else that had been lodged in the numerous gaps between the roof and walls. Newspapers in tightly packed sheaves had also played their part in excluding the furies blasting the house and out of curiosity I cut one open. Unfolding the tattered pages I found articles on the progress of the war, confirming along with a few visible trimmings on some of the clothing that these D.I.Y. defences had been in place for a very long time.

Then, after six days......Eureka! We had a new roof, a weather-proof one for the cost of a few pounds. Gutters, drainpipes and weatherboarding entered the scene and the warm winds from the Azores could transform themselves into whatever they pleased on their passage across the Atlantic. Our little house could withstand anything.

CARRIE ON REGARDLESS

Ten days after the roof was mended I picked up a rather unpleasant virus. In my younger days I had a friend who would turn deathly pale at the slightest indisposition whilst I on the other hand retained my healthy complexion whatever ailment assailed me, and I envied my friend and everyone who could look as ill as they felt, or even more than they felt for all I knew. I envied them to the point of jealousy. But this time my luck was in. I turned a yucky shade of greenish-purplish-white and I was thrilled.

'Oh, you look really ill' were words to gladden my heart, and I demanded that a hand mirror be handed to me so that I could thrill at the sight of my pale and wan self. I thought my complexion resembled that of an Elizabethan noblewoman, without the noxious substances.

Some years previously Dulux brought out a range of colours with names like Apricot White, Almond White and Apple White. Where did the inspiration for that come from? But I always knew I had produced the best shade of all and that Dulux had missed a trick for I don't recall a Yucky White ever appearing on the market.

Anyway, this happened at a very inconvenient time as Angela and I had planned to go to a sale at Llanybydder the following day. She was going to buy a foal having saved by various means a very respectable sum. Now it was impossible for me to go, so Gordon who hated auctions had been wheedled into taking her in my stead. However I couldn't let them go without one very strict instruction.

'Angela, do not buy a colt, buy a filly. Gordon make sure she buys a filly,' I instructed in an ailingly bossy sort of way, and off they went while I lay in bed thinking about my glorious complexion.

Dusk was falling when they arrived home, Gordon looking exhausted. He sank into a chair gasping that he'd never go to an auction with Angela again. He'd already vowed that he wouldn't go to one with me either, and as Louise and Jessica weren't auctiony sort of people I suppose that in spite of the day's events he felt relatively safe with his decision.

***

161

When she was quite young Angela knew she wanted to work with horses. She was a natural rider and young as she was seemed to have an understanding of what was going on in an equine's head, so trading on this natural talent she had come to us some months earlier with an ingenious proposition. If she started saving really hard, she told us, she'd have enough money to purchase a foal, gain valuable experience handling it and when it was old enough she'd gently back and school it. By the time she left school to go as a working pupil she'd have quite a bit of knowledge tucked under her belt.

'But there are always horses up here,' we said. 'Different horses all the time.' This we were told was not enough. Bringing on a foal was what was needed. Desperately.

The seriousness with which we were forced to view her plans to widen her knowledge was reinforced shortly afterwards by the arrival of a letter addressed to her with the word 'Tattersalls' printed on the back of the envelope. For days I was apprehensive about going out to the yard for fear of what I might find in the stables, yet being in the house wasn't all that relaxing either, for every time the phone rang I was convinced it would be our bank manager enquiring with polite sarcasm whether I really thought our account would stretch to dealings with bloodstock agents.

So seriously was this scheme taken that Angela cut down her spends to five pence a week, and in the middle of November came to me with my current collection of Green Shield stamp books. 'What are these worth, mother dear?'

I wasn't at all sure, but thinking I might be at the receiving end of a bargain said all too smartly 'Two weeks washing up and the goat house washed out every Saturday for a month.' So with dishes and goat house washing swapped for stamp-books she thumbed her way through the Green Shield catalogue, wrote out a list, and informed me that as soon as she could get to the Green Shield centre her Christmas shopping would be done. With this accomplished, she was able to ransack her Christmas savings box, count out the cash no longer needed for presents and transfer it to the foal fund.

I'd never seen money grow like it in my life! I always had at least one theoretically workable savings idea on the go, yet however hard I tried, something always seemed to stop me proving myself a financial wizard. My grandfather had a firm belief that if you looked after the

162

pennies the pounds would take care of themselves and my daughter was well and truly proving it.

Money sent as Christmas presents was added and immediately after Christmas all prospective birthday present donors were politely contacted to see if it were possible to have cash rather than gifts and could it be in advance please, for the target date had been set..... January 21st. Work was being done for anyone willing to pay for it and the piggybank was bulging. We were she felt, as family and general overseers of juvenile frolics, entitled to a several times daily account of how every penny was achieved and what precise part of the foal's anatomy it would purchase. We were all rather thankful when the day before the sale the total was announced, and that was when the dreaded virus attacked me.

So an excited daughter and a reluctant father set off for Llanybydder. As Gordon described it later, she looked over dozens of foals without making a single comment, so he had no idea of what was going through her mind. He pointed out various reasons why one might be better than another: confirmation, colour, the 'look in the eye', but still not a word was spoken by this child whose volubility had been non-stop over the previous weeks.

They went into the auction ring and she watched in silence as horses, ponies and foals came and went. After a while nature dictated that her father left the ring, and it was during those few minutes that Angela saw what she just knew was the right foal.

Now a twelve year-old wafting a catalogue aloft in a auction ring is not the sort of thing a parent wants to know about, but still less is it something a parent doesn't want to know about, and whether or not she bore in mind her limit of twenty-nine guineas we would never know, for at twenty-seven guineas the little iron grey foal was knocked down to the...... 'Young lady, your name please?'

It was all done and dusted when her father returned.

Of course, I knew nothing of all this excitement lying as I was on my sick-bed, until suddenly the door burst open and shouts of 'He's here, he's here,' filled the air.

He?...............He?

I crawled out of bed and struggling into my dressing gown joined Louise and Jessica in the kitchen and saw framed in the doorway the sweetest most adorable face a foal ever had atop a near black body. He

163

seemed so tiny and after the strange experiences of the day, so vulnerable. We fussed over him, admiring his beauty and adorable expression and telling him how happy we were to have him with us and that he would be well looked after, little knowing that Caradoc Machod Bach, Carrie, as we called him, would become the most loved of all our equines, such was his endearing personality and sweet nature.

When quite exhausted by all this exertion, I staggered back to bed, vaguely aware of Gordon slumped in a chair, head in hand, murmuring 'Never again, never again, never again.'

***

In the 1990's a book was published entitled The Man who Listens to Horses, written by an American named Monty Roberts in which he described his method of training a horse. He was appalled at the brutal method commonly used to break-in young horses, and even as a young boy he knew that there must be some other way for these beautiful creatures to exist with humans without the physical and mental distress inflicted on them in order to be controlled. He suffered with them as he saw their spirit broken and watched them obey through fear, the first steps in a life of unwilling compliance.

He was determined to do something about it, and he did. He learned their language. He gave demonstrations in many countries, showing owners that by using the body language of the horse a rider could be on the back of a calm and willing animal which had never before had a saddle on its back let alone a bit in its mouth, and all this within twenty minutes or so.

What he witnessed in his youth was excessive, but the general method of 'breaking-in' was frequently less than sensitive, the very phrase having the suggestion of force in it. Many people went to his demonstrations, a specified number having booked-in their young horses for his attention. Some were already believers; many were sceptical......until they saw with their own eyes what happened and how it was done.

But on that January evening in the 1970's when the little iron-grey colt stood in our doorway and captured our hearts we'd never heard of Monty Roberts. Nor had it entered our heads to divine horse language

164

in terms of training. One thing we did know however was that our new arrival would grow to maturity knowing nothing but kindness and that he would learn without knowing he was learning. The following day Angela put a soft head collar on him and took him into the meadow, where after the usual exhibition of authority from Bess which was very brief as he was no threat he settled into life with the other animals. Almost immediately a friendship was struck between the foal and Bill, a retired racehorse which we'd bought for Louise some months earlier; a kind and gentle creature. Wherever Bill went Carrie would follow, leaving his side only to come for a pat or a cuddle from anyone who entered the meadow, until he latched on to the idea that my daily trip to the vegetable garden for the day's requirements would generate a tit-bit held in my hand, just out of his reach. Carrie would follow me as I walked the short distance to the gate where he would be given the goodies.

With the approach of spring and serious work to be done in the vegetable garden, he became a frequent companion on the other side of the fence although I had no illusions as to the real reason for so much flattery. As the day warmed up I'd discard my jacket and sling it over his back, then maybe a jersey would follow. If I was wearing a woolly hat he'd pull it off and I'd put it on him. He looked particularly rakish one day when I found him wearing Gordon's old green tweed trilby. Whilst mending some fencing Gordon felt his hat whisked from his head, so he plonked it on the little chap who made no attempt to remove it. Taking hats from heads became a great sport.

A couple of weeks later we borrowed a horsebox from a friend, leaving it in the yard with the ramp down. Angela put a few goodies into a bucket and placed it just inside the box. She brought Carrie into the yard and we all sat down on the log under the ash tree wondering what, if anything, would happen. The foal joined us, accepted a bit of biscuit and wandered off. He stopped near the box but didn't approach further so Gordon and I left to attend to other things, leaving Angela to clean a pile of tack and keep an eye on Carrie.

After a while she appeared at the door. 'Come and look.' The empty bucket was on its side some way from the box but there was no sign of the foal.

'He just walked in, ate the goodies and chucked out the bucket.'

The little chap turned his head to give us a perfunctory glance but stayed where he was.

'Will he be alright when he wants to come out?'

'I'll keep an eye on him.' But no sooner were the words out of her mouth than he began to back out, slowly and carefully with the caution of a veteran. He was so small that he could have turned round inside but evidently something told him that this was the way to do it, and although Angela moved forward in order to catch his head collar in case he should put a foot wrong no help was necessary. For several weeks the horsebox remained with the ramp down and when one of us was about the yard we'd call Carrie from the meadow and he'd wander in and out of the box at will. Boxing was not going to be a problem.

Sometimes I'd deliberately leave the garden gate open and before long he'd appear at the kitchen window knowing that a few succulent bits of vegetable would come his way, and if he found the door open, well, that was an obvious invitation which he'd always take up, clopping up the two steps and onto the flagstones. As he grew bigger the heavy oak table and dining chairs had to be moved to enable him to turn round and get out, but that was something he was never in a hurry to do.

As the seasons came and went we continued the game of draping things over him. We'd use him as a prop, leaning on or over him while we chatted or admired the view. We picked up his feet regularly and as he got older we'd rest a saddle on his back or tease him with a bit, jigging it gently in his mouth, then one day when he was approaching his third birthday, Angela draped herself across his back, raised her feet from the ground and hung there for several seconds. The pony flicked an ear but remained motionless. The following year he stood quietly while she saddled and bridled him then climbed aboard. Off they went. He had grown into a fine pony, well fed by our glorious old pasture and the goat's milk that had nourished him in his first year with us. Although he'd reached 13.2 hands his beautiful small head and neat ears reflected his Welsh Mountain heritage while his slender body and height confirmed the 'some thoroughbred' which his previous owner had said was in him. What else had contributed to his make-up we knew not. His iron-grey coat shone. Nothing fazed him.

166

One day some young girl or boy was going to have the perfect riding pony.

We could never have laid claim to the intellectual approach of understanding the language of the horse, but I don't think Monty Roberts would have been too dismayed at our simple method, although it did take somewhat longer than his!

**

When Carrie was four years old, the friend who had lent us the horse box phoned. She was selling it and the gentleman from Hereford who was buying it enquired if she knew of a really reliable pony. His youngest daughter, aged twelve, was not as bold as his other children and whilst she longed to take part in horsey activities with the rest of the family she was always nervous. Several promising sounding ponies had been tried out but none of them assuaged the child's anxiety. Well, Laura knew of one alright, but whether it was for sale was another matter.

Should she give him our phone number?

That evening I phoned Angela, who by this time was working in the Cotswolds. It was decision time. So Mr Walters and his daughter came to Tironnen bringing with them their box. We liked them very much and for the little girl meeting Carrie, well, it was love at first sight. She fussed over him and I could see that she wanted him to be her pony, although for all I knew she'd acted in the same way with all the others she'd met, but her kindness was obvious. We saddled him up, she climbed aboard and her confidence grew as she rode him round the field. Being the perfect gentleman he was, he walked straight into the box and they took him home for a fortnight's trial.

Three days later the phone rang. 'We don't need a fortnight. He's just perfect. Such a character, he's one of the family already.' Well of course. He always was.

SURGICAL SPIRIT

Once the smell of spring emerging had permeated the innermost regions of urban life our guests began to arrive, and we soon found out which ones appreciated that spring beckoned us also, only in a more demanding way, for the 'doings' on a small-holding didn't just stop because we had visitors. Most were happy to enjoy what was going on around them, giving a hand here and there or just relaxing, and we would cut our work to a minimum so as to be able to spend as much time as possible in their company, exchanging news and enjoying reminiscing. Generally it was well worthwhile coping with a couple of frenetic days catching up on tasks after they'd gone. Having friends to stay was just a continuation of what went on every day but with less work, more food, and plenty of laughter. Nothing out of the ordinary really, until James and Eleanor from South Carolina arrived.

Never in my wildest imaginings could I have dreamt up anything like the twenty-four hours spent in their company......well, Eleanor's company.

It wasn't that they didn't fit in. Far from it. They were at great pains not to impose, quite appreciating that we had tasks that necessitated short absences from time to time. James was a darling and he and Gordon got on really well, and we both voted him a super person; the sort you really wanted to put yourself out for.

Eleanor?......well, Eleanor was different. Eleanor was different from anybody I'd ever met. Wherever in the world she might have been: standing in the Acropolis, walking through the catacombs or watching big game on the Serengeti, her attitude would have been the same. Her observance of all that was close to hand was completely blotted out by the subject which obsessed her whole being and on which she extrapolated with vigour, knowledge and an unbelievable vocabulary......her health.

We had been aware of the existence of these elderly American relatives for only a couple of years but we had exchanged letters. Perhaps because James was considered to be the more accomplished correspondent Eleanor always sent her good wishes but never put pen to paper. Certainly he wrote most interestingly, his letters being very descriptive and full of chat on many subjects relevant to life in his part of the world, so we were always pleased when his familiar handwriting appeared on the blue airmail envelopes. Then one day in December we received their Christmas card and with it came news of their Grand Tour. They were going to 'do' Europe, starting in early spring the following year and wanted to include a visit to us in their itinerary.

Being familiar with the spontaneity so beloved by Americans I dispatched a letter asking them to let us know when they planned to come. However had we known James and Eleanor more intimately we would have known that they were not the sort to diminish the delights of surprise by giving prior notice.

It was the third week in March and a bitter east wind had been blowing for several days. Gordon was reading by the fire, recovering from a dose of flu that had laid him really low. Although he insisted he was feeling much better he was still far from well and looked terrible, his pallor not enhanced by the red and green check of his dressing gown. Just to make sure I wasn't left out of the drama stakes, a couple of days earlier whilst rooting for something in the barn I'd trodden on a nail that pierced through the sole of my wellie into the sole of my left foot, which inconveniently had me limping about on my heel, 'ooh-ing' and 'ow-ing' as pain thundered up my leg with every movement. That was the situation when the phone rang.

'Is that you Jenny?' I knew at once that it was James. He sounded just as warm and chatty as his letters. 'James, oh, it's lovely to hear you.'

The kind, faintly rasping voice at the end of the line sounded enthusiastic as he said, 'And it's great to hear you and we'll be seeing you real soon.'

'Yes, yes, that's lovely, when do you want to come?'

The answer seemed a little odd. 'Oh, we've come; we're here.'

He did sound very near. A moment laced with panic took over and then passed. He was probably calling from a hotel, or maybe Heathrow.

'Here?' I asked, 'You mean you're in London?'

'Oh, no, much closer than that. We've got Brit-rail tickets and we've come by rail and we're in Llan....Llandovery. Now you just tell me where we find you.'

Watching my expression, Gordon quickly got the gist of things and signalled to me from the fireside. 'Are they here?' he mouthed.

169

I nodded, mouthed 'Llandovery', and whispered 'I'll tell them to get a taxi and I'll meet them in the lane.'

'Are you still there Jenny?' enquired the voice in my ear.

'Yes James, we're making arrangements. Hold on a minute.'

'You can't do that,' said Gordon, 'You know you can't put any pressure on your foot. There's no way you'd get down there safely.'

'I'll be alright,' but Gordon would not hear of it.

'You are not driving down to the lane,' he said, sounding very 'master-of-the-house' in an illish sort of way. 'We can't let them come on their own anyway. Tell them we'll be there in thirty minutes. I protested in vain. Considerate as ever, Gordon repeated as he heavily climbed the stairs, 'Tell them we'll be thirty minutes.'

***

The journey to and from the station was marred by anxiety about Gordon, but he didn't have to contribute anything verbally as our guests were in a chatty mood, interspersing information about themselves with concern for my foot and exclamations at the loveliness of the countryside through which we were passing. At one point James remarked that Gordon looked a bit peaky, to which he replied, 'Just a bit of a cold,' but I think James thought it more than that because when we arrived in the village he insisted on stopping, and emerging from the local pub with a bottle of whisky cradled in his arm announced 'I guess this will help.'

We left the road, drove up the steep track and ushered them, against the stinging east wind into the warmth of the house. I put down the large carpetbag I'd brought in, and Eleanor placed beside it a small leather case, which I assumed to be a vanity case. She immediately began rummaging through the carpetbag until, finding what she sought, kicked off her shoes to replace them with the obviously welcome softness of sheepskin slippers.

'It's ma feeut,' she announced. 'Oh, ma Gad; ah have such trouble with ma feeyut. They get so swollen on long journeys. It's always been the case when ah'm sitting for long,' and she gazed at the troublesome wool encased extremities for a few moments, then soothingly rubbing the upper part of her right foot not hidden by

170

slipper, said slowly and with much feeling, 'Ma feeyut are the bayun of ma laaf.'

I muttered something sympathetic and hobbled off to make coffee as Gordon ushered them into the sitting room where they made themselves comfortable by the roaring fire. As I passed the carpetbag I noticed that the leather case was no longer with it and when I took in the coffee saw that Eleanor had placed it beside her chair. They spoke of their life in South Carolina, well, James did the talking while Eleanor leaned over the fire nodding absently from time to time, seeming quite happy to stare at the blazing logs, until James mentioned Maine. They had lived for several years in Maine and at the mention of that northern-most state Eleanor shot up from her recumbent position to throw up her hands in horror.

'Oh, ma Gad; that was a terrible place to be. Ah felt the cold so. Ah used to get awful cramps, you have no idea how awful. Ah just don't know how ah stuck it for so long. Cramps raat insaad, all the taam. We had to leave in the end you know, ah was in such constant payun,' and she clutched her abdominal region, adding in case we were in any doubt that the removal of her person from inhospitable Maine had lessened her suffering, 'Ah get them steeyall from taam to taam.'

I gazed at her for a moment, her dramatic reaction to a name on a map being something not hitherto in my experience, then I muttered something jokey about pain in Maine, which observation was justifiably ignored and James continued the history of their northern sojourn without further interruption by Eleanor of things anatomical. She returned to her fire gazing, the warmth no doubt comforting the memory of her latent agony and I passed round a plate of sandwiches and mugs of coffee. It was as Eleanor was reaching for a piece of chocolate cake that I noticed a wince of pain on her face. James noticed it too.

'You alright honey?'

The reply was weak but determined. 'Oh yes dear, I'm alraat. You know how this payun attacks so suddenly.'

Eleanor felt an explanation due. 'It's ma rheumatism.' She looked at each of us in turn. 'Ah get it in ma arms, and it starts from hayur,' she indicated the source of the complaint somewhere to the left of the nape of her neck, 'and it travels across hayur,' the instructing finger

171

traversed her shoulder, 'and continues on down to theyer,' the finger obligingly followed the river of pain to a point half way between her shoulder and elbow. 'Ah have it in ma hayunds too. Why......' she held the word for several seconds and once more looked fully into each face around the fire indicating quite clearly that what was coming next would require our full attention. 'Why, sometimes ah can't even hold a cup and if ah'm suffering in the other hayund as weyull, oh ma Gad,' and she paused for a further moment to let the significance of such affliction sink in, then with perfect timing which precluded any change of subject being made without obvious callous disregard for her condition, continued, 'But of course, ah have ma ayuds,' and she leaned down to pat the small leather case that I'd first noticed. 'Ma ayuds,' she informed us, 'are heyur.'

I longed to see inside the case but just thinking about her 'ayuds' seemed to do her a power of good so she didn't offer to open it but gazed fondly at it nestling beside her sheepskin clad feet. She clearly gained much comfort from its presence, and I wondered if it had some curative value for she reached out for another slice of cake, this time without the agonizing spasm of the previous gesture.

After a while I got up saying that I'd better prepare dinner and had just removed a chicken from the fridge when I was joined by Eleanor holding the little leather case.

'How're your feet?' I asked just stopping myself in time from saying 'feeut'.

'Oh, they're O.K. I guess,' she replied absently, her mind apparently elsewhere, her gaze centred on the pale plumpness of the chicken, which evidently reminded her of something.

'In naanteen forty-faav, naanteen forty-eight and naanteen fifty-six, ah had three very serious abdominal operations.' she announced. I didn't know whether to scream with laughter or appear solicitous but decided on the latter, which was just as well for she continued, 'And what a clever girl you are. You must have known that this is the only meeut ah can eat without suffering ill effects.' She leaned towards the dish, her voice dropping to a confidential tone and I wasn't sure when she next spoke whether she was apologising to the bird for the enthusiastic manner in which she was anticipating its succulence, or explaining to me.

172

'Ah get no payun at all when ah eat chicken, none at all, but ah have to be real careful with other things.' Her voice began to climb back to normality as she forgot the honoured carcass on the plate. 'Beef and lamb, ooooh,' she held up her hand and tipped her head back a little, 'Just the teeniest, weeniest bit, and pork......ah dare not touch it ma dear, ah just dare not. Ma stomach you see, after those operations, oh ma Gad, I thought ah would not leeuv, but the doctors were wonerful, they...were...just...wonerful. Ma own doctor, Dr. Komanski, warned me after ma first operation. 'Eleanor,' he sayed, 'Eleanor, you will have to be watchful of your eating habits for the rest of your laaf,' but ah thought ah could cope with that. No, what worried me was having unsightly scarring, and as though he could read ma thoughts he sayed immediately, 'don't you worry Eleanor, ah will ensure that any scarring will be minimal,' and he was raat. It was the same with ma next two operations. Ah was so anxious, but each taam he reassured me and he was raat. 'Ah can assure you that scarring will be minimal,' he sayed, and she contemplated the unblemished bird in silence for a few moments then murmured softly, 'He was a won'erful, won'erful mayun.'

I put the chicken in the Rayburn, peeled potatoes and carrots, made a salmon hors d'oeuvre, took a bag of peas from the freezer and picked out what I thought to be a raspberry tart (it was!). I skimmed the cream from the morning's milk and whipped it thick, set the table and made up meals for the dogs, all the while being regaled by Eleanor's reminiscences which were delivered with a profusion of medical terms which left me baffled by a mind that could or wanted to remember them, and limp from their bombardment. By the time I'd done the preparation and was ready to relax while the cooking went on, I was as familiar with the revered Dr Komanski as I was with the various stages of Eleanor's triple surgery, but the recitation continued and it was not until some time later that the narration culminated in the emergence from hospital of the soon-to-be-scarless Eleanor.

When she had finished she sat down on a dining chair and placing the little leather case on her knee opened it. She was facing me and the lid was up so my curiosity was still not satisfied regarding its contents and I had to conceal my nosiness whilst she quietly immersed herself in examining whatever was within. I thought I might as well make use of her pre-occupation so I pulled on my wellies and slipped outside to

173

give the goats their evening meal, thinking that a few minutes of their carefree company would be the perfect antidote to Eleanor's hypochondria. When I returned she had two bright blue pills in the palm of her hand.

'My, ah didn't hear you go out.' Her tone was of surprise but in no way aggrieved that she had been left.

'Now which place is maan, honey?' and acknowledging my reply placed first one pill beside her wine glass and the other, with precision immediately below it. Without haste she screwed the cap on the bottle and returned it to the case, then a second bottle was brought out and a tiny yellow pill set beside one of the blue ones in an equally precise manner, then a large white one. So it went on; a routine reminding her of her afflictions and healers, leisurely performed and evidently satisfying, which continued until I saw, my eyes nearly popping out of my head, that eleven 'ayuds' made up a pattern beside her glass. She gave a little sigh, closed the lid of the case, sat back in the chair and looked at me, smiling.

'Theyur.' She put the case on the floor. 'Ah always put ma ayuds in the same pattern then ah know ah've taken them all.'

'Do you just have them with your evening meal?' I asked, for something to say.

'Oh honey, ah take ma ayuds with all ma meals. They are ma laaf. Ah have to.' and she repeated, 'They are ma laaf.'

Gordon was bearing up very well for it was obvious that he enjoyed James's company but even so I could see he was using all his will power to be attentive. The dinnertime conversation was enjoyable because James liked talking and we enjoyed listening to him. He was most interesting and although I noticed that once or twice Eleanor seemed to want to break into the discourse, he skilfully managed to avoid the intrusion; something that had come with long practice I imagine. So we managed to steer clear of all things medical until the raspberry tart unaccountably drew forth some affectionate musings on a broken femur and slightly more understandable reminiscences of severe blood clotting.

All aspects of their life, every place in which they had lived, the work they had done, the holidays they had taken, the people they had met, helped Eleanor recall her precarious physical condition of the time, but as the evening wore on we found ways of over-riding this flood of disorders that were drawn from an apparently limitless storehouse of medical episodes.

Gordon offered his apologies and retired early. James dozed by the fire and Eleanor insisted on helping me clear away. As I washed up she resumed her reflections, the sounds of cutlery and dishes being deposited on the stainless steel draining board making an appropriate background to the stories of kidney stones, gall bladders and various conditions of heart, lungs and stomach. But not all Eleanor's life was wrapped in such high drama. The more mundane side of her existence consisted of bouts of sinusitis, migraine, intestinal problems of a more prosaic nature than those requiring surgery, and a variety of other ailments, each and every one of which she had studied in great depth. An epidemic of some sort and a handful of accidents gave a certain roundness to her autobiography and after years of practice she was able to wax lyrical about every aspect of her sufferings. From the first symptoms, through the periods of anxiety when her life hung in the balance (even an in-growing toenail seemed to have her suspended between now and the hereafter) to her recoveries, which were never, but never, one hundred per cent, for after each narrative she would give a little sigh. 'Ah just never felt quite the sayum.'

The following morning was bright and crisp and our guests slept late, for which I was thankful as it gave me the opportunity to get on with various tasks in my laborious hobbling way, but as soon as I heard movement above I took some coffee up to them, then set about preparing breakfast. They came downstairs making appreciative noises as the aroma of bacon, sausages, eggs and potato cakes met them on the stairs, and as on the previous evening Eleanor went through her ritual with the little leather case, setting out the coloured pills in the same orderly fashion beside a glass of water, then swallowing a selected two before commencing her breakfast. I saw that some of the pills differed from those put out the night before and wondered how on earth she remembered which to take at which meal but then I thought, this is her hobby......her laaf; in fact it's more than a hobby, it's her whole existence, her reason for living and when something's of that much importance one does remember.

Gordon and I only ate a cooked breakfast when visitors were present and the tantalizing smell was too much to resist, so I thought I'd have an egg and fried bread. By the time I'd taken it to the table

175

our guests had progressed to the toast and marmalade and Eleanor was munching with a rather inattentive air as though her mind was elsewhere; almost as if she was expecting something to happen. I poured myself some coffee and thought how good it all was and wondered why we didn't always treat this early meal as one of the necessities of life instead of hurriedly downing porridge and toast. 'We really should indulge more often' I mused as I slowly cut through the egg into the bread beneath and raised the portion on my fork to admire the brilliantly coloured yoke, part of which had begun to trickle down the edge of the golden bread onto the fork, when Eleanor emerged from her reverie and pushing back her chair in order to stand, announced, 'Jenny dear, ah must leave you a minute while ah go and evacuate ma bowels.' James unconcernedly helped himself to more coffee, Gordon came downstairs looking as sickly as he had the previous day, and I regarded in silence the egg on my fork, enthusiasm for it suddenly at a low ebb.

Whilst Eleanor was fulfilling her obligation to nature, James expressed a desire to see the animals and we had a pleasant twenty minutes or so touring the estate. I was most impressed by the pertinent questions he asked and some of the observations he made and I wondered how he managed to put up with the constant talk of infirmity but then I thought, perhaps it's not like that when the two of them are on their own. Perhaps he's learned to shut himself off or maybe Eleanor is only like this with other people. Anyway, it was none of my business. I'd have liked to have talked to him and listened to him much more but time was pressing as their train left shortly after twelve o'clock, taking them on to Shrewsbury where more unsuspecting relatives were waiting. I offered to pack a lunch box but having had such a substantial and late breakfast it was declined and we climbed into the Land Rover to retrace our drive of the previous day. The bright winter sun was shining through the leafless trees to throw lacy patterns on almost every stretch of road and we arrived at the station several minutes before the train was due and stood chatting in the old fashioned waiting room.

'Ah just love it hayur,' remarked Eleanor, 'Ah just so love it hayur. We've had such a lovely taam and you've made us so welcome. Ah know you have a lot to do but you took taam off to make us comfortable and we really do appreciate that, don't we, James?

James, ah do so love being with these lovely people, don't you?' I could hear the sound of the approaching train as she warmed to her theme.

'James, don't you just love being with these dear people in that dear liddle ole' house?'

The train rounded a bend and slowly drew to a halt.

'Oh, James, wouldn't it be lovely to stay a few more dayuz?'

But sensitive James had the cases on board and was already bidding us goodbye. We helped Eleanor up and watched as they turned to go down the corridor, when she unexpectedly reappeared at the open window in the door.

'It's been lovely. Really, really, lovely. Ah just can't say......' Her voice trailed off as she looked at Gordon as though seeing him for the first time.

'Ma Gad,' she exclaimed, a look of admiration, possibly even envy on her face, 'Oh, ma God, you look dreadful. You oughta be in bayud.'

We could see exactly what Gerry meant. Suzanne sat smartly astride the pony her face turned towards us as she listened to her father, her expression alternating between regret and anticipation as Gerry talked. Regret at the thought of parting with her much loved friend and anticipation at the thought of getting a larger mount, for there was no denying it; her pony Punch, was far too small for her.

'Of course,' continued Gerry, stepping forward to stroke the pony's neck, 'We'd never sell him but we'll be looking for a good home for him shortly,' adding as he patted the animal, 'Won't we m'boy?'

Talking about it later it seemed to us that Gerry had made a point of letting us know about the pony's imminent redundancy but neither Gordon nor I had said anything at the time, and as Suzanne had been diverted by other goings on and had cantered off, the conversation changed.

We got on very well with Gerry and Pamela. Gerry was an ex-military man whose usual gentlemanly demeanour could when roused, bristle in apoplectic rage against laziness, cowardice, pig-headedness, vulgarity, unpunctuality, low standards in general and most of all stupidity. Anyone at the receiving end of this maelstrom would feel as though they had been slapped across the face with a very wet rag, yet on many instances when expressing his irritation at human frailties his irascibility was tempered by an ungovernably wicked sense of humour.

He had done everything, although a great many aspects of the colourful life he sometimes described were gloriously exaggerated, for he seemed to have won the war single-handed. He had been everywhere, could, but seldom did quote the classics and poetry, read copiously, had a passable talent as both water-colourist and writer, was interested in every subject under the sun, kind to the old, the young and animals and a countryman to the core.

Every Monday morning he drove reluctantly to London, where once entrenched fought commercial skirmishes with vigour, then every Friday he would return to the countryside he loved, to re-charge his batteries in the pleasure of meeting friends, hunting, fishing and doing whatever had to be done with his bees.

The time spent in his company could range from a serious discussion on anthropology to a side-splitting description of some small incident which would have passed unnoticed in most people's experience, but Gerry had a gift for latching onto the crucial point of any trivial event, dressing it up and embellishing it to give the better telling. He was larger than life and we loved him.

He was also the possessor of the most infectious laugh. One August evening Gordon answered the phone. I heard him roar with laughter and some time passed before he regained his breath in order to say something, but before he could get the words out laughter overtook him again and the merriment became more and more hysterical. I guessed it was Gerry who'd phoned; he was the only person we knew who could cause such a reaction. I opened the sitting room door hoping to join in the fun, to find Gordon on his knees bent double, howling as though in pain. I could hear Gerry's voice hooting down the phone, words hindered from clarity by prolonged guffaws and gales of laughter.

I couldn't tell whether the story was being repeated or if it was just taking long in the telling, but clearly whatever the joke was it was mighty funny. The sight of Gordon's tear-stained face set me off but I hadn't a clue as to what I was laughing at. I leaned over to get my ear closer to the receiver but all I could hear was a great roar of hilarity interspersed by the odd word 'bee-sting......get home......missis.' It was as though the words were strung out like pieces of washing on a long line of laughter. We were both in a state of collapse, tears streaming, stomachs aching, facial muscles likewise and still the guffaws came non stop down the line. What a great joke it was, except that I wasn't party to it.

I had to remedy this omission. Grabbing the receiver from Gordon I managed to piece together through the guffaws the story of a farmer who was at a local show and on visiting the Gents and been stung by a wasp on the exposed part of his anatomy. Afterwards Gordon said that if only he'd known what was coming he'd have had the tape recorder ready and whenever we felt like a 'dose of Gerry' we could have just switched him on.

Pamela, who was a great W.I. lady, lived life at her own pace and in a quietly determined way organized her weekdays as she chose. The lovely Georgian house always seemed to me to be in two parts......the

179

part where Gerry loved to be, and the part where never in a million years would he venture, this latter being the nether regions where in the kitchen Pamela enjoyed her idea of domesticity. This consisted mainly of creating glorious flower arrangements with which to enhance the exquisite furniture on which they were placed. The kitchen seemed to be given over to this activity.

Chests, cupboards and chairs were always piled high with vases and bowls at the ready for the lovely arrangements of flowers that always ornamented the house. Papers, magazines, jars, boxes, and goodness knows what else were put on or into every available space and when the space ran out or things could no longer balance with safety they were deposited on the floor. The kitchen required a strong heart to withstand the permanent disorder, but against this colourful background Pamela calmly concocted Gerry's favourite dishes with dexterity and imagination. She prepared for his weekend home-coming by making sure everything was as tranquil and comfortable as possible so that her husband could sink back in his favourite chair and relax against a background of antiques, water-colours and object d'art, while three lively Jack Russells leapt at him effusively in between bouts of ear-shattering combat as they fought pitched battles with each other on the Persian rugs at his feet.

So it was at the Saturday morning pony club rally which had brought them to admire their daughter's equestrian skills that we found ourselves listening to observations about the future of Suzanne's pony. On the way home we talked about the somewhat pointed allusion to 'a new home', agreeing that he'd be fine for Jessica and we wondered if they really thought we'd be suitable people to look after him. The following week the subject was again brought up, so I hesitatingly suggested that if they thought we'd be fit guardians we'd love to have him until Jessica outgrew him. They both leapt at the suggestion and said they'd immediately begin to look seriously for another mount.

Several weeks later Suzanne rode the little pony up to Tironnen. Knowing that she was riding him for the very last time must have brought many memories flooding into the young girl's mind as they sauntered through the lanes. The pony had been bought as a foal when Suzanne was small and they had grown together until in his fourth year the two of them had assumed the roles of rider and mount. Many happy years had followed during which both had increased their skills, with Suzanne's natural exuberance overcoming her pony's somewhat lethargic attitude to exercise. Such a parting as this one could only have been a sad event but no doubt softened by the pleasant ride over to Tironnen and the knowledge that she would still see a great deal of him.

Her parents had come ahead by car and while we all waited at the yard gate for her to appear at the bottom of the field an impatient Jessica stood a little way down the meadow the sooner to get a view of the arrivals. I saw her crane her neck and take a few hurried steps further down the field, then she half turned towards us and began to jump up and down waving her hands.

'Here they are.'

Suzanne appeared through the lower gate, cantered up the remaining distance, quickly dismounted and with a courtly flourish handed the reins to his delighted new owner. The child gazed at the little chestnut gelding, stroking the dense forelock, which hung between two neat ears. Although her asthma had greatly lessened she was still painfully thin from years of torment but her face glowed with happiness in sharp contrast to the pony's long-suffering expression. She passed her hand along the broad back which bore a distinct resemblance to a billiard table, smoothed the thick cascading mane and patted the firm shoulder, then putting her arms gently round his neck, whispered 'Oh Punch, you are so beautiful.'

So Punch joined Bessie in the meadow, and after submitting to her furious but brief signals of seniority carried on life much as before, pony clubbing in the village and hacking through the lanes and up on the moors. A not very arduous existence. However, although capable of giving a good ride and doing all the exciting things ponies and their riders normally enjoy, Punch had one great interest in life.

Food.

He was a glutton.

He ate all day and presumably all night. The only time he ever rested from eating was when he was being ridden. An outward ride would be made with a great show of reluctance and any stopping on the way made use of by a smart head down to grab any blade of grass that offered itself to his accomplished jaws. Once pointed in a

181

homeward direction it seemed he couldn't move quickly enough, head up and ears alert, for home was where the food was.

In winter his affections were directed solely to the bearer of victuals. The sound of the food store door being opened brought him into loud penetrating voice, and the sight of a bucket in someone's hand ensured that his small weighty body would be pushed hard against the gate, thus delaying immediate access to the nosh-up. It took Bessie's greater size and top dog mentality to move him and he never learned to associate jamming the gate with the delay in getting his food. We could hang over the gate, shouting, shoving and waving our arms around yet he would remain straining his neck towards the elusive bucket until the sound of Bessie's thundering hooves sent him scampering to a safer pitch. He ate with the frenzy of a millionaire disposing of his cash assets against the inevitability of a Wall Street crash

Left unchecked on rich spring pasture, Punch would have kept up his gorging until he became ill, very ill, for gluttonous ponies are highly subject to a painful affliction of the feet called laminitis. Apart from not being rideable during this period, the cure is near-starvation, and whilst being frightful for the animal, it can I imagine be most distressing for the owners. So every morning before Jessica went to school she led Punch into a small corral in the yard which Gordon had made. No grass grew there but there he stayed until Jessica returned from school in the afternoon, when he would be turned out into the meadow. The bucket in the corral contained only water and those early spring weeks were a time of terrible torment for the little gelding. I felt sorry for him all on his own so I made a point of visiting him from time to time, sometimes with few dates or a carrot.

On one of these occasions I was stroking him on the nose. A warm breeze was blowing across the yard and maybe this, coupled with the soft movement of my hand gave him a feeling of well-being. His eyes closed as he sank into a pleasant reverie and I was just beginning to get a bit that way myself when a hen flew up onto the fence right by his head. Startled by the sudden flapping he jerked his head upwards opening his mouth as he did so. He then closed it. This all happened in a split second but in that fraction of time Punch's mouth and my hand somehow met. The hen settled down on the fence clucking contentedly to herself and I juddered as the pain in my forefinger rose

182

to an excruciating pitch, trapped under the pressure of Punch's front teeth.

The eyes that sleepily looked at me from under the thickly spread forelock bore no malice. Throughout the whole encounter I doubt whether he was ever aware that my finger was in his mouth, and just as no conscious thought had caused the action so no conscious thought came to my rescue to suggest that he should do other than remain as he was......dozing in the warm sun with my finger between his teeth.

'Punch, let go.' I suppose it was just something to say and it sounded as stupid as it was. I wiggled my hand very slightly. Every movement sent signals racing to my nerves, not only in my finger but also up the length of my arm, across the shoulder to my neck and throat, where I had a strange desire to swallow something that wasn't there.

'Let go Punch, let go,' but my hissing met with no response. Well, what was I expecting!

'You bloody thing,' and with eyes closed Punch acknowledged my exasperation by flicking one ear forward and the other back, and the hen perhaps feeling a little anxious roused herself with dignity and moved a couple of feet down the fence before settling once more.

I was in a fix and there appeared to be only two ways out of it. Either I would remain as I was until either Gordon missed me or Punch let go, and I reckoned I'd pass out before either happened. I pictured myself fainting, my limp body leaning against the wall, and wondered if its weight would cause the dozing pony to release his grip and if he did what would happen when I crashed to the ground. About a foot away was an old Belfast sink, which I filled each day during the summer when the duck pond looked like drying up. It now contained a murky broth, which had neither the appearance nor bouquet of a Malmsey butt and did not look a delicious thing in which to drown. Maybe if I fell straight down I'd miss the sink altogether and just crash my head on the hard edge. It was all very dramatic but positive thought was needed not drama.

On my left was the stable door that opened into our food store. I slipped the bolt off the top half and pulling it open leaned over the bottom half as far as I could. I knew that if I could grab a handful of whatever was nearest, Punch would let go, but both sacks were well out of reach. I felt behind the door in case a stick or some implement was leaning there but the reachable inside of the store was as bereft of help for my plight as was the outside. My head was now throbbing in unison with my finger, and the part that was visible had turned a greenish white. My reflections about drowning in the sink surfaced again. I reached into my pocket and pulled out some paper handkerchiefs, baling twine, a hoof-trimming knife and a Crunchie Bar wrapper with a sticky piece of my favourite goody wrapped in it. (Comfort food would come later.) I examined the items in my hand none of which appeared to carry the hallmarks of rescue. Then I thought, if I could get the hen off the wall, which was bound to be a noisy affair, then Punch would probably wake from his reverie and all would be well.

I slipped the knife and other bits back into my pocket and examined the baling twine. It had been cut so that the knot was more or less in the centre, so holding the knot between my teeth I caught hold of the two lengths of twine about eighteen inches away. Releasing my toothy grip I flung the knotted end with as much force as I could from left to right across my right arm, the forefinger of which was still confined in Punch's mouth but the knot caught the crook of my elbow and the hen only extended her wings a fraction in surprise before settling down again. I tried a second time but the same thing happened, except that this time the hen didn't even move.

Well, the easiest thing in the world is to have an idea but it's only good ideas that are any use. I had to think again.

What was I trying to do?

Answer: disturb the hen.

Why wasn't the baling twine idea working?

Answer: because there was no weight involved.

Weight was needed and weight was in my pocket in the shape of the hoof-trimming knife. EUREKA......

I dropped the twine and took out the knife, which had suddenly become an article of infinite value, aimed the blunt end at the hen and threw. She screamed her objections as it landed against her well-upholstered wing, flapped speedily and noisily into the air, taking the pony completely by surprise. He removed his teeth from my finger and with a feeling of hideous nausea I gently withdrew my right hand, cocooning it in my other as I tenderly raised it to my mouth where I gently blew on it in an effort to try and relieve the pain. I stood there,

184

shoulders hunched and convinced that if I moved the throbbing would increase a hundredfold. After a while it dawned on me that the whole episode couldn't have lasted more than twenty or thirty seconds although it seemed as though I'd been standing there for ages.

Over the next few days the finger sported a variety of colours: yellow, green, purple; all very pretty.

Punch said goodbye to his grassless corral when spring turned to summer and stayed with us for another five years, never losing his reluctance to ride out nor his eagerness to return and certainly not his voraciousness. When Jessica outgrew him he went to an adoring family who couldn't bear the thought of confining him each spring. He got laminitis which fortunately was caught in the early stages but we never knew which he suffered from most: the pain in his feet or his starvation as he endured the cure.

PUT IT ON THE SLATE

For nearly three years the Slate Cameos had kept us financially afloat and although Gordon was well and truly tired of engraving and of having an aching arm after each morning session, there was little hope of anything else taking their place. They were our safety net and were serving us well.

Things had gone from bad to worse as the decade progressed with inflation climbing at an alarming rate, at one point reaching 16.5% in 1976. The country was staring bankruptcy in the face and the Labour government had to call in the International Monetary Fund which immediately forced it to control the money supply in order to stabilize the economy and stave off impending disaster.

We were well aware that the economy was in chaos for that was the reason Gordon had begun engraving in the first place, and listening to the news we were reminded constantly just how bad things were, yet we felt strangely removed from what we heard, for apart from the expected quiet time in January there was no cessation of orders for the slates.

We attended several country shows and the Royal Welsh Show and as well as selling the standard selection of Cameos, we'd taken commissions. The proud owners of champion bulls being particularly keen to have their animals immortalised in slate. Photographs would be presented and Gordon would engrave the likeness with the name, occasion and date beneath. These commissions were engraved on thick pieces of slate of a good size and always looked very impressive. Whatever hardships were being experienced in the rest of the country, a champion was a champion, and had to be commemorated.

Occasionally a phone call or letter would elicit a request from someone who had bought a Cameo on their travels but one morning we received a most unwelcome missive.

A complaint.

A complaint?

This came from a man living somewhere in the Home Counties and a very sarcastic letter it was too, the sort of letter that had obviously given the writer much satisfaction in composing and even greater delight in visualising the quaking terror with which we would read it the following morning. I forget the actual wording of it except one phrase. Apparently whilst on holiday his wife had purchased the Cameo of a bird and when she later cleaned it 'the bird had flown.'

Gone.

Completely vanished.

This had apparently marred the recollections of what had been a delightful holiday in Wales.

We were, it seemed, charlatans preying on the unsuspecting and we deserved to be shown as such to the world. To this end he was going to contact Esther Rantzen, who at the time had a popular television programme That's Life, which highlighted a variety of incidents, most of which were consumer orientated. Sad, funny, despicable and preposterous people and a good few we considered just plain stupid were all featured in her programmes.

Evidently we were to be thrown to the lions along with the fraudulent, lying, mercenary band of criminals regularly thus exposed. Miss Rantzen brought many sharp practises to the public eye but we didn't think we deserved to be included among them.

Gordon replied with a polite but marginally frosty letter requesting that the offending slate be returned and that he would have it analysed. This would show, he wrote, that rather than being cleaned as instructed on the reverse - *to clean simply rinse under running water and leave to dry* - some form of polish had been used. It was our guess that his lady had thought to improve the slate by making it shiny and had polished it.

Of course we never heard any more and I felt quite sorry for the man's wife who had obviously not told him what had happened.

Downtrodden I reckoned.

We had friends who on receiving a letter from the Prime Minister congratulating them on their successful business had it framed and hung in the loo, and another whose notification of a forthcoming knighthood had been deemed worthy of the same honoured place. Now we had a letter that whilst not being in quite the same league was definitely worth making sure our visitors enquired about it's significance. It remained there for several years until having milked as much hilarity from it as we felt we could, it was thrown out. I do hope its author is reading this.

Orders kept coming in and we enjoyed our regular drives to Snowdonia to buy slates, but as well as being arm aching the

187

repetitiveness of the engraving was getting to Gordon. He knew that the financial climate prohibited any experimentation but longed to become involved in something else. Then one day late in '76 the phone rang. Someone of whom we'd never heard but who had heard of Gordon, required artwork for a training video for Lloyd's Bank. Meetings were held, agreements arrived at and work on the house was put on hold, except of course for those times when it was necessary to exercise a 'different set of muscles'.

Were things beginning to look up at last? Were the IMF's restrictions beginning to have some effect?

An audio-visual. This was something involving techniques entirely new to Gordon but quickly grasping the principles involved he thoroughly enjoyed this foray into new territory and was delighted to be working on the cartoon characters required, something for which he had a great talent. This commission took a few weeks to complete and he was sorry when it was finished. However, shortly after, we had a visit from a couple who had purchased several Slate Cameos from our outlet in Solva in Pembrokeshire, and as they were travelling back home along the A40 thought they'd try to find us. Amazingly, without directions they did. Over tea and Welsh cakes it came to light that they were involved in audio-visuals. Another opening had landed in Gordon's lap.

Some weeks later when the bank opened the door of the rented front room of one of the village houses for its once a week stint of business and chat, I was thrilled to be able to hand over a cheque for a mammoth fifteen hundred pounds.

'Ooooh,' said Sian as she laid the cheque on the counter before flicking through the cheque book until she came to the relevant payslip which she stamped with vigour. 'Ooooh, that's nice. Is it work or something you've won?' This sort of conversation didn't happen in Southampton!

'Work' I replied, unfazed by her question and I told her about the audio-visual for Lloyd's bank and she said what a pity it wasn't for 'our' bank as it would be nice to have seen something home grown, as it were.

Then a chance encounter in the village with some newcomers who ran a company that constructed large exhibitions and were looking for a designer brought another dimension to Gordon's work. This proved

188

highly remunerative and rather than producing drawings he constructed scale models of his designs which was right up his street.

So began the slowing down of the engravings, which had saved our bacon when things were so dire; when we both knew the other was harbouring the question, do we really have to pack it in, but refusing to vocalize it.

Orders for more Cameos kept arriving and each parcel sent out contained a short note saying we were slowing down production and thanking the recipient for their custom over the years. Nearly all our customers phoned or sent a short note with their cheque, saying how sorry they were and what excellent sellers the Cameos had been, and if Gordon ever started doing them again would we contact them. Very nice, I thought, but we both knew it wouldn't happen.

Twenty years later while shopping in Hay-on-Wye near where I live, I was walking towards a woman who appeared to recognise me and she also seemed familiar to me. We stopped.

'I know you from somewhere' I said. She however, was smarter than I. 'I used to buy Slate Cameos from you when I had my shop here.'

Of course. It was a shop in a beautiful 16th century building where massive oak beams spanned the ceiling, and lath and plaster walls were intersected by timber framing, all of which presented a suitable background for the interesting crafts displayed.

'I retired many years ago but when you said there would be no more Cameos I kept six back and they're on my wall still. They were one of my best sellers, you know.'

DOWN THE LINE

Our telephone number was not dissimilar to that of an auctioneer in the nearby market town of Brecon and because a prefix had recently been added to the Brecon numbers we quite frequently got calls to his office. These misfired dialings escalated to quite significant numbers a few days before an important livestock sale but generally the caller offered a speedy apology and rang off. Occasionally though, we would get someone who was completely nonplussed at finding someone other than a representative of Bennet & Thomas on the other end of the line, or at least temporarily nonplussed, as was the elderly gentleman who rang through to us several days prior to the Christmas fat stock sale.

I'd just put a batch of mince pies in the Rayburn and was preparing pastry for some more, when the phone rang. I went to answer it, picking up the receiver delicately with a thumb and forefinger so as not to transfer to it the sticky pastry mixture that adhered to my hand.

'Hello, Pontbrynach 340.'

A rich vibrant voice asked, 'Is that Bennet & Thomas?'

'No, you've got the wrong number.'

'You're not Bennet & Thomas then?'

'No, I'm afraid not.'

Normally at this point if not before, it would have been obvious that I was not the person required but this gentleman needed more convincing. The next question was innocuous enough but each word was delivered separately from its neighbours and encompassed such resonance as to do justice to a Burton or Olivier.

'Not to do with the mart then?'

'No, sorry.'

After the glorious expounding of the previous sentence what followed rather took me be surprise.

The sound began on a very high note and descended very, very, slowly. Oooooooooh.'

I listened fascinated. Never before had I heard incredulity expressed in such an expansive way.

'What number are you then?'

'Pontbrynach 340.'

Puzzlement now crept into the voice as it resumed its lyrical delivery.

'Well now, I dialled Brecon 340 so how did I get you then?'

I explained that to get through to the auctioneer, the prefix 43 had to be added and if that wasn't done only the three digits registered. That way people got to us instead. 'It happens frequently since the codes were changed.'

Obviously impressed by my technical knowledge he resonated, 'Well, well,' and pondered on what I'd said for a few moments.

'43 you say. Well, I'll do that now.'

I thought this would terminate the conversation but he was evidently feeling chatty.

'Where are you then?'

'Pontbrynach.' I warmed to his friendliness whilst keeping a mental note of the length of time the mince pies had been in the oven.

'Pontbrynach?' then after a pause, 'In the village?'

'No, on the hill, not far from the common.'

To my delight the high-pitched sound began again, descending slowly as before to a deep baritone, then there was another pause.

'On the hill? It's beautiful up there looking over the Beacons.'

'Yes' I said, 'It's very beautiful. You know it then?'

'Well, you tell me where you are on the hill and I'll tell you if I know it.'

'Tironnen.'

This time the sound was different. It seemed to encompass complete knowledge of our whereabouts, the house we lived in, its surroundings, our lifestyle, indeed the sort of people we were. It was a warm brown sound and it lingered long on the same note, dropping slightly before blending into the words that followed.

'Aaaaaaaaaaaah. I know it. I know Tironnen.'

The name was delivered as though it was cocooned in softest silk and I thought how my own rendition of it had been so banal and lifeless. The man was speaking slowly now, more I felt to himself than to me, and the words rose and fell on a sea of music, sometimes hurried over as if time was of the essence, yet others were drawn out and lingered over as though their very individuality deserved special attention.

191

'I remember. Yes. I remember going to Tironnen with my father. A long time ago that was, yes a long time ago. I was four, maybe five at the time and I don't know why we went but I remember it as clearly as I do getting out of bed this morning. After we'd been to the house we climbed up the hill behind, right to the top, yes, right to the top we went. I was so tired when we got there but when we did I thought I was looking out over the whole world.'

From where I stood I scanned the great panorama stretching from the Black Mountains, across the Beacons to the flat topped Carmarthen Fan in the west, aware of how even more dramatic it was from 'the top'.

'It's so lovely up there,' I offered but sensed he wasn't listening. A long silence followed and I knew he was recalling the tired little boy and maybe many other memories associated with that visit long ago. Suddenly his voice became livelier as though the recollections of that youthful hill climb had vanished. 'Some time back, when there was no one living there, I was told someone kept a horse there, in the house. Funny keeping a horse in a house,' and he sighed slowly and after a pause said, 'Fancy you living at Tironnen. Fancy now,' and after another pause, asked 'You like it there?'

'Oh yes, we love it.' I hoped that the warmth in my voice assured him that the house was in caring hands.

Another silence, then fully back in the present he queried 'What was that number you said?'

'Forty-three, before the number you want.'

'I'll do that then.'

I was just about to say, 'Come and visit us. Come and have tea,' when the pungent smell of burning caused a hitch in my thinking and already the man was saying 'It's been nice talking to you,' and he was gone.

Slowly I replaced the phone, then with nose a-twitching rushed into the kitchen. Smoke poured into the room as I opened the oven door, telling me that the mince pies were beyond saving. I pulled out the baking trays and with eyes smarting from the fumes I hurled the cinder-like contents through the door onto the garden where they could cool while I made some more.

But what did a spoilt batch of baking matter, for how can you value a few mince pies against an encounter with a poet?

There are days when everything I do is not only well done but also magnificently done. Every task, however complicated is completed effortlessly, any problem resolved speedily, any extraordinary happening settled with efficiency and style. Needless to say, these days have a rarity value akin to a miss-printed Cape of Good Hope Penny Red, and a night's sleep will generally ensure that the following morning sees a return to my normal fingers and thumbs approach to whatever tasks face me.

It was halfway through the afternoon of such a super-efficient day. Gordon had gone to Brecon for some glass to mend a broken window in his workshop and I was at the top of the garden doing battle with an overgrown hawthorn hedge when the phone rang.

I walked quickly down towards the house pulling off my thick gardening gloves as I did so, then throwing them casually onto the garden wall went inside, at which point the ringing stopped. 'Oh well, I suppose you'll call again if it's important' I said out loud, as though addressing the caller, and pulling on my gloves returned to my hedge husbandry. But no sooner had I placed the secateurs round a spindly branch than the ringing started again.

'O.K. I'm coming, I'm coming,' I called out in a singsong voice as I repeated the walking glove-removing exercise, but before I'd gone a few yards the sound again stopped.

'Oh bother,' I muttered irritably as I did a rather smart about turn on my right heel and marched back whence I'd come to continue without I hoped, further interruptions. Hawthorn being prickly stuff needs to be treated with a certain amount of respect and as I gingerly extricated a particularly thorny bit of growth the phone rang yet again.

'I don't believe this,' I said, standing motionless with the secateurs held aloft in one hand and the branch I was just about to remove in the other. 'Who on earth is doing this?' and I was about to run down the path to express my displeasure when I thought,   'No, I'll let it ring.'

Well it did. It went on and on and on until I felt obliged to answer it in order to restore peace to my world. So it was not in a state of equanimity that I lifted the receiver.

'Hello,' I said trying to keep my annoyance in check.

'I've got an extra entry for the mart,' announced a very gruff voice.

Realising that the man thought he was through to the auctioneers I answered, 'I'm sorry but you've got the wrong number.'

'You're Bennet and Thomas aren't you?' This was said in such an uncivil and demanding manner that I could almost feel the words being spat down the phone at me. Even so my super-efficiency kept me courteous.

'No, I'm not but if you........'

An exasperated expletive blasted into my ear before the sound of the phone being slammed down terminated the call.

I was shocked

I was speechless (almost!)

I was angry. Boy, was I angry. You're not going to get away with this, I thought.

This was in the days long before 1471 was in use, so I dialled Bennet & Thomas's number but it was engaged. The ignorant fellow had no doubt got through to them and the number remained engaged for several minutes but eventually someone answered.

I introduced myself, then continued, 'Would you mind, and I quite understand if you don't wish to, telling me who has just called you? It may be someone I wish to speak to.'

'No, I don't mind.' The man was obviously puzzled, 'but would you mind telling me why you want to know.'

So I told him, becoming almost as hot under the collar in the telling as I had been in the hearing. He roared with laughter. 'It was Newton-Jones from Tressiliog. Going on about being told he'd got the wrong number when he knew he hadn't. Known to be a bit short on civility. Don't be upset by him though, he's the same to everyone.'

I assured him I wasn't upset, just furious. I thanked him for his co-operation and began thumbing through the directory for Mr Newton-Jones's number.

My dialling was immediately answered as if he was waiting for a call. This was a good start. It would make him all the more irate when he found that this was not his expected call.

In a clear voice dripping with sweetness I asked, 'Is that Mr Newton-Jones?'

'Yes.' A lack of civility was thickly spread on this one word.

'Oh, I'm so glad,' I cooed slowly. 'I do so want to speak to you. Please listen very carefully Mr Newton-Jones. Five minutes ago, you made a phone call and by mistake got through to me. I'm sure you remember.' I paused for a second or so to let him digest the unexpectedness of my message. I thought I was doing awfully well and it flashed through my mind that I was giving a very passable rendition of Fenella Fielding. 'Well the next time you get a wrong number and are answered with politeness, please don't display your lack of manners by behaving in the way you have just done. I don't like it.' Then, still dripping syrupy sweetness added softly, 'Goodbye,' and was just about to replace the receiver when a thought occurred to me and I put the phone back to my ear. I could hear him breathing deeply and I had to stifle a strong desire to call a melodious 'yoo-hoo'. His complete lack of reaction was something of a surprise. No protests, interruptions or shouts. Nothing at all, yet it seemed that my little speech had had some effect if only to produce a temporary paralysis of mind.

What on earth was he doing I wondered but the seconds passed without a sound apart from the breathing, and I pictured him looking at the phone as though expecting something more tangible than a disembodied voice to ooze from it. There wasn't much chance that he'd taken in my number when I'd answered his call earlier, so my identity would forever be a secret and he would never know who I was or how I knew who he was. No wonder he was perplexed for that is surely what he was. But one thing he did know as he held the telephone in his hand was that someone somewhere, thought he was a rather nasty individual and was prepared to tell him so with overt civility and politeness. It was very satisfying.

I couldn't resist another 'Goodbye Mr Newton-Jones,' the mellifluous tones of which surprised me in view of the fact that I was trying to stifle giggles, and before my mirth exploded I gently replaced the receiver.

I was well pleased, for that was definitely 'style'.

BAGGINS

The winter of 1974/75 produced some harsh easterly blizzards, which relentlessly blew the snow into massive drifts, causing the countryside to lose its natural contours in the face of such onslaughts.

High on the hillside of the next valley lived a friend Sarah, who bred rough collies and shelties and one February morning on a day when all but the most intrepid remained indoors, she was out with her dogs in the snow-covered fields. After going only a short way, she was intrigued when one of the collies came bounding through the snow towards her, then darted away to a spot beneath an evergreen hedge where the branches were hanging down with the weight of snow they carried. The dog ran back to her only to shoot off again. Aware that something unusual had occurred her other dogs joined in and soon they too were either plunging excitedly back and forth to Sarah, or staying by the hedge looking expectantly while waiting for her to join them. Reaching the animals she immediately saw the object of their interest.

Two large brown eyes looked up at her from the base of the hedge. Gently she picked up a shivering puppy from where it had lain half covered in snow, slipped it inside her coat and retraced her steps to the cottage, the dogs leaping about her. She gave the puppy a brisk rub down with a warm towel, fed him warm milk from a pipette and settled him in a hay lined box on top of the boiler, not giving much for his chances. Then she phoned me. 'I need some goat's milk for an invalid,' and I listened to the story of finding the puppy.

'His eyes are open, but he's so small and weak. He's very emaciated. I'll do what I can for him, you never know.' She sighed, then added, 'He's one of mine, well, one of Bamber's. Exactly the same colouring. Obviously the result of an illicit meeting with one of the farm bitches.' Bamber was Sarah's blue-merle rough collie, a magnificent animal whose colouring always attracted attention.

'How on earth did it get in the hedge?' I asked.

'Oh, I think I can guess. There's a farmer not a million miles from here who doesn't give a damn about his dogs. Just leaves them to fend for themselves and I reckon that some poor little bitch gave birth to her one and only, fed him for as long as she could, then took him to where she thought he would be safe. She probably went off to die somewhere. I had the dogs out late yesterday afternoon and the puppy wasn't there then. Anyway, you're not holed up in your place are you?'

'We're O.K. here' I replied. 'Gordon's taken the Land Rover down to the lower farm just in case but so far all is well. I assume you're alright else you wouldn't be thinking of us getting milk to you.'

'Oh no, I don't want you to do that,' Sarah said hastily. 'Robin's hoping to leave early today, so I'll ring and ask him to pick the milk up on his way. If he can't get off I'll come over.' Five minutes later Sarah rang again to say that Robin would be with us around midday.

I bottled up three pints of fresh milk, then in case the weather got worse and cut us off from the outside world, decided to send some frozen milk as well. Then in large letters I wrote a note that read 'FREEZE.' This note I pinned to my jersey, which was my normal way of making sure that somebody would remind me of whatever I needed to be reminded of, and sure enough when Robin arrived later he stood in the open doorway as though he'd been turned into stone.

'What on earth are you doing?' I asked irritably as the cold air filled the room. 'Ye gods, get in and shut the door; are you trying to kill us?'

'I was only doing what I thought you wanted me to do,' he replied with mock offence. 'If you'd had 'WELCOME' writ large across your bosom the confusion wouldn't have arisen.'

'Ohhh, silly me. Must remember in future not to let reminders conflict with the elements.'

***

Against all odds the puppy clung to life thanks to Sarah's devotion, for she was feeding him every three hours day and night. Slowly he gained strength and slept most of the time. He whined when he was hungry and little by little gained weight, and although Sarah was pleased at his progress her comments were guarded.

'I'm hopeful, but it's too early to tell.'

Then one afternoon ten days later she phoned. Although it was still very cold, there had been several days when the winter sun had been strong enough to thaw a good deal of the snow.

197

'Do you feel like coming for supper? Now that the roads are pretty clear I want to come out of purdah don't you?'

'I didn't know you'd been hemmed in?'

'Well no, we haven't been, but it just takes so much longer to do anything when in order to get anywhere you either have to lift your feet over six inches of snow or concentrate on not falling in the slush. There's no time for anything other than getting the necessary things done is there? I feel socially deprived.'

'Well, supper would be fine. Thanks very much. Usual time?'

'Yes, everyone welcome. By the way, puppy dog is gorgeous. You'll love him. Bye.'

***

As soon as we arrived at the cottage where Sarah, Robin and their young family lived we were ushered quietly into the heavily beamed living room. On the floor, to one side of the wood burning stove was a box with a piece of blanket draped over its edge. In the box was the puppy, his head resting on the blanketed edge, his ears pricked. His eyes showed nervousness, which wasn't surprising, yet he didn't move at our entrance. We all knelt or sat on the floor so as not to appear too daunting and just looked at him, ooooing and aaaaing in a whispery sort of way.

'I can't believe he's grown so well,' said Sarah, 'I really didn't think he'd make it.'

'He's gorgeous,' said Louise, leaning forward and slowly extending her hand in the direction of the box. The puppy drew back slightly but after several seconds resumed his original position resting his chin on the box edge, eyeing Louise's hand as it ever so slowly moved towards him. 'Is it alright to hold him?' she asked, and at that moment, almost as if in answer to her request, the puppy stood up and stretched.

We were then able to have a really good look at him, 'ooooing' and 'aaaaing' again, which evidently disturbed a couple of cats who roused themselves from their chosen spot in the inglenook, glared disdainfully at the assembled company and returned to their slumbers. The girls desperately wanted to make a fuss of the puppy but when

Louise attempted to pick him up he shied away curling up again in his box.

'It's going to take some time to sort him out,' said Sarah.

'Whoever has him will need a lot of patience.'

Angela was incredulous? 'Aren't you keeping him?'

'Oh I can't. A house where there are small children running round is not the place for him and he couldn't go out in the kennels. He needs somewhere where he can get used to his surroundings in his own time. All young animals need quiet times, this one more than most. I'll keep him until he's physically fit and in the meantime I shall find a suitable home for him.'

There was silence for a few seconds, then Jessica piped up. 'We can.'

Her announcement didn't seem to make much sense so we let it pass, then Angela, having evidently homed in on her younger sister's wavelength said, 'Yes, we can.'

'What are you going on about? What's all this 'can' about?' But as I said it I'd knew that two parents were being ambushed.

'We can look after him.'

'He'll get used to his surroundings with us.'

'We've already got two dogs,' said Gordon.

'Plus a goat that thinks it's a dog,' I added.

'Please......please?'

'Well Mum,' said Louise in a wise eldest-daughter sort of way, You've always said if you've got one animal you might as well have two, so surely if you have two you might just as well have three.'

Why had I opened my big mouth!

***

We called him Baggins. He very soon got to know his name and made a friend, for Tigger the cat, having inspected Baggins's bed evidently decided it to be a good billet and within minutes of the puppy's arrival the two were snuggled up together. Although at first Baggins was too timid to venture beyond the confines of his box, after a few days he began to sit up whenever something was going on, so his life became more interesting. In between times he slept and grew.

199

We had decided on a programme of keeping him warm, fed and taking him outside when he needed to go. Other than that we would speak his name whenever he looked up from his box and say something in an encouraging tone but leave him to take the initiative. We just hoped that by this gentle persuasion he would become more trusting. As Sarah had said, leave him to become used to his surroundings in his own time.

Then after he'd been with us for a week or so, he stretched, looked about for some while, clambered out of the box and padded over to the dish that Dylan had just left empty. I'd just come in from doing the morning's milking so I poured a mugful of warm milk into the bowl which Baggins quickly lapped up, then as though realizing he was far away from the safety of his bed, scuttled back. But his courage was now awakened. After this visit to Dylan's food bowl he was emboldened to explore the big kitchen further, scuttling behind a chair or into a corner or back to his box if any sudden movement occurred but we felt that our methods were bearing fruit. Gradually he began to investigate the world about him, venturing outside provided one of us was with him. By early spring our gangly youngster was romping with Dylan and chasing any stray hen that appeared in the garden. The timid puppy was becoming able and slowly gaining confidence.

Jessica particularly played a great part in his rehabilitation, encouraging him to be adventurous and consoling him when he was frightened. As the months went by his permanent coat of many blue/grey hues began to oust the puppy fur and thicken and lengthen. Four white socks and a partial white ruff gave him a most striking appearance and the collie features and shape were so marked that it was obvious he was going to become a very handsome dog. As summer came and waned his body filled out and the proportions began to refine themselves, each week showing more of the elegant appearance which he would have when fully grown and I rather regretted our choice of name for him. In a few months time he wouldn't look much like a 'Baggins'. Still the name would have to stay. His manners were impeccable and he was enjoying his lessons of simple obedience, delighting in the effusive fussing when he did the right thing, eagerly accepting some reward. Not only was he beautiful; he was very intelligent.

Then one Friday in late summer, when Baggins had been with us for seven months, Gordon and I drove down to the village. It was a fine day and the dogs and Bluebell's kid Blossom had spent the morning alternately careering around the garden or lying exhausted on the grass. We often left them outside if we expected only to be away a short while, as there was no way they could get out of the garden. We returned forty minutes later to find Dylan, Bouncer and Blossom still enjoying themselves but of Baggins there was no sign.

Where could he be? Could he have hurt himself and be lying injured somewhere? Gordon went round to the front of the house where the garden was so small he could see at a glance that Baggins wasn't there. Could someone have wandered up the hill, opened the door and shut him in? That was quite a ridiculous idea but nevertheless I went into the house calling his name.

'Where's Baggins, Dylan?', but the black dog only looked expectantly at us and wagged his tail.

We called the dogs and searched the outbuildings and behind the barn. We walked up the old cart track above the house and through the fields beyond, calling his name but all the while knowing that it was a futile exercise as there was no way he could have left the garden and even if he could he was still too nervous to have done so. Yet we kept up our search.

'Baggins' I shouted at the top of my voice, 'Baggins, Baggins.'

We set off across further fields, Gordon going towards the woods south of the house and I going eastwards, making my goal the stretch of trees and marshland which marked the boundary between our neighbour and the farm beyond. I stood listening for any noise that would indicate Baggins was about. The chirruping of birds, the occasional scuffle of a squirrel as it hurried about its business through the early falling leaves, the faint sound of a tractor high on the hill and in the distance Gordon calling and whistling were the only sounds to be heard. What on earth had happened? It just didn't make sense.

Normally a walk through the trees was a joyous thing, a time to relish the interest or excitement of whatever time of year it was, but not this time. I felt no curiosity towards the inhabitants of this tranquil place as they organized their lives to withstand the coming winter. Even the sound of the stream trickling over stones that had always been so great a part of the enchantment was now just a sound of no

201

consequence. Down through the wood I walked, calling and stopping to listen, frequently diverting my path to take in the fields beyond, or the marshland on the homeward side, all the time hearing Gordon's voice in the distance. I sometimes backtracked via another route for in order to cover as much ground as possible, every step accompanied by the agonizing fear of finding the dog in an old snare and I didn't know whether this would be worse than not finding him at all. Yet all the time I was certain of one thing; we were on a wild goose chase for there was no way Baggins could or would have got out of the garden on his own.

I met up with Gordon at the bottom of the wood and sadly we walked back up to the house, trying in vain to find some reason for Baggins's disappearance. Dylan ambled beside us, no ground scent giving him reason to stray or get excited. And it was a puzzled and unhappy pair who arrived back at Tironnen.

We made a pot of tea which we quickly downed and set off again, straining our eyes and ears, alert to any slight movement or sound which may have indicated the presence of the young dog but all was still. Lingering for a few moments in the yard, I kept repeating to myself, but he can't have got out, he can't have got out.

The direct route from Tironnen to the moors is where the land slopes most steeply and the going was quite hard on that warm September day. Before we reached the top we had to push our way through masses of copper coloured bracken calling all the while, hope rising occasionally as some shifting of the bronze fronds would send us hurrying to the spot, but a bird would fly up or some unseen creature scuttle off at our coming and stillness would return, the brief moment of hope dashed and our risen spirits would drop like a pebble in a pond.

The girls came back from school and were distraught to hear our news. Refusing their customary drinks and biscuits they set off to search, hoping no doubt that they would succeed where we had failed. Dylan followed them and I watched the little group crossing the fields until it vanished from sight. I phoned our nearest neighbour but there was no reply, then made more calls to friends and neighbours asking that if they heard anything about a stray dog to let me know. I mechanically began to lay the table in readiness for a dinner that I was sure none of us would want. The thought of Baggins filled my mind, not in any particular way. Just his name really.....Baggins......and his eager face hovered before me as I set out the cutlery around the mats on the oak table. Come home Baggins, please come home. My eyes were hot with unshed tears. Oh, Baggins, where are you?

I didn't hear the sound of anyone approaching and was startled when a knock on the open door broke in on my brooding. Our neighbour stood on the step and I wondered how long he'd been standing there and if my whispered pleading had reached beyond the table over which I'd been bending.

'Oh, Elwyn, I'm sorry. Have you been there long? I was deep in my thoughts.'

Looking at his face, normally jovial but now set hard, I realized that something was wrong. 'What is it?'

'Have you seen Jess about?'

'No, she's not been up here for ages.'

Elwyn shook his head in a perplexed way. 'Well, something's wrong. I put her in the shed when I went up to plough the top field and now there's no sign of her.'

Jess was not a wanderer and had only ever made two appearances in our yard. Even if our gate was open Baggins would never even go into the meadow or the yard without one of the family, yet these two dogs had disappeared and on the same day. One a highly trained sheep dog mysteriously missing from its shed, the other, to anyone who didn't know otherwise, a young sheep dog confined in a fenced garden. Bells were beginning to ring, although at the time I didn't know what tune they were playing. Gordon left his work when he heard Elwyn's voice and joined us as I was saying that we also had a dog missing.

Then suddenly a tune began to play. Friday is market day in Brecon, and there is a general exodus from the farms as people go into the town for most of the day. Meeting friends to discuss the happenings of the previous week and the fates and fortunes of mutual acquaintances is an enjoyable event for communities kept very much at home by the nature of their work, and going to the mart covers a variety of activities crammed into this excursion. It's a fair bet that on a fine September day anyone left on the farms would be out in the fields, ploughing or sowing. The outdoor tasks to get everything ship-shape before winter are numerous and lengthy and no opportunity

203

would be lost to get on with them. So farmyards would most likely be unattended and anyone coming into the lower farm would have heard the sounds of Dylan and Baggins barking as they played, and if they so wished followed the track up to Tironnen. Somebody had done just that and Jess at the farm below was there for the taking.

'They've been stolen haven't they?' It was more of a statement than a question, adding, 'That's what's happened isn't it?'

'I think so. I've heard of this going on in other parts and some dogs have disappeared from down towards the Swansea road. Sheep dogs are fetching a lot of money. I'll have to pay at least two-hundred pounds to replace Jess and a youngster like yours would be just the right age for someone to start training.'

I picked up the phone and dialled the police house number. The policeman's wife answered. 'That makes three today,' she answered, confirming our suspicions. 'We've heard several dogs have been reported missing down Swansea way last week. It looks as though these people are spreading their wings.' I gave her descriptions of Baggins and Jess and replaced the receiver. We were dealing with an organized gang here.

Gordon walked over to the big inglenook and filled a glass with beer from the stone cask. Silently he offered it to Elwyn, then put another glass under the tap and I watched as the golden brew jetted into it, rising up the sides, forcing the pale froth ever upwards until it reached the rim. The squirting sound ceased as Gordon turned off the tap and some froth overflowed, coursing down the outside. I observed this homely operation, outwardly attentive but not really seeing, for I was numb at the thought of what had happened.

That evening we searched again and the following day also, but of Baggins and Jess there was no sign. Returning from that final search I put on the kettle. My actions were slow, my attention to what needed to be done made sluggish by dwelling on the unhappiness which pervaded the house. I thought of the many days and nights that Sarah had dutifully spent willing the starving puppy to live, of the months during which Jessica had returned from school to give priority to encouraging his confidence and how he had repaid a hundredfold the time invested in him. Just to look at him was reward enough. And now, some bastards had just scooped him up so that they could make easy money. By this time, wherever he was, it would be a long way from us and I knew we'd never see our beloved dog again.

I drew a breath and quickly expelled it, bracing my shoulders and straightening myself up as I did so. Life had to continue; work had to be done; Baggins would never be forgotten. I could but hope he would find a home where someone would be kind to him.

ANGLO-NUBIAN RELATIONS

'She's a very large goat,' Frances said, 'Bigger than many Anglo's. So many seem to have lost the big body but Miranda is what I call a really good old-fashioned goat. I'd keep her myself but I've no room.'

We were getting so much milk from Bluebell and Snowdrop but not enough cream for more than a small quantity of butter each week. British Sannans can give an enormous amount of milk but the butterfat content is not as high as with Anglo-Nubians whose milk yield is generally somewhat lower but has a high percentage of butterfat. It seemed sensible to think about getting an Anglo and we'd talked about it for quite some time but hadn't made any enquiries. There was no rush. Then one evening I phoned Frances, from whom we had bought Bluebell and Snowdrop, to request a registration form so that Blossom could become a bona fide member of the British Goat Society's herd book and mentioned that we were interested in finding a good Anglo.

'Well, it's strange that you should ask' said Frances. 'I'm going to collect one next week from Sussex. It's rather sad really. She's been kept as a pet and I rather think they've got tired of her, although they won't admit it. I know the goat well. She's five now and had a couple of kids before she went to these people. Both kids went to some Arab state for good sums of money to improve the stock.'

That sounded promising, although as we didn't exhibit our goats nor have much in the way of Arabs knocking on our door asking for foundation stock to improve their native herds, I didn't think any future offspring of Miranda's would be likely to be that remunerative. Anyway, it was butter we wanted, not money.

Frances described Miranda in detail, finishing with 'She's a grand old thing......a real character. I think they want a hundred pounds for her.' Reeling back from this, I told her I'd see what Gordon thought and put down the phone.

Hoping that my enthusiasm would in part nullify the sound of the sum required, I described Miranda to Gordon in glowing terms, stressing the importance of such an investment. To have enough of our own home produced butter was a lovely thought and of course there'd be milk as well and kids to sell, so forking out one hundred pounds for her would be but a temporary hitch in our bank balance. With my

206

usual optimism, I said I felt that this was an opportunity not to be missed.

'Well it's up to you' said Gordon, which of course meant one thing. I phoned Frances to say we'd come over to Worcestershire the following week, by which time she would have collected Miranda from Sussex.

***

When we arrived I opened the wide white gates for Gordon to drive through and thought how beautiful Frances's yard was. Freshly pink-washed loose-boxes ranged both sides and tubs of flowers and hanging baskets ornamented the paving and walls outside office and tack-room, for Frances was not only an enthusiastic goat breeder but great in the show world of the native Welsh Mountain pony.

'Hello,' we said to two heavily forelocked heads peering enquiringly at us from open stable doors and as Frances emerged from the house, we said 'hello' to her as well. In the homely kitchen we drank coffee and talked about the many things that had happened since last we met, mostly goaty and horsey, then having enjoyed this pleasant ease-taking we went outside to be introduced to Miranda.

At the sound of the door opening and voices emerging we once again became the centre of interest to the stabled ponies as Frances told us about the important show to which she was taking them the following day. We walked down past the boxes towards the big purpose built building that ran the width of the yard at the far end. This was the goat house, light and airy, partitioned into a dozen or so stalls, with two larger ones for kids and goatlings and a small milking parlour at one end. It was very organized, spotlessly clean and no doubt very snug in the cold weather. We passed empty stalls and went out the other side into the exercise yard from which an open gate led into a field.

'She's out there. Wait here and I'll get her,' and Frances opened the gate and walked across the grass calling 'Come on come on,' to the browsing herd of Saanans. Every head looked up and when another 'come on' rang out the merry crowd swarmed towards her, eager to find out what the excitement was about. Just one lone figure sauntered well behind the group, seeming only to move because everyone else was moving but showing no interest in why the herd was on the run. The inquisitive Saanans crowded round and with a pat for this one and that Frances pushed her way through to the solitary creature that stood several yards away.

As she took hold of the goat by the collar the animal surprised us by bursting into life, and with a rolling gait sprinted across the field with Frances jogging by its side. When the goat noticed us it applied the brakes with such suddenness that Frances was cannoned forward before the weight of its large stationary body whisked her back to a more or less standing position. She regained her balance and with a degree of composure, brushed her hair from her eyes and smiled ruefully.

'She's quite strong.' This sounded like the understatement of the year and I made a mental note that Miranda had the capacity to pull a ten-ton truck and would be required to walk with a willow wisp wafting in front of her nose until she learned who made the rules.

'I think she's been allowed to get away with too much,' observed Frances, putting my thoughts into words. 'I suppose a couple of children would think this funny. But she's a really good type you know.'

I had no doubt of it. If Frances said she was a good type then I knew she was.

I looked at Miranda. She was certainly some hefty lady. A roomy goat with a coat in various shades of mushroom and chestnut mingled with patches of cream and black, which looked like the sort of rug one could buy only at Harrods. With a head held high, long floppy ears and half closed eyes gazing down a nose that would have made Julius Caesar tremble with envy she looked straight ahead, surveying the world with an air of aristocratic boredom. I patted her neck. 'Hello Miranda,' but she responded to neither the pat nor the voice.

'Well, do you want to take her?' Gordon hated hanging about and as he knew I'd already made up my mind couldn't see any reason for delay. Frances explained that it was three years since Miranda had last kidded and that the amount of milk she was giving was not worth bothering about. 'If I was keeping her I'd dry her off.'

Soon however, she would come into season and could be mated with Frances's own Anglo-Nubian stud goat and in the early part of the following year we should, with luck, have at least one female kid to continue the line. It was all very exciting. So we completed the necessary paperwork and prepared for the journey home.

'Come on Miranda.'

'I'll take her.' Gordon reached for her collar and the goat, springing once more into action, attempted to move off at high speed but Gordon stood his ground and she gulped and spluttered under the tension of the collar. Gordon refused to move at her pace but she wasn't going to give up her bat-out-of-hell act so easily, quite unable to realize that from now on this was a game she was not going to win. She choked her way to the Land Rover and I was amazed that she allowed herself to be lifted in and seemed quite content to settle down to eat some hay. We bid Frances goodbye and set off for home.

All went well until a few miles outside Hereford, when a most peculiar noise impinged itself on our senses. A cross between a high-pitched moan and a whistle came at fairly regular intervals and Gordon cursed the Land Rover for whatever expense this latest irregularity would cost.

We listened intently, trying to locate the exact source of the trouble when eventually I realized it was coming from where Miranda lay in the straw. Climbing onto my seat I turned round and leaning over as far as I could to reach the back of the seat behind me I pulled it down so as to get a view of Miranda in the back. Closer investigation revealed her head on one side buried in the remains of the hay, with her tongue protruding slightly from her mouth. Her eyes were closed.

'It's Miranda,' I yelled, 'She's ill, she's ill.'

'God, don't scream like that, you'll have us in the hedge. What's the matter with her?'

'How do I know? But will you stop please, then maybe we can find out.'

We decided not to stop on the road, remembering her ability to go from nought to sixty in seconds, so we turned in at the next opening and drove up a stony driveway to find ourselves on a circular forecourt bordered by beautifully tended flower borders. I knocked on the house door and explaining the situation to the intellectual looking man who opened it asked if we could attend to our goat on his drive as we thought she might be ill. He showed no surprise whatever at my request, told us to go ahead and shutting the door apparently took no further interest in us or our goat. Maybe he watched what was happening from behind the curtains but I thought it very trusting to leave strangers with a goat, even an allegedly sick one, among such an array of obviously prized plants.

We lifted Miranda's head and she looked beyond us with that faraway look. The moaning noise had stopped and her tongue had gone back inside her mouth.

'Up you get.'

It was easier said than done. We tried to get her up, pulling and heaving but she seemed totally oblivious to our energetic manoeuvrings and remained motionless.

'Come on Miranda.' I prodded somewhere underneath her, at the same time trying to encourage some movement in her rear end by giving weak jerks under her back legs. I was getting a bit irritated by now. 'Oh, come on you wretched thing, how can we find out if anything is wrong if you won't even move.'

We tried persuasion of one sort or another for a bit longer but to no avail and with perplexed sighs stood back and looked at her. As we looked something must have signalled in her brain that here was an interesting situation, for without any warning she transformed from an inanimate object to an Olympic sprinter and was already halfway through the door before Gordon flung himself at her, grabbing her collar and whatever part of her anatomy he could get hold of in order to halt this bid for freedom. At the same time I leapt into action and pushed like mad while Gordon leaned all his weight on her. She held her ground for a while then slowly began to retreat and with eyes closed, sank down onto her bed of straw.

'Let's get along. I don't thing there's much wrong with her.'

I was beginning to think the same.

'We'd not gone many miles before the noise began again. Her nose was once more half buried in the straw, her tongue protruding to one side.

'Ooooooooh,' I joined in the moaning, 'There is something wrong, I know it.'

'Maybe the travelling is upsetting her,' suggested my spouse without much conviction, 'In which case the sooner we get home the better.'

'But perhaps it's not that. Perhaps there really is something wrong. I think we should call into the vet's.'

So we stopped at the next phone box and called the surgery which was just about to close but Mr Edmonds said he'd hold on until we arrived which we did ten minutes later. Gordon and I tried to rouse Miranda who did not wish to be roused and remained reclining in her vapid attitude in the straw. We tried to lift her, pushing and pulling as before, muttering jokily about getting some sort of pulley on board to make light of this seemingly impossible task. I don't know what our elderly vet thought we were doing all this time. He was probably getting a bit impatient as I did notice him come to the door once or twice.

'Just a minute,' Gordon pulled my sleeve, 'I've got an idea. Just stand back from her.'

We stepped back a foot or so. Seconds passed and the vet sauntered towards us. Used to the eccentricities of man and beast he stood beside us, silently contemplating the prostrate goat. Suddenly the eye visible to us opened. A glassy look appeared. Then it happened. She was on her feet and about to shoot through the door but we all flung ourselves at her, our vet having the presence of mind to think that this explosion of energy might be better contained by as many people as possible and in the scrum of human arms and goat legs Gordon somehow managed to grab her collar. Pulling for all she was worth and choking against the collar we entered the surgery where Miranda came to a halt as suddenly as she'd started, remaining quite motionless between us, oblivious to the aura of fury about her. I explained that she might be suffering from the trauma of the journey.

'She's been making a very peculiar noise,' I said, 'Like this, and I gave what I thought to be a fair rendition of Miranda's moaning, although Gordon said later that I overacted in the most ridiculous way and that a noise such as I made could only have come from something with lungs ten times the size of a goat and there was no need for such exhibitionism anyway.

Well, sucks to him; I thought I was pretty good.

Something was bothering her I insisted as the vet peered into her eyes and mouth. He felt her pulse and shoved a thermometer up her rectum.

'Without a complete examination, she seems in perfect condition,' he said. 'There are no signs of stress but to be on the safe side I'll give

211

her something to see her safely home,' and he turned away to pick up a syringe which he began to fill from a small bottle.

It was then that I became aware of a tightening round my hips, and looking down saw the bottom of my voluminous jersey disappearing in thick folds into Miranda's mouth. I gave her a wallop on her quarters and began to yank the jersey out, watched by a fascinated husband and vet. It emerged barely recognisable as part of my still handsome if old Aran, covered in the green mulch which I suppose is the permanent coating of a goat's throat and stomach, and with as much dignity as I could muster removed a few amorphous objects which had transferred themselves from some deep part of her interior.

Mr Edmonds held up the syringe. 'Right.'

I wanted to yell 'no no, it's not right at all. We don't need this costly injection. This animal is nothing but a joker,' but I didn't have the nerve and watched with deep regret as about three pounds worth of something slowly trickled into Miranda's vein.

'Out you come.' Gordon gave a tug on her collar but Miranda stood firm on the tiled floor, having sunk into another reverie. Another tug, this time more forceful and suddenly she was up but Gordon was prepared and although they entered the lengthening shadows outside at a somewhat unseemly gait the head-long dash of before was not evident.

Inside the Land Rover once more, she settled down, head in straw to begin the now familiar lament. Determined this would trouble us no more we ignored her. It must have dawned on us both at about the same time just what the sonorous rhythms were.

'Do you realise we've just incurred a vet's bill because we have a goat that snores?'

We burst out laughing, but I thought just you wait my girl, just you wait. I didn't really know what, if anything, I could do about a snoring goat. It didn't matter anyway as only Bluebell and Snowdrop would hear her and for all I knew they might snore as well. Maybe it was a goat thing but I resolved there and then that there would be no more false alarms culminating in vet's bills.

I was still muttering to myself when we arrived back at Tironnen. We sat for a few moments congratulating ourselves that in spite of such a journey we'd got home with our sense of humour more or less intact. Evening was rapidly turning to night. The hens had put themselves to bed and the ducks were enjoying a late puddling in the pond. Gordon reversed the Land Rover closer to the out buildings bringing into view our unlovely muck heap which, because of the amount of recent rain, had collapsed well beyond its normal boundaries and was a horrible sodden mess where it had descended into the gully. I was gazing at this mess when I became aware that Gordon had got out and was opening the rear door.

'I'll take her,' I called as I climbed out.

'She's very strong.'

'Well I've seen that with my own eyes,' I said 'but I've got to get used to her.' In a sudden surge of indulgence I thought maybe I'd misjudged her. Perhaps she was used to being handled by females and Gordon had just frightened her. For some reason I chose to obliterate from my mind the earlier performance with Frances. Anyway I would give Miranda the benefit of the doubt. I smiled at her ingratiatingly but it seemed to be her habit to stare straight ahead; seeing or unseeing I couldn't tell.

'Up you get.' I jigged the collar a little but Miranda held her ground. I waited then jigged again. With a sudden rustle of straw she was on her feet, out of the Land Rover hauling me across the yard, her aim apparently to be anywhere other than where she was and to get there at the greatest possible speed. My legs were shooting up and down like pistons as we careered towards the barn, my fingers locked around her collar and I fleetingly wondered whether to chance turning to catch a last look at Gordon before we bolted through the great barn doors.

Abruptly Miranda diverted her course and I was swung sideways, losing my footing and letting go of her collar. I hoped that I could contain my fall but to no avail. I landed with a splosh into the mire of our extended dung heap and watched as my hands disappeared up to my wrists and beyond, feeling the gunge seep into my wellies, where it slithered about to search for the spaces between my toes and boots.

I didn't know whether to laugh or cry.

Gordon had caught Miranda and was standing a few feet away, evidently having difficulty controlling his hilarity.

'Don't laugh,' I screamed. 'I'm stuck and I hate you.' But in spite of my invective I began to giggle.

He opened an empty stable door and shoved Miranda inside.

213

'Hold out your hand.'

'Can't. I'm stuck here forever. I might as well be in the sinking sands of Dee.'

'You're not going all dramatic are you? Although on second thoughts this is as good a time as any.' He held out his arm.

'Give me your hand.'

I eased my left hand free to the accompaniment of a soft swishy sound and flicked some of the attached muck towards him, then withdrawing the other reached out to grab the sleeve of his jacket. I began to try to prize my muck covered footwear from the mire and Gordon chivalrously placed a foot in the muck in order to get a better balance as he hauled me out, but having reached a more or less standing position all I could do was lean perilously towards him. My wellies, filled as they were with sludge stayed put in spite of all my attempts to extricate myself, remaining firmly where they were. Trying to get a grip inside them by scrunching up my toes was impossible. Clearly some other tactic was called for.

'You'll have to leave your boots. Just step out of them.'

'Step out of them? Into that?' My indignation was rife and somewhat misplaced considering my situation. 'I don't know how you can suggest such a thing. I'm not walking wellieless in that.'

'But you're in it already! It's oozing out around the top of your boots; you're knee-deep in the stuff.' I knew he was trying not to laugh at the apparition facing him.

It was true. I must have looked grotesque, for the parts of me that weren't encased in wet rotted manure were liberally splattered with it for I could feel it on my face. But I wasn't giving in to the hilarity stakes just yet.

'I didn't come to live out here to spend half my time walking barefoot through dung-heaps.'

'Well you said you could manage her. Come on now; take the plunge.'

I glared at him, not knowing whether the word was deliberately chosen, but whether it was or not I considered it singularly inappropriate.

I was determined to remain humourless.

But I couldn't.

214

Laughter overtook us and for several seconds I held onto Gordon's arm as tightly as I could for fear of toppling from my less than upright stance.

'Right,' I said, cautiously withdrawing one leg from my boot. My sock, gunge-encrusted and unlovely was draped over my toes by about five inches like a sort of glove puppet that had given up hope. It weighed about a ton.

The giggles began again as Gordon put his arm round my waist to help me balance as I drew out the other foot, a duplication of the first, and with one step I was on the cobbled walkway.

It was now payback time.

Since my mishap had been the cause of so much mirth it was appropriate I thought, to have a bit of fun myself.

'Oh, thank you my love' I purred, rubbing one manure splattered cheek against his as dollops of the stuff slid from other parts of my person. 'What would I have done without you?'

Then my thoughts turned to Miranda. Don't let it be like this Miranda. Please don't let it be like this.

How little did I know!

SOME CHICKEN – SOME NECK

After nearly a year of hell living in cages where they'd been unable to move from the standing position in which they'd been placed at ten weeks old, the battery hens we'd purchased had tasted freedom for two years. They'd spent their days enjoying dust-baths in the yard, scratching in the dung heap or searching in the field for tit-bits. Their meals arrived on time and every night they were shut up in the safety of the hen house for protection from any marauding fox.

In exchange for this they had supplied us with eggs. Sadly, however, there comes a time in every hen's life when one end stops functioning and it isn't the end where the beak is. They eat with the enthusiasm of a production line super hen but somewhere along their internal wires the message 'make an egg' doesn't get through, at least not very often. One way or another surplus birds have to be culled, so along with several of our other birds the battery hens had become redundant.

It would have been sensible to have fattened them up before killing them but we were a bit squeamish about the whole business, so this first time, faced with the task of culling we were not interested in making a meal of it, as it were. All we wanted to do was to get the numbers down, the quicker the better, with no reminder of the job once it was done.

Some people, I'd heard, slit the throats of their poultry, leaving them to bleed to death, but we found that idea horrifying. The most common way was to wring their necks. Several people told us how to do it, one neighbour giving a graphic demonstration. 'It's quite simple,' she said. 'Just pick the bird up by its feet,' she clenched her right wrist with the thumb pointing down, 'then bend the head up, and push the neck down,' and grasping the imaginary neck with her left hand she held it aloft then thwanged it downwards. 'That's all there is to it see?'

It didn't seem simple at all.

We were not yet convinced of our ability to carry out all this bending and pushing, so our helpful postmaster said he'd show us when he was culling next but somehow we never got round to taking up his offer. An article on the subject confirmed neck wringing to be painless, as this way the bird will die instantly. But what if it didn't?

216

What if, after all this picking up and bending and pushing, it wasn't dead? Or worse, wasn't quite dead? The birds had to be killed but the idea of causing pain was repellent to both of us. We had to be sure.

'Perhaps,' I offered, without much conviction, 'we could practice on a piece of plastic tubing shoved into the end of a hot water bottle.' But if we didn't do it properly first go, how would we know? No pathetic squawk would issue from a hot water bottle to inform us of failure. There seemed no solution except to practice on the hens themselves, so we discarded the idea of neck wringing, which is why we prepared to enact one of the more gruesome scenes from the French Revolution.

The girls had set off for school but a couple of minutes later I heard the garden gate bang again, the door open and Jessica's voice calling, 'Mum, I've put a red marker on Boadicea. Make sure you don't kill her,' then the door slammed and she was gone. I was on the landing at the time in transit between rooms collecting bedding for washing and although I heard her words they didn't really register, but I automatically called out some sort of acknowledgement and continued stripping the beds then lugged everything downstairs to put them in the washing machine.

Having milked, mucked out and fed the goats my most pressing need was a cup of coffee. As I sat at the table waiting for the drink to cool a little thinking of nothing in particular, I stretched out along the table to gather empty cereal bowls and plates, stacked them and collected the cutlery, which I dropped into an empty mug. Then I lapsed into idleness for several minutes, while my finger absently played with a Biro that had been left on the table.

Coming out of my reverie I focused on the pen. There was something about it that my mind latched onto in an unclear sort of way. It was a red pen. What about a red pen? Hadn't someone said something about a red pen or a red something? Oh well, I thought, if it was anything important it would come to me sooner or later and I let my mind continue drifting until Gordon joined me for a leisurely chat before we began the grim task that faced us. I stood up, gulped the last of my drink and pulling my ancient wax jacket off its peg, followed Gordon through the door.

I stood on the step shrugging into my coat. It was a grey, dank morning and a mist hung thickly in the air beneath low cloud. Not a leaf stirred and if I'd had a superstitious nature I'd have said a sense of foreboding was in the air, recognising that if I'd been a hen my superstitions would have been well founded. Gordon passed by on his way to the side of the house farthest from the yard, carrying the implement with which we were going to despatch the birds. It was an enormous straw-cutting knife with a blade about twenty inches long, its newly sharpened edge gleaming obscenely bright.

'Oooh, that's really vicious,' I remarked.

'Painless and quick,' he countered. 'Are you ready?'

'Ready? Do you mean ready to have my head chopped off? Has the cooking not been too good of late then?', and with that appropriate witticism I set off towards the hen house to collect the first of the hens. The previous evening I'd tagged each doomed hen with a red marker and it wasn't until I'd almost finished doing it that it dawned on me that it would have been a good idea to separate them from the survivors at the same time, but I hadn't, so they were all shut in the hen house as usual. I cautiously opened the door and the first bird I caught had the marker on its leg so I closed the door, much to the indignation of the remaining occupants and with a strong sense of betrayal took it to the garden where Gordon waited. I collected another then a third, each time opening the door and managing to let out some of the unmarked hens that were battling to be about their daily business, before taking the doomed bird round almost as quickly as Gordon was despatching them and throwing them into a large bin.

I had just delivered the fifth bird when something nudged my memory; well, not so much nudged, as shot into it like a bullet. My hands slapped against my cheeks and I froze as I stared in horror at the sight of Gordon about to decapitate another bird.

'What's the matter?' he asked, the bloodied blade raised for the next execution.

'No, no, something terrible has happened,' I screamed. 'Don't kill that hen, don't kill that hen.' I peered into the face of the creature he was holding for any sign of recognition then rushed into the yard followed by Gordon, understandably perplexed at my agitation.

'What is it? Tell me.'

'I put red markers on all the hens which have to go' I yelled as I ran towards the hen house 'and Jessica's put one on Boadicea and I don't know which one she is.' I flung open the door and the remaining occupants tumbled out.

'What have you done that for? What's going to be achieved by letting them out?'

'Oh, maybe I might just……oh, I don't know' I whined as I scrutinized each hen. Perhaps, I thought, a glimmer of hope rising within me, Jessica had so named it because it had some obvious warlike expression but if that was the case I was not astute enough to observe it, for no matter how intently I studied them, each bird was large of size, red-brown in colour and seemingly devoid of any characteristic different from that of its peers.

'Boadicea,' I called in a tremulous voice, 'Come to me Boadicea,' and as one they rushed forward, squawking and flapping their wings, bustling into one another in the usual hen like way. There was nothing I could do about it. I'd just have to leave one out and hope that at sixteen to one the odds would be in my favour, although it wasn't something I'd have made a bet on. So we continued, taking a bit longer than before, because having let the birds out they were now all over the place and didn't take too kindly to having their freedom curtailed and it was then, as we got into the swing of things and relaxed a little, we became aware of something strange going on.

Gordon had just picked up a head and was about the throw it in the bin when a headless body emerged, taking a gargantuan leap in the air winging sightlessly for a couple of yards before descending with a thud to earth and stillness. Not only did this apparition fly but it emitted a short squeaky cackle and we stood rooted to the spot, staring at the awfulness of it all while the overcast sky and misty drizzle contributed to the Hammer Horror in which we were playing such a reluctant part.

We knew that the nerves of newly dead chickens caused some movement but we'd never expected anything like this and how was that banshee-like noise accounted for? Gordon must have chopped its head off above the voice box, which was now making its last involuntary call. We looked at one another in horror, then Gordon took the hen I was holding, despatched it smartly and dropped it in the bin, where it immediately rose up to flutter past us, knowing nothing of where it had been or where it was going. A couple more carcasses had a last fling but the remaining ones stayed where they were thrown thank goodness, although as each body was deposited in the bin, I watched nervously out of the corner of my eye for further macabre happenings. Ye gods......I wondered if something like this had inspired Dante to write The Divine Comedy.

'Let's get a move on. The sooner we get this job finished the better,' said Gordon, then added, 'Ouch,' as the head he was still absently holding raised itself up and bit him on the finger. Well, that was his story!

The brown hen we saved from the slaughter was not Boadicea and Jessica was dreadfully upset when she arrived home to find that she was no longer with us. I felt terrible for causing my child such distress. However, she soon decided that the one we'd saved was suitable for pet status along with a one-eyed hen which, because of its affliction spent its days pecking in clockwise circles, and Donald one of our recently hatched Aylesbury ducklings. Donald had been born with a deformed right leg, which had left him further and further behind his siblings as they grew and became faster as they followed their mother down to the pond each morning. Donald didn't grow much at all and certainly didn't know what speed was. In order to try to alleviate his misfortune, he was subjected to mustard baths before and after school, with attendant massaging of the faulty limb and it did seem that after a few weeks his limping waddle became slightly less pronounced. One day Donald decided to take a nap beneath the curve of the front wheel of the Land Rover. The wheel was wide but Donald was small. Gordon was going down to the village. He fired the engine and drove off.

Poor Donald.

Jessica called the brown hen, Lucinda, after Lucinda Prior-Palmer who had just won the Badminton Horse Trials again, and the hen, which had spent almost the first twelve months of her life cooped in a cage before she came to us, defied all the rules of selectivity by going broody. I queried this phenomenon with several people. No-one had heard of such a thing but then no-one I'd asked had ever kept battery hens. Lucinda, unaware that she was possibly making history, returned to the half-hidden spot in a pile of timber where she had been laying her eggs and in due course emerged, clucking to her thirteen chicks. She was so proud of them and we were very happy for her. She lived with us for many years, frequently spending spring and summer days

220

sitting at our open door, a privilege allowed only to her and a fair match for any dog or cat that passed too close for her liking.

A sort of Cinderella hen.

THE STALLION

Everyone agreed that Bessie was a fine mare. In the land of the mighty Welsh Cob her conformation caused no jarring to the eyes of any native horseman and over the years she was much admired for her good bone, serviceable feet, capacious chest, fine head, good free action and not least her unusual dun colouring. She could spend a day hunting or hacking over the moors yet return home in high spirits, as alert as when she had set out, and after a brisk rub down and a good meal she'd stand with her head over the stable door as if to say, 'Well, where are we going now?'

Several people thought she was a good part Connemara, even purebred Connemara was mentioned, but we knew nothing of her antecedents and if there were papers proving her lineage they didn't come with her. But whatever breed or breeds had made her the good all rounder she was, her genes were too good to lose. We'd often talked about letting her have a foal and because of her powerful build our minds had turned towards a thoroughbred as the most suitable type of mate. We even got as far as attending a stallion show at Cardiff where a fine looking horse named River Poaching caught our attention, but having jotted down his name and number we postponed any further enquiries until a later date. We were in no hurry.

Then one day during the summer holidays we were down in the village at a Pony Club rally and I was in a relaxed mood. Leaning on the bonnet of the Land Rover with the combination of a warm breeze and the heat rising from the bonnet I had become quite somnambulistic. I must have had my eyes closed for I was quite startled when I felt a nudge on my arm.

Gordon said, 'Oh sorry. Feeling drowsy?'

A quick upward toss of my head shook away the cobwebs and I was all attention. 'What is it?'

With two slow backward movements of his hand he indicated that I should look behind me. My attention was riveted. A blonde young woman whom I'd never seen before stood several yards away, her face animated as she watched the lesson in progress. In her hand she held reins attached to a bridle, and the bridle was on the head of a horse whose beauty took my breath away.

The animal was a bay but a bay such as I'd never seen before. His short straight body glowed brown-red like a freshly fallen horse chestnut. The lustrous skin stretched over the muscles of his neck and quarters, down incredibly long limbs becoming black at the lower joint and on down to well-set fetlocks. Over his arched neck hung a luxuriant mantle of shining blue-black mane and great dark eyes peered between a spread forelock. He stood quietly beside the young woman, his attention on the energetic goings-on in the school. There was an undeniable gaunt look about him but he towered above her and it wasn't just his size that seemed to make him look big. There was something else......a majesty......a presence about the animal that is difficult to describe. Forty years later the impression is with me still.

Over the years I've met many vital, superb animals among countless hundreds but only one other has demanded so strongly to be looked at in the way this one did simply by being there, and as I looked at the lovely horse my allegiance to the Cleveland Bay got a slight dent in it. Not that there was any comparison really. Whatever this creature was it certainly wasn't bred for pulling gun carriages. Yet on the grounds of pure unadulterated beauty I had never seen anything like this. The horse emanated a magnetic spell and I had to find out about it.

As we approached the young woman turned towards us, smiling.

'We're curious about your horse,' said Gordon without further ado.

'We've never seen anything like him. We're Jenny and Gordon by the way, we live up there, a couple of miles away,' indicating by a gesture the northern hills. She smiled and introduced herself. 'I'm Laura. I'm on the other side of the valley, thataway,' and she indicated the opposite direction. We remarked on the beauty of the animal and Laura seemed pleased at our comments. She stood back from the horse in order to admire him with us.

'Yes, isn't he just.'

I stroked his head, which he lowered, the more to enjoy the fussing. The dark eyes that looked at me were kind, almost pensive and I had the conviction that I was privileged. 'What is he?'

'He's a desert Arabian racing stallion from the royal stables,' was the unexpected reply. 'I lived in the middle-east for several years and he was given to me by a sheik. His name is Hamdany Al Shamaal. It means The Desert Wind.'

The Desert Wind....... how beautiful.

From the royal stables...... how amazing.

A present from a sheik......how intriguing.

This was pure Hollywood!

'I smell a story here,' I remarked and Laura chuckled mysteriously, then without thinking I added, 'What do you have to do to acquire a horse like this from a sheik?' immediately wishing I hadn't because although the question was asked in all innocence it wasn't the sort of thing you'd say to someone you'd only just met. But Laura only laughed and said, 'Oh, I know how it sounds but it wasn't like that at all. I'll tell you about it sometime. Eight weeks ago I was at Dover meeting my lovely boy after two years quarantine in Austria and he's not looking too good after it either, but in a few months we'll have you ship-shape won't we old chap,' and she gave the horse an affectionate scratch under his chin.

During the following months we became very friendly with Laura and her husband Phil and we enjoyed watching cine-films of much of their life in the desert, especially of the races, seeing the tall elegant racing stallions and soft doe-eyed mares who could in the twinkling of an eye become imperious chargers flying with their brothers over the sandy race-track. Films of the royal stables showed the frisky young stock, some of them pointed out by Laura as full or half-brothers and sisters to Hamdany. It all seemed a far cry from life on a Welsh hillside. So we saw a lot of this beautiful horse and if at our first meeting we had been struck by his majesty, dignity......even now I'm not sure what it was......to see him move was pure magic. With extravagant strides, mane flowing and tail flying out behind him, he would race round the fields, sometimes breaking into what seemed barely a movement at all, floating over the ground rather than on it. Pacing, Laura called it. He was a dazzle of colour flying by.

I'd still not found out how she'd come to own the horse, until one day, when we were leaning on the gate watching him, I said, 'Come on now. Tell.' She looked at me questioningly. 'Tell me about Hamdany. How is it that he's here? I know about your social life out there and what your work was but I still know nothing of how or why he was given to you and unless it's something that will send me fainting to the ground in horror, I'd like to know please.' So she told me the story.

One day, whilst riding along the seashore of one of the royal beaches, dreamily dwelling on the pleasures of life, her attention was caught by a small child standing some way out in the bay.

'I was looking towards the shore and I could hear faint cries of distress,' said Laura. 'There were very few people on the beach. Most were families occupied with their own amusements but I'd noticed a young woman on her own, sunbathing, seemingly oblivious to all else. The water is very shallow for a long way but the child was so far out that the waves were beginning to get quite strong and I could see that a disaster was about to happen.

I yelled in the general direction of the people on the beach and turned out to sea but horses don't go very fast in water so I slid off and started running, vaguely aware that the sunbathing woman was on her feet, waving and screaming for all she was worth. I kept my eyes focused on the child but suddenly it vanished under a wave and by the time I reached where I'd last seen it, it had been washed several yards away. I grabbed hold of it and held it upside down to get rid of as much water as possible. I could see it was unconscious. A man from the beach had joined me and he carried the child, which was about two, back to the shore, because there was nothing we could do in the water and to this day I don't know how he ran through the sea so quickly. Fortunately I knew how to give artificial respiration to the child although I'd never had cause to use it in an emergency before. Its wretched mother stood by wringing her hands and screaming. Oh how I wanted to slap her. The man got his car engine running and drove us hell-for-leather to the hospital, with that woman jabbering and leaping up and down in her seat the whole way, literally the whole way. The child survived and I hope its mother gave up sunbathing.'

I could picture it all. The limp child, its agitated mother, Laura trying to keep calm in an un-calm situation against the background of glorious sand and brilliant blue sea. Now where was all this leading I wondered.

'The following day,' she continued, 'I had a phone call. The sheik who owned the beach wanted to meet me.'

'I expect that he'd heard you weighed twenty stone, were completely bald and had a moustache.'

'Probably,' replied my friend, who was the epitome of the English rose. So Laura met the sheik. She explained to me that it would have

225

reflected badly on his family had there been a fatality on his beach and he wished to express his gratitude for her prompt action. 'He handed me a small box. It would have been unthinkable to refuse and when I opened it I was looking at a beautiful gold watch. I said what I hoped was the right thing and we got on really well.' Shortly after that an invitation was issued to her and Phil to spend a day at the races, where they met his wife to whom Laura took an instant liking which appeared to be reciprocated. The two couples became good friends and spent much time in each others company.

When after a few years Phil's assignment was completed and they were preparing to return to the U.K., the sheik expressed his wish to present her with another gift, 'To remind me of the time I saved his beach,' quipped Laura. 'We had this incredible picnic out in the desert in a tent complete with drapes, carpets, everything, so I assumed that this experience was the gift he had referred to but when we'd returned to his palace we found ourselves being taken in the direction of the royal stables. Well you know me, always happy to look at horses. When we arrived, one of the grooms was standing there holding a stallion. The sheik took hold of the bridle and I could hardly believe what came next. He lifted my hand, put it above his on the bridle and......I'll never forget his words. He said (I get a lump in my throat just thinking about it Jenny) he said, 'This is my gift to you, Laura. Perhaps sometimes when you are riding in the English countryside, you will think of us.' Well, you can imagine I was lost for words. This horse, this beautiful horse was mine and I couldn't think of anything to do or say I was so choked.'

It seemed a glamorous life but Laura's highly developed sense of the ridiculous always kept things in proportion. It had been a wonderful experience and of course she had a permanent reminder of it just outside the door. It was quite a story.

I had been wondering for some time if I could broach the subject of mating Bessie to Hamdany. I didn't want to put Laura in the position of having to refuse my request but I knew without a doubt that any offspring of this elegant stallion and our beautifully put-together mare would be something worth looking at. Then one autumn evening after a leisurely supper in the garden at Tironnen, Laura remarked on Bess's excellent conformation and almost before I'd had time to agree with her she repeated what she'd said, adding 'It seems a pity not to have a foal from her.'

This sounded like an opening. Could it even be an invitation I wondered, so I asked in a deliberate sort of way, 'Now, why would you say a thing like that?'

She grinned. 'Well, I'd like to find out what sort of foals Hamdany would produce from different sorts of mares.'

I could hardly contain myself. 'Are you saying we could put Bess to him?'

'Well, yes; if you'd like to,' sounding almost apologetic! 'She's a fine pony.'

Would I like to!

'Oh......that's wonderful. I've been thinking about it since I first clapped eyes on him but hadn't liked to mention it in case you were only thinking in terms of thoroughbreds and Arabs and other posh stuff.'

'Goodness no, not yet. I really want to find out if he'll put his mark on foals from a variety of mares. I'll use Ballet Girl of course (her own thoroughbred) but three or four good mares will give me an idea of what to expect.'

So we found a mate for Bess. No ordinary mate but a prince, and a prince of the desert. A Rudolf Valentino type horse. Gosh!

***

Bess came into season early the following year but it wasn't until late spring that she and I set out to walk the nine miles to visit her princely suitor.

Already signs of early summer were reaching the higher hills and our amble through the lanes was a delight. Early buttercups were beginning to monopolise the fast growing vegetation which banked either side, and sweet smelling violets, dark and light were massing where the grass grew less strongly. But spring was not giving up so easily for bluebells and delicate wood anemones still lingered, exquisitely pale in the bright sunlight, before the stronger colours of summer overtook them.

Bess stayed with the stallion for three weeks and then we repeated our journey in reverse. By this time the hedgerows had changed beyond all recognition so it was as though we were walking a different

227

route. Massed banks of bright yellow and brilliant pink were growing up around comfrey and delicate wands of cow parsley. Sometimes we'd be walking in brilliant sunshine, almost dazzled by the gaudiness of it all, then overhanging trees played shadowy games and everything would change becoming cool and slightly mysterious. Some experiences one never forgets.

Generous extra rations and plenty of goat's milk were allotted to Bess during the following autumn and winter to ensure her foal would be as healthy and strong as possible. We thought that as long as the weather was reasonably clement the small paddock above the vegetable garden would be the best place for her to give birth. In the meadow was a large pond, fed by springs welling up from the water course below, which also created small, marshy places, unsafe terrain for the new-born although in all probability Bess's native intelligence would have warned her about these things but we didn't want to take any chances. The paddock was on a slope, which was good, for a mare will seek out a slope when birth is imminent and also she would be separated from our two curious geldings. If the weather was bad she could go in the stable.

The foal was due on the 29th of May, so a couple of weeks before we began taking her up to the paddock in the evening......just in case. Each morning there would be a rush to the paddock by whoever was first dressed, but for several days each child would return indicating her disappointment at not being the messenger of exciting news by a shrug or comment. 'Never mind,' we'd say, 'It'll happen soon.' and with breakfast over they'd set off for school no doubt hoping that the longed for event wouldn't occur during the day.

May 29th passed, and three more days. The skies began to cloud over but the weather held, until late in the afternoon of the fourth day an ominous south-westerly gusted up the valley, hitting us smartly, ruffling the feathers of browsing hens and causing the cats and dogs to look up from their basking on the lawn. It passed beyond us to work itself out elsewhere and all was quiet for a while but the calmness had a threatening feel about it and shortly after, another blast stronger than the first swept across the hills, this time breaking small twigs off the sycamore tree, sending them skimming down to float on the ruffled water of the duck pond. In the distance I could see great clouds hurrying across the sky, blotting out the few remaining glimpses of

228

blue, and the dogs roused themselves, stretched and went into the house while the cats chose to seek warmth and comfort in their favourite secret places.

The brief respites were becoming less. Anticipating what was to come I filled buckets with water, pushed hay into hay nets and hung them up. The horses had already taken shelter at the far end of the meadow in the lea of the wood and by the time I'd finished and walked round to the field gate rain was falling. Big, big drops.

'Come on, come on,' I yelled, 'Come on,' but the strengthening wind carried my words away from them and I had to walk halfway across the meadow before they were aware of me.

'Come on, come on.'

Now the rain was lashing my face, making me impatient because I knew they were watching, wondering whether greater protection lay with me or where they were, then Bess, nudged by the notion that my appearance in such conditions meant I was offering hospitality started forward. Immediately Punch, Carrie and Bill moved as well, overtaking Bess and her load. I slipped a halter on her, and our little procession urged on by the strong wind behind us hurried towards shelter.

Before going to bed I made my usual late night check that all was well. A serious gale was now blowing and I stood on the step waiting for a lull before attempting a swift race to the gate, which I held onto until another respite enabled me to race across the yard to the shelter of the buildings. Carrie and Punch lay dozing in the part of the barn that they shared on these occasions, and Bill, warm in his thick blanket, appeared from the shadows to put his head over the stable door as I passed. Bess was eating hay, and the raging elements outside could barely be heard through the thick walls. I stayed for a minute or two, savouring the stillness, the smell of the hay which in the beam of my torch had become the colour of straw, the sweet smell of Bess and the sound of her contented munching. All was well.

I looked in on the goats snug and chewing the cud, and shepherded seven reluctant ducks from the pond closing the hen house door behind them. Later, snug in my own bed I forgot the sounds of fury and the buffeting that Tironnen was getting. I grew drowsy and slept like a log. By the next morning peace had been restored. Gordon had put the kettle on and gone outside for a perfunctory look at the storm battered house. I chivvied the girls then went down to prepare breakfast. We were so relieved that all appeared to be in order outside that neither of us had given Bess a thought.

'Have you been to look?' asked Louise as she came into the kitchen followed by Angela and Jessica.

'What? Oh, Bess? No......no, I've given up thinking it'll ever arrive.'

'Well, we'd better go and see.'

There was a sudden scramble for Wellingtons, a surge towards the door and they were gone. Within seconds the door slammed back on its hinges.

'It's here.'

'It's a little bay like Hamdany'

'I knew it would come during the storm.'

***

That tranquil morning when the only evidence of the previous night's disturbance were numerous twiggy branches scattered about the yard we all gazed over the stable door at the beautiful scene within. The foal, which could have been born only minutes earlier, lay in the straw, Bess nuzzling around it making loving snickers of reassurance, reassurance that its sudden departure from the warm place in which it had lain for eleven months had not brought it into an alien world.

Lifting its head the foal tried to rise on giraffe like legs, falling and trying again, falling and resting a while, till after several attempts it succeeded, wobbling precariously as it searched along the line of its mother's belly for the food which it instinctively knew was there.

Time passed and still we watched, making occasional observations but generally silent until suddenly with a jolt, I realised the time and that if the girls didn't leave quickly they'd miss the school car at the end of the lane.

As soon as I'd seen them off I made a bran mash, placed a round of apricot jam sandwiches on top and took it out to Bess. I stood by while she ate the sandwiches, throwing up her head after each piece and curling her lips back to make that wonderful horsey grimace which I think means delight, before finally getting her head down into the warm bran. The foal was lying in the straw, its head resting between its spindly forelegs, seeming, like his mother to be content and I left them together ...... Bess and her fine son.

***

Laura was delighted with all Hamdany's foals although our youngster seemed to have a special place in her affections. Time passed, the woolly foal coat disappeared, the body filled out and the promise of a fine youngster became increasingly evident. He had his mother's spirit but his colouring was Hamdany's, and although the deep chestnut coat was slightly less vibrant there was no mistaking the blue-black of his luxuriant mane and tail. It seemed that in this young colt we had the best of both parents, and we celebrated his first birthday watching him career round the meadow in an imperious gallop, then slow to pace elegantly, his coat gleaming, the blue-black tail held high over his back, just like his father.

We had an Arab prince in the meadow and were well pleased.

SAY CHEESE

My first attempt at winemaking was a long time ago when we were living in the city and the children were very young. I'd been making cordials for them, orange and elderflower and lemon barley water and it seemed a natural progression to move on to winemaking. It would be interesting and a challenge.

Well it was interesting all right and I certainly made it a challenge. Slavishly following the recipe and referring to other parts of the book for each individual instruction explained by copious diagrams for the uninitiated, I'd pour boiling water onto my chosen fruit or vegetable, cool it, add yeast and nutrient, do whatever else I was bid. I'd stir it each day for several days, by which time the concoction was ready to pour into a special glass jar which would be fitted with an air lock, to be left for weeks or months to more or less look after itself. But by the time it was ready to be transferred to the glass jar I'd have wafted my nose over the liquid and convinced that anything that smelt so revolting could ever become drinkable, I'd throw it onto the compost heap. I had followed the book word for word yet couldn't make out where I had gone wrong.

I didn't know anybody to ask and was considered a bit 'freaky' by those who knew me for doing such a thing anyway. My grumbles were received either by an indulgent assertion that next time I'd probably succeed, this assurance generally accompanied by a silly grin, or a blatant burst of laughter followed by the silence of one who obviously considered me beyond the pale. So I just kept quiet, continued my quest for perfection and carried on confronting catastrophe.

Why I never consulted the man who ran the shop where I bought the various items for my hobby I'll never know. In one of the less salubrious parts of town he presided over a large shed which was neatly stacked from floor to ceiling with bottles, cans and boxes, the latter being full of miscellaneous articles in a bewildering variety of shapes and sizes. He probably knew everything there was to know about his subject and as I never once saw another female in the place thought he might well be disposed to share his knowledge with a young woman who was clearly pretty incapable......especially if he had an audience of male customers to impress. Yet I'd go in, select

232

what the book told me I needed and leave with no more than the usual 'please's 'and 'thank you's'. It was probably shyness that kept me mute but in such circumstances. I think the word stupidity would have been more apt!

Puzzled, frustrated but undaunted, I'd study my instruction book, searching for clues as to why I always seemed to end with failure. This went on time after time, with my dreams of cheap plonk receding. Then one day, whilst waiting at the bus stop for a visit to town, I got into conversation with an elderly gentleman. Somehow or other the chat turned to wine-making and to my delight I found myself talking to a master of many years experience, who had made wines from almost every variety of vegetable and fruit. He could quote the vintage years of carrots and rose petal, elderflower and nettle, yet remained modest enough to admit that he too, had failures, so I poured out my troubles to an ear that listened with sympathy and understanding.

When I'd finished, he held up a hand, put his head slightly on one side and smiled kindly. 'Well now, my dear,' said he, 'I know exactly what the matter is. You're not doing anything wrong. Do just as you have done before but when you are going to put it in the storage jar, do just that. Pour it in. Don't on any account smell it. That's the only problem you have….you're too eager to find out how good it is, and believe me, at that stage it seldom is good. Everything changes.' His blue eyes twinkled. 'Looking at me now, could you ever have imagined what a dashing young blade I once was? Well, it's the same with wine, only it works in reverse; you'll see.'

Oh, what a sweetie he was, and yes, I could imagine the dashing young blade of earlier years. How fortuitous to have met him. My heart had leapt at his words of encouragement, sank rapidly as visions of all my wasted efforts flooded before me and rose again with equal speed, as I mentally added a few pounds of pears to my shopping list and planned a foraging trip at the weekend. It was good preparation for the life style of which I then knew nothing. So with enthusiasm again at fever pitch I began the process once more, seeing it through from beginning to a reasonably successful end.

Once we had moved to Tironnen our favourite varieties became elder (flower and berry) blackberry, damson and nettle, these all free for the picking. But when there was a glut of something either home

233

grown or wild, lots of other fruits and vegetables were used. I always hoped that one day we'd have enough rose bushes to provide rose petals for another delicious wine but we never did. I'd enjoy the beauty of the blossoming bushes in the gardens of friends, at the same time longing to tear off the petals and put them to use. How paradoxical.

When one morning a couple of months after Snowdrop and Bluebell had kidded, I opened a book on farmhouse dairying at the chapter entitled Cheese-making, you would have thought that some memory of past disasters would have surfaced.

It didn't.

In order to have all the milk available for our own needs, I had begun a few days before to transfer the kids from their mother's milk to a substitute. Gordon had already made a cheese press with three concrete weights, each with an iron handle set in the top for ease of lifting. A small one weighing about three pounds; a medium one of six and a half pounds and the largest weighing in at ten. Everything was ready: wooden spoon, curding knife, skimmer, ladle, thermometer, measuring jug, muslin, mould, jam pan, cheese rennet, starter, salt; all laid out in operating theatre style. I'd been looking forward to making cheese for so long and now I could begin.

A cheddar-type sounded a good homely one to start with and determined to get everything right in preparation to actually doing anything I studied the recipe with neurotic care. Even this didn't ring any winemaking bells to dint my confidence.

Pour into your pan two gallons of whole milk and one of skimmed milk.

I considered the jam pan. This looked like a 'quart into a pint pot situation', which a speedy check with a Pyrex jug confirmed. My jam pan held only two gallons.

Brain cells unaccustomed to vigorous exercise struggled with the maths and came hesitantly to the conclusion that ten and a half pints of whole milk plus a bit, and five and a half pints of skimmed milk less a bit, equalled two gallons. This would fill the pan. I checked again. Same result. I lifted the bucket containing Snowdrop's morning offering and measured out just over six pints and then made it up to the required ten and half pints plus a bit, with Bluebells milk. I'd put the previous evenings milk into a wide dish and scooping off the risen

234

cream with the skimmer (a sort of large flat spoon with holes in it) placed the cream in a bowl, set it on one side and added five and a half pints, less a bit, of the skimmed milk to the jam pan. The two gallons came to within half and inch of the top and I was thrilled that within hours my first homemade cheese would be taking its initial steps to maturity.

'Warm it very gradually to 83 degrees Fahrenheit.' This I did and then added the special cheese making rennet. I stirred it slowly, oh so slowly, with a sterilized wooden spoon, covered it and left it to set for about thirty minutes. Taking my time, I cut the curds towards me in lines about half an inch apart then cut more lines at right angles to the first. Using an angled curd knife I inserted it down the side of the pan and made horizontal cuts through the curd so that the pan now contained lots of ½" squares floating on top of the whey. I was thrilled.

Following the book exactly, I obeyed a few more instructions, then ladled off the whey and tipped the curds into a muslin cloth, which I tied up like an enormous plum pudding. This I hung from one of the old ham hooks in the ceiling and left it to drip into the large stone crock I'd placed on a table beneath. I was enjoying myself immensely. Cheese making was something I was taking to like a duck to water.

The following morning I unwrapped the cloth and tipped out the curd onto a large scalded board. Now devoid of most of the liquid it held its shape.....round and smooth at the bottom, then ridged where the cloth had folded as it gathered in ever tightening creases to where it had been secured at the top. I looked at it with some misgivings, picked up the bucket of drained whey and took it to the horses, tipping some into a pothole for the hens en route.

Returning, I studied the white polystyrene-like substance. It looked very odd and I wondered what the first cheese makers had thought when confronted with such an unpromising substance. Why had they continued? It could surely only have been desperation, or were they, unlike me, blessed with second sight, which afforded them a vision of the transformation of the despondent looking object into a culinary delight?

Hard cheese was what I wanted but as I broke up the curd some of my enthusiasm vanished. I mixed in some salt and tentatively tasted the stuff. It was like leathery cottage cheese but I already made unleathery cottage cheese simply by allowing milk to sour in a jug. Something had gone wrong, so picking up the tray I marched outside and flung the lot over the wall onto a group of hens, setting off a chorus of annoyed clucking which ceased when the object of their annoyance turned out to be edible. A great misery settled upon me. I phoned Hilary, a friend also the owner of a newly kidded goat.

'Have you tried making cheese?'

'Not yet. I've not put the kids on bottles but I'm about to any day now.'

'Have you read anything about it?'

'Well I've got a book on it which I've looked through. It doesn't appear to be that difficult. Why? Have you made any?'

'Oh,' I moaned, 'I've tried but all I've ended up with is a horrible spongy mess that I know would never turn into cheese. I don't know what it is I'm doing wrong. I've got all the right things, I'm not hurrying the job, everything is spotlessly clean and I can recite the instructions backwards but all I manage to get is this awful gunge. It tastes simply dreadful. The hens think it's wonderful but that's not much comfort. For thousands of years people have been making cheese. Simple people have turned out cheeses day after day, week after week, year in, year out and here am I, ready and willing, and I just can't get it right.'

Hilary was suitably sympathetic and threw out a lifeline. "I've heard of someone who makes cheese and butter and I believe she has people over for dairying sessions. I must say it would probably be much easier to watch someone than try to follow it from a book. And it would make a nice day out. These people are very well set up I believe. Even grow their own cereals. I'd thought about trying to find this person; now you've spurred me on. She makes a small charge. Would you be interested? If I can find her shall we go together?'

Would I be interested! I'd long been aware that my ability to follow the written instruction was not of the best. If I were handed a sheet of paper with details both worded and illustrated on how to stick a stamp on an envelope, I'd probably send out a cry for help.

'I'll find out about this then and call you'

As good as her word Hilary rang a few days later to confirm that we could go for a demonstration in cheese and butter making one day the following week, so she'd plumped for the Tuesday and was that

236

alright for me? If she'd organized it at two o'clock in the morning it would have been fine. All I wanted was to be shown where I was going wrong.

Now there was light at the end of the tunnel.

Forget about the mistakes of the past.

I was about to be enlightened.

So I met a most delightful lady. Mrs Seeley welcomed us as though we were old friends. She had drifted into late middle age carrying an abundance of youthful beauty and energy and armed with these morale-boosting attributes quietly and efficiently ran her side of a highly organized self-sufficient holding.

We were, it seemed, just two of many who had asked for her help, which was why she'd set up these small classes and of the four novices who were to be her pupils for that day we were the first to arrive. It was clear that she was delighted to show others the skills of the cottager and when I muttered something about not getting it right from a book she soothed my battered pride saying that an hour's instruction was worth any amount of study where practical matters were concerned.

By now the other two pupils had arrived and after introducing ourselves and giving a brief summary of what kind of animals we kept and where we lived, we followed Mrs Seeley into her lofty kitchen.

A red Aga presided over an array of ancient stone crocks and jars of all shapes and sizes. They sat on the tops of cupboards and work surfaces, while others, too big to be lifted down from any height, rested on the flagged floor against a background of dark wood panelling. A collage of a country girl feeding her chickens occupied nearly half of one wall. Made mostly of string and twine of varying thickness and texture on a background of hessian, its beautiful design and honest workmanship embodied an air of rural living. This was a very professional piece of work and whoever had created it certainly put into it the spirit of Mrs Seeley's environment.

Round about the kitchen various implements of everyday use hung on strategically placed hooks, and ceramic tiles, their design picking up the vibrant red of the Aga, covered part of the walls. The warmth given off from the cooker reflected the feel of this homely room and I began to feel that in this encouraging atmosphere even I could not fail.

237

An enormous pan stood on the edge of the hob; filled to the brim with milk from the Jersey cow I'd seen grazing in the orchard when we arrived. Mrs Seeley checked the temperature with a thermometer and our lesson began.

We washed our hands with operating fervour.

Under her tuition we put the milk through an identical regime to that I had followed during my lone trials, stirring and setting, cutting and warming then hanging up the curds. That being done, Mrs Seeley produced another muslin wrapped curd, which had been draining for several hours and was now ready for salting. Now, I thought, I'll see where I've been going wrong. She undid the tie and tipped the curds out of the cloth onto a scalded board. Its appearance was not unfamiliar. I waited for our instructor to give a cry of horror and was already composing words of consolation after she was forced to acknowledge that even with years of experience in the dairying arts she could be faced with public failure, but not a flicker of concern disturbed her serene expression.

'Now, we break this up with our hands into small lumps......would one of you do that? And then we salt it.'

I was dumfounded, rendered into complete inactivity but I forced my voice to studied casualness.

'That's, er....that's it is it?'

She gave me a questioning look but quickly turned back to oversee the salting of the curds.

'Yes, that's it. Quite simple really. The golden rule is to treat curds gently, always working them slowly.'

Oh, misunderstood and unloved curds. What a ghastly fate had been yours, to be hurled over the wall to the merciless scrabbling of chickens. I was about to tell my sorry tale but decided otherwise when Mrs Seeley, as though intuition was allowing her to be party to my blunders, said, 'It really does help if you can be shown.'

We ladled the salted curds onto a piece of muslin and placed the bundle in a mould, which was then put in the press.

Having a cow, Mrs Seeley made big cheeses. So she explained to those of us who had less milk about appropriate weights, and a question and answer session brought forth more information about pressing, bandaging and curing. It was all so engrossing. However, there was nothing more to do to the cheese so we went into the cool

238

dairy and bashed cream about in a small wooden churn, which was quite a change from the gentle attitude we'd had to adopt towards the cheese. Butter quick, cheese slow, was a simple enough maxim. We learned to listen for the sound of the butter 'coming' as the fat grained and reached the stage for draining off the glorious buttermilk. We washed the butter time and time again, churning it with fresh water, and like small children, laughing at the sloshy sound as it hit first one side of the churn and was then tossed over to the other. Then we pulled the squidgy stuff out, put it on a clean board, pressed out any remaining water, added a little salt, and after sampling the fruits of our labour patted it into a neat shape with butter pats.

We were shown several sturdy cheese presses constructed by Mrs Seeley's husband and we admired cheeses in various stages of maturity set out on scrubbed wooden shelves in the dairy. A tasting followed from several cut cheeses laid out on the table, with explanations of how to obtain different types, then we finished the morning asking questions and exchanging ideas over coffee and biscuits.

Mrs Seeley's demonstration was not wasted. From then on my familiarity with the art of cheese making increased. At first I had a few failures, mainly due to trial and error in dealing with the weights on the press but most were very tasty and some were deemed worthy of praise with almost every mouthful. Cheeses came thick and fast. I became more confidant and worked on the theory that as goat's milk is different in construction from cow's milk, slight variations on Mrs Seeley's recipe might be permissible. I began to experiment with setting times and time taken for maturing, eventually finding what seemed best for my particular milk and method of working, until failures became almost non-existent.

Cheese making became one of my happiest and most rewarding activities. Even on the days when making didn't take place the little two and a half pound cheeses needed some attention. Those in the press had to be turned and wrapped in fresh cloth and I loved to feel them getting dryer as the last remnants of whey were squeezed out under pressure from the heavy concrete blocks. Those on the wooden shelf had to be turned daily for a few weeks, and any mould wiped off, and again I could sense the maturing taking place as each day they felt a little firmer. There was always an air of mystery about a home

239

produced cheese. As the flavour was dependent on what herbs were growing in the meadow at the time, not one ever tasted quite like any other although the overall flavour and appearance was of a Cheshire......a creamy, crumbly Cheshire, and I was confident enough to wrap a tartan ribbon round one from time to time when a special gift was to be given.

Lunch at Tironnen was generally a simple affair. Wholemeal bread, with oats and honey in the baking, well-matured chutney, and of course, a wedge of our gorgeous cheese.

Simple indeed, but I doubt anyone ever had better.

A BIRD IN THE HAND

Many times I had gone up to the vegetable garden eager to tackle some particular task only to find several gaily coloured, feverishly energetic little birds scuffling and scratching among the rows of growing things, leaving limp and broken casualties all over the ground. This, I realised, was what bantams did if they got half a chance. Chickens also enjoyed demolition work but a fence of sheep netting, the holes of which were small enough to keep them out, surrounded our vegetable garden. It was different for the bantams, they just popped through.

I had accepted them from a neighbour who had more than she cared to keep and I had to admit they made a lovely splash of colour as they scurried about. The black bantam we'd had for a couple of years treated their arrival with indifference, preferring the company of the hens she knew, wandering with them up the old cart track above the house, making occasional sorties into the field. Like them she generally confining her daily doings to the yard, which, with its luscious compost heap and large patch of nettles below the grassy bank offered all the excitement a hen required.

The new bantams though, were not to be indulged so easily, flying up over the garden wall to enjoy dust-baths beneath the fruit bushes that grew beyond the small flower garden. This I would not tolerate. I'd rush out, wafting whatever implement came to hand, yelling for the dogs to give chase and the birds would fly back into the yard, leaving dusty holes and liberal deposits of visiting cards.

The dogs, quickly appreciating this new sport, would be ready and waiting each morning for the first contingent to fly over the wall, which proved all too much for the bantams. Jumping, barking dogs greeted them as they flew up and in mid-flight they'd turn, squawking their annoyance and flee. After a few weeks most of them were not prepared to face such an enemy every morning and gave up, although a persistent few kept up the battle a little longer. That's sorted that out, I thought. But it hadn't.

They went west.

They found the vegetable garden.

Something had to be done, which is how 'the catcher' came into being. It was one of Gordon's more simple inventions, consisting of

241

two large net vegetable bags, each split down one side then stitched together to form one large bag. This was then attached to a circular wire frame, which in turn, was fixed to a long pole. It looked like an enormous butterfly net and my demeanour as I swung it wildly around in mid-air when shooing the trespassing bantams was as composed as the bearer of a machete in a tribal war. A sight guaranteed to send even the most brazen bird fleeing for safety. I never caught one in the net; there wasn't any need to try. Waving it around was enough. I don't know whether my neighbours way down the hill ever heard the whoops and yells from on high as they went about their business but if they did they must have wondered what on earth was going on. Nothing was ever said.

But it was impossible to keep the bantams away from the vegetable garden and the speed with which we could chase them out bore no relation to the amount of damage they could have done before we knew they were there. To their credit they laid small white eggs with great regularity and proved excellent sitters on clutches of hens eggs but the balance did not weigh in their favour, so one day when Gordon held aloft several cauliflower seedlings which had been scratched up I decided enough was enough. I replaced the seedlings, firming them into the ground, hoping I wouldn't be doing this sort of thing for much longer and went down to the house where I wrote a short notice advertising them free for the taking.

The following day we put the notice in the post office and late that evening the phone rang. Mr Horner introduced himself. He lived some way off on the Abergavenny road but a friend stopping in the village that evening for some fish and chips, had seen the advert in the post office, and knowing that he, Mr Horner, had spoken recently about acquiring some bantams, had noted our phone number on the back of his hand. Mr Horner waxed lyrical at the idea of having bantams, 'and wasn't it an amazing thing that his friend had chosen to stop in our village and wasn't it extraordinary that we had an advert in the post office window just at that very time?' Bantams were, it was obvious, about to become the most exciting things in his life. Eventually he drew breath.

'How early can you come?' I asked, 'Because we'll have to box them first thing before they wander off and I don't want them hanging around like that for long.'

242

'Eggggggggggggzaklymam,' came the reply. 'I will be there before 10 o'clock. Will that suit you?'

I said it would suit me well, and gave directions as to how to find us, my information being frequently responded to with 'Eggggggggggggzaklymam, the 'eggggggggggg' part of which was delivered in a drawn-out crescendo, culminating loudly on the zak, followed by a crisp lymam which was clipped off almost before I'd had time to hear it. It was an unusual way of speaking, especially as the phrase seemed to be interjected quite randomly, as though it was slipping out without him knowing.

'Now mam, would you mind repeating those directions?'

I was about to do just that when I had an idea. 'Look, people do sometimes have difficulty finding us, so I'll draw a diagram of where we are in relation to the village and when my husband goes down there in the morning he'll leave it at the post office for you.'

'That's very kind of you mam, very kind. Ten o'clock then.'

'Yes, we'll tell Thomas the Post you'll be calling.'

'Ten o'clock. Eggggggggggggzakly.'

I faithfully repeated the conversation to Gordon, trying to imitate what I thought to be Mr Horner's Herefordshire accent but he thought I was making it up.

My first thought the following morning was that the bantams would be away within a matter of hours and although I never liked parting with animals I knew that this was going to be the exception. The loss of seeing golden feathers glinting in the sunlight as a dust bather rose to shake itself amid a bed of beetroot would not tug at my heartstrings. It was definitely a case of, if it's going to be thee or me folks, it's going to be me.

After discussing the modus operandi over coffee I distributed the morning ration of corn about the yard and opened the hen house door, standing behind it and peering round as the hens, already gossiping amongst themselves, pushed their way forwards, eager to be out and about. I was aware that some of the bantams would linger on their perches for a few moments and I reasoned that if I shut the door after all those who wanted to be out were out, we could go inside and behind closed doors catch the remaining bantams with ease.

Actually I was banking on Gordon catching them because I never liked handling birds as small as bantams and on the rare occasions

243

when any had needed to be caught I had, through a mixture of clumsiness and design, missed them first go anyway.

Sure enough, as the birds crowded through the door, five bantams obligingly remained on their perches, and I quickly nipped inside. Gordon joined me, bringing in two cardboard boxes. At once the birds realized something was up but he deftly caught one and lowered it into a box, slowly drawing his hands out as I carefully folded over the lid. We had learned from previous experience that haste during this operation can result in torn hands, frayed tempers, and, standing in a corner with a crafty glint in its eye, an escaped bird now knowing what the game was all about, waiting for round two to begin. Soon Gordon had another bird firmly in his hands and I gingerly opened the lid of the box, keeping my free hand close to the aperture in order to forestall any attempt to escape by occupant number one.

Within minutes the bantams were in the boxes and we went outside to review the situation. The remaining eight birds mingled with the other poultry and I wondered if we'd ever catch them. The idea was to entice them back and proceed as before. We waited a while for the last remnants of the morning feed to disappear and then I threw a handful of corn into the henhouse. As one body the hens rushed madly inside but all eight bantams remained pottering about the yard. Could we induce them somewhere else perhaps? I threw more corn into an empty stable. 'Come on,' I encouraged, and getting no response, unthinkingly shrilled my usual call of 'Henny henny henny,' whereupon deducing that more exciting things were afoot, all the hens abandoned the corn on the henhouse floor and flapped across the cobbles to where I stood. They looked at the ground, at me and about them, until one, brighter than the others, got the idea that goodies lay in the stable and made for the door. The others immediately swarmed forward reminiscent of the crowd outside Harrods on the first day of the sales, while the bantams continued their exploration of the yard.

Speed in completing the task was essential, for any minute they were sure to wander off towards the meadow where they'd all go their separate ways and be impossible to catch.

'Perhaps I'll try the catcher. D'you mind fetching it?' Gordon asked, then he called Dylan who came eagerly leaping over the garden wall to be sent to the top of the yard beyond the henhouse.

'Sit,' commanded Gordon and the dog turned to look at us expectantly as he obeyed the command. He wasn't often called upon to do anything in the way of work and probably wondered what it was all about, but judging by the way his tail swept from side to side over the powdery soil was quite happy at the prospect. I fetched the bantam catcher, handing it to Gordon who stationed himself opposite the henhouse, while I moved down just below the barn doors. By more or less surrounding the birds, we reckoned we would achieve one of two things. Either they'd be persuaded to return to the henhouse or else they'd fly into the barn. The former would ensure capture of all, the latter of at least some.

I stealthily crept to the henhouse door and threw in a handful of corn, then returned to my station. Amazingly two of the birds stopped pecking at the ground and moved over to the doorway. The others, their curiosity alerted, followed, and the little party stood on the threshold, considering its next move. With bated breath we waited, Gordon holding the catcher at arms length, I, poised for a leap should they make for the barn and Dylan holding his position at the top of the yard, thumping his tail wildly on the dusty ground if one of us glanced his way.

The bantams still hesitated going into the henhouse and I was telling myself that it was only a question of time, when I heard the familiar sound of the postman's van starting up from the bottom gate at the far end of the meadow. Dylan heard it too and pricked up his ears, wondering whether it was in order for him to embark on his daily routine of noisily escorting the post van up the track. He half stood and instinctively I yelled 'Sit'. As though a gun had been fired in their midst the bantams flew, most into the barn but two or three were up and away over the roofs towards the meadow.

'That wasn't very bright,' observed Gordon.

'There's nothing very bright about this whole enterprise,' I retorted testily, furious with myself. 'Chasing these bally things like this is ridiculous; there must be an easier way.' We advanced on the barn and closed the big doors. There was enough light coming through the slits to see bantomy shapes on bales of straw.

'Well, I can't give much more time to this,' said Gordon, 'I've got to get on,' and he surreptitiously swung the catcher around at the birds, deftly enmeshing two of them. They squawked and screeched but in seconds we had them out and into a box. The remaining three had flown up to the top of the bales, several feet higher, from where they regarded us warily. Gordon approached stealthily, manoeuvring the catcher to just below where one stood, then swiftly enveloped it.

'Two to go' Gordon laid the catcher against the wall. 'But I really must get on. If you can't catch them we'll have to tell Mr Whatsisname he can have them another time. We can take them to wherever he lives,'

I lined all the boxes up in the cool of the barn and dropped some corn into each one, then thankful to be able to get on with other things, I did just that.

By lunchtime I was very annoyed indeed.

'I'm not keeping them like this any longer,' I said, 'people who say they'll be here at a certain time and don't come are a bally nuisance.'

I opened the boxes. The bantams, apparently now accustomed to their new quarters, were not in any hurry to leave, so I left them to disembark at their pleasure.

Shortly after one o'clock the phone rang. Mr Horner announced himself.

'What happened?' I asked immediately.

'I'm afraid I'm not where I ought to be.' came the reply.

I was on the point of saying that how anyone could wander round the Breconshire hills for three hours before realizing they were lost was pushing credulity too far, and why couldn't he just admit that even though he was lost now, never in a million years would he have been at Tironnen at ten o'clock, but instead I reminded him tersely that I'd given him perfectly clear directions, even a diagram showing where we were in relation to the village.

'Eggggggggggzaklymam. I'm at Tirabad now. Are you near here? Somehow or other I must have missed your lane.'

'Tirabad?' I couldn't believe my ears. Not only had he missed the lane he'd practically missed the county! 'You're miles away, miles. If you want the birds Mr Horner, I'm afraid you'll have to come for them another day.' By this time the humour of the situation was getting to me and it was all I could do to contain my giggles. 'They were all ready for you at ten o'clock but I've since let them out. I couldn't keep them cooped up like that waiting for you and I really can't catch them again today. You do still want them?'

'Oh, I do ma'am, I do indeed and would it suit you if I call tomorrow morning at about ten o'clock?'

He was blissfully unaware of the nervous energy, which had been expended catching the birds and the idea of repeating the morning's activity the following day was not welcome, so I nearly told him not to bother but fortunately common sense overpowered cussedness. Besides, I was curious about this character and the humour of the situation had not escaped me.

'If you can't make it, please let me know before eight o'clock.'

'Eggggggggggggzaklymam, eggggggggggggzakly. But I'll be there. Before ten o'clock. Well before ten o'clock.'

'He's at Tirabad' I reported to Gordon. 'Can you believe it? He must have gone across the range. Says he got lost but how he could have misunderstood my instructions I don't know. I presume he picked up the map you left. Must be a bit dim although he sounds sharp enough.' I had a mental picture of Mr Horner driving over the firing range, ignoring the red flags, while twenty-pounders whizzed over his head!

A charade not dissimilar to that of the previous day took place the following morning, although experience played a part in shortening the task, and it wasn't long after the birds had been boxed that we heard the approach of a vehicle grinding its way up the track and an ancient Land Rover hove into view coming to a noisy halt at the meadow gate. It was just after nine-thirty so our visitor was taking no chances with the time. The elderly occupant climbed out and came towards us.'

'Horner's the name, ma'am, and it's a lovely view you've got here.'

The breezy voice came from a cheerful face, roughened and brown, the signature of a lifetime of outdoor working. A greasy looking brown beret was pulled firmly down on his head and an ancient black jacket, possibly once part of a Sunday best suit and decorated with several lengths of straw covered what appeared to be the remnants of a fair-isle pullover, the exposed part of which displayed as much hole as knitting. A length of orange baling twine was threaded through one of the buttonholes of the jacket and knotted, presumably to be tied round Mr Horner's person in the event of inclement weather, thereby solving the problem of the jacket having no buttons. Below the jacket a pair of

247

flamboyant check trousers shouted loudly before vanishing into Wellington boots, while a red and white kerchief adorning his neck gave an air of studied casualness to the ensemble and the whole outfit proclaimed Mr Horner as a man of individuality.

I tried not to stare too hard at this vision as the three of us walked towards the barn. I indicated the boxes to him and explained that three had not been caught but we'd let him have them next time we were going in his direction, which would certainly be within the next ten days.

'Eggggggggggzaklymam,' said Mr Horner, looking directly at Gordon. 'I know how it is and if you don't mind I'll come for them tomorrow. At ten o'clock.'

Gordon didn't answer, being slightly nonplussed at the unusual mode of address.

'It seems a long way to come specially,' I remarked, stifling a giggle. 'We'll be round your way in a week or so and it'll be no trouble to drop them off.'

But Mr Horner was adamant, so it was agreed that the three remaining birds would be boxed and waiting for him the following day and with that settled he resumed the eulogy of the bantam that had been my introduction to him when he had phoned two evenings ago. They were bright (well, all except our dull black bird); their colours were beautiful (undeniably); they were good egg layers (definitely); it was lovely to see them about the place (no it jolly well wasn't). I thought the conversation to be getting a bit dangerous and managed to steer him away from the subject by suggesting some refreshment but bending down to pick up a couple of the boxes he indicated that he was anxious to be on his way. Gordon and I picked up the others and between us carried them down to the Landover.

'See you tomorrow then.'

'As early as you like.'

'Eggggggggggzaklymam, eggggggggggzakly,' and with unexpected vigour he swung into a three point turn across the uneven terrain of our meadow causing shrieks of annoyance to issue from the back of the vehicle, and with fumes blowing on the wind towards us, shot down the track. The following morning he was early on the scene to collect the remaining birds. His clothing was identical to that of the previous day, even, I would have sworn, to the wisps of straw on the black jacket, and I gazed fascinated at one bent in a V shape which I was sure had been in the same spot on his lapel the day before.

We chatted for a few minutes, Gordon again finding himself addressed somewhat unconventionally, until our visitor picked up the box and announced his departure. We walked with him to the Land Rover where he placed the bantams in the back. He hoisted himself up and turning, looked directly between the two of us, called out cheerily 'Thank you and goodbye ma'am,' before shooting backwards and up into the meadow to turn towards the lower gate. He waved from the window and the screeching of disorientated birds floated back to us as the elderly vehicle rocketed down the track.

Some days later I was telling a neighbour about the trials and tribulations of catching the bantams, exaggerating the details to become acts of some drama in order to give a tad more excitement to the story. He was a most appreciative audience, chuckling at the saga which encouraged me to build on the tale even more.

'You did have fun,' commented he, 'But you know, in the unlikely event of you ever having to do such a thing again, just wait until they're asleep. I think you'll find you can pick them off their perches without too much bother!'

'Eggggggggxackly!'

DEAD LOSS

I had always assumed that all goats ate with the enthusiasm displayed by Bluebell and Snowdrop. As soon as their feed buckets were put before them the contents were attacked and devoured, every last morsel scooped up and the buckets licked clean, so I was a little disconcerted to find that Miranda did less than justice to her daily ration of dairy mixture. In fact she did a good deal less than justice; she ignored it.

The morning following her arrival I took in her breakfast and found her looking at the apex of her pen where the partition joined the wall, as she had been when I'd left her the night before when I'd done my 11o'clock nightly round. She delicately poked her aristocratic nose into the bucket, barely penetrating the surface of the food and then finding it not to her liking, returned to her former position. It was very strange. I tried to persuade her to taste a little but she turned her head to one side, refusing to acknowledge the presence of either the bucket or me. I tipped the mixture back into the bin and replaced it with some crushed oats. Maybe she'd never tasted dairy mix before but she was sure to have had oats.

'Come on Miranda,' I coaxed.

Without much interest she once more obliged by sniffing round the perimeter of the bucket, withdrew her head almost immediately to return to the wall. I did a bit of tut-tutting, went to the food store at the far end of the goat house again and added some flaked maize. This she would not be able to resist. All animals loved flaked maize.

'Oh, Miranda, you're going to love this,' I announced, putting down the bucket. She inclined her head as before, then in a desultory way circled it within an inch of the food but the companionship of the wall still outshone any pleasure to be gained from the contents of the bucket and I scratched my head in exasperation and knelt down to stroke her.

'What's the matter with you?' I asked irritably. 'Are you behaving like this because you're new here, is that it? I don't understand you Miranda. Just tell me what you've been fed on,' and I got up and looked at her but the spectacle of her large bony body gave me no clue.

I returned to the sacks stacked against the far wall. A couple of handfuls of bran added to the oats and maize might do the trick, so once again I carried the bucket back to her and watched as she followed her routine of looking and turning away. I picked up her drinking bucket and poured some water over the food, just enough to dampen it and mixed it with my hand but that didn't suit either. My patience was fast evaporating.

'What do you think you're playing at? Is this some sort of game? If this is a daily ritual you think you can play you've got another think coming,' And I grimaced at her, continuing my useless tirade, 'One more chance, just one more chance for you to eat this morning, then out you go.' I was warming to my oratory and early in the morning when so many things had to be done with both animals and children, persuading a perfectly able goat to eat its breakfast was most provoking. 'I don't care. Starve for all I care,' I kept on, behaving like a bolshie two-year old and temporarily forgetting the depleted bank balance caused by her purchase.

From the neighbouring pen came the satisfied sound of crunching, as Bluebell and Snowdrop, having cleaned out the last crumbs from their buckets, began on some greens, all the while watching Miranda and me through the slats. Every so often, one of them, thinking the burlesque next door worth closer inspection, would put a yellow eye close up to the gap, then having seen enough, retire to continue searching for the tastiest pieces. Again I picked up her bucket, opened the gate and hissed, 'Once more, just once more,' and made for the kitchen where I poured enough hot water onto some molasses to make it runny and ferociously stirred it into the food, muttering to myself as I mashed the stuff together. Doing this for a sick animal was one thing but this was ridiculous.

Marching into the pen for what I determined would be the last time, I flung down the bucket and watched as Miranda sniffed a couple of times then selected a morsel..... and returned to look at the wall. I took hold of her collar; quite forgetting the reflex action triggered off by this and was immediately taken for a spin round the pen. I let go, to find myself on a level with the ladies next door, who, having finished their greens were standing on their hind legs, their forelegs draped over the wooden division, the better to observe what

251

was happening. Remnants of marigold and various leaves hung from their oscillating jaws, vanishing slowly as I watched.

I patted each white head. 'You,' I said, 'Are normal greedy goats, thank goodness and if you have any ideas as to what I can do with this one I would be very glad to hear them.'

I leaned over, undid the latch on their gate and they hurried out, eager to enjoy another day. I ushered Miranda out after them but she stood on the cobbles radiating indifference and once more I took her by the collar but this time, with feet firmly on the ground I resisted the violent reaction. She seemed surprised by this and walked with reasonable decorum by my side to the meadow, where I shut the gate and returned to tidy up the goat house.

The hay which I'd left for her to nibble overnight had mostly been pulled from the rack and strewn liberally on the floor as though she'd tugged it out mouthful by mouthful but found it not to her taste. Oh my, I thought, she even turns up her nose at the hay. This really was pushing things a bit far, for our meadow was that rare thing, an old pasture, and many herbs made up the hay we took from it. Every year our neighbour combined it taking half in payment and one of the great delights of winter was to pull a wedge from the end of a bale and inhale the sweet smell of summer as it drifted from the cut. The flowers, whatever their original colour, all dried to a uniform brown or orange, but the grasses maintained their colour right through the winter. It was probably some of the finest hay in the country, causing occasional comment from one of our neighbours who, whilst consenting that goats, as milking animals deserved the best, considered it criminal to 'waste hay like that on bloody horses.'

But even such luxury did not impress Miranda. During the following couple of weeks she picked at her greens, pulling a leaf of this and a stalk of that, never allowing herself to appear anything but obliging and on my late night check she would always be standing in her usual 'face to the wall' position, although during the course of the night most of the bunch of stuff I'd hung up would be eaten. We were getting somewhere but clearly Miranda was used to better things. But what? Every day she'd select a few morsels but no more, so I began to mix in a few chunks of wholemeal bread, which were always eaten and as our bread contained honey and oats, at least she was getting a bit of nourishment. Fortunately she enjoyed her mineral-lick. It was

252

the only normal thing she relished and it was just as well, for on magnesium-starved land like ours it was essential that the animals made full use of the large blocks put out for them.

Out of curiosity I decided to see if she had any milk. I wanted to know what it was like and certainly the bare cupful lived up to the reputation of the Anglo-Nubian as a butterfat producer, for the cream lay thick on even this small yield and I longed for the day when the milking pail would fill and I could retrieve the cream from the steel setting pan and put it daily on one side until there was enough to churn. But milking her for such a small amount was hardly worth the trouble, apart from the fact that on her self-imposed diet I didn't want her to be spending her energy producing milk, so after a few days I dried her off.

I wondered about Miranda.

She was a well set-up goat, strong as an ox and her coat had a shining healthy appearance. So what did she eat?

I phoned Frances. 'What do you mean, she doesn't eat?'

I recited the list of offerings, which Miranda had found unsatisfactory.

'Well, this is peculiar. I went to fetch her from Sussex one day and you came for her early the next so she was only here for one night as you know and she was picky with her food that morning. The long journey could have unsettled her for a while so I didn't think anything was amiss. I tell you what, I'll phone the Barlow's, they were the people who had her and ask them what she's been fed on. Perhaps she's been sharing the dog meal.' In our innocence we both laughed, then she added, 'The only goat I've ever come across that doesn't eat is a dead goat.'

'We're getting there,' I interjected jokily.

'I'll call you as soon as I've anything to tell. It's very odd.' I put down the phone, hoping that it wouldn't be long before some light could be shed on Miranda's eating habits.

As I was working in the yard that afternoon I let the goats in to eat patches of nettles, which liberally grew amongst the stone remains of some former buildings. They were only allowed in the yard when I could keep an eye on them, for in one nimble leap they'd be up on the wall and over the fence to commence destruction of our soft fruit and herbs. They always seemed to enjoy this change of scene, for it was a

253

pleasant diversion for them to scrabble among the piles of stones for which we'd as yet found no use, biting off the plants which grew profusely and then when enough eating had been done, play on a large tree stump or spread themselves like a couple of sirens on the bank to cud, a picture of contentment.

So that day as I worked I kept a close eye on Miranda. I wanted to find out what, if anything made her tick. She ambled about, daintily picking out a morsel here and there, which she then cudded endlessly with her eyes fixed straight ahead, unaware as usual of the world about her. The other two tackled each clump of nettles, jaws opening and closing with relish as they moved and very much aware of what was going on around them. The difference was very marked.

I went into the house to make a pot of tea, keeping an eye on them through the window. I called Gordon and we settled on the great log under the ash tree for a welcome ten-minute break. The white goats bounded down from the bank towards us and Dylan sauntered up wearing the expression of one who was just passing by. Miranda slowly followed and stood well behind the trio.

'Biscuit?' I handed the tin to Gordon and bent down to pick up the two mugs of tea and at the sound of the tin being opened Miranda's lethargy vanished. She sprang forward, knocking Gordon backwards. Several biscuits fell to the ground and I hastily put down the mugs, slopping most of the contents on the tray in the process, as Gordon heaved himself up from where he'd been pushed part way down the back of the log. I reached out to grab Miranda's collar but missed and she swivelled away from me to begin greedily devouring the spilt biscuits. Regaining his balance, Gordon reached out and caught her, then I took over trying to pull her head away from the ground while she hung forward in her collar, straining to get her head down again in the direction of the biscuits. My goodness, she was strong, although where her strength came from on her diet I couldn't imagine, and raising a finger in a 'don't you dare' gesture towards the three witnesses, I marched her, protesting down to the goat house. But once in her stall her animation departed and she stood facing the wall as before. I patted her on the head and left.

Gordon emerged from the house with a fresh drink, having cleared up the debris except for a few pieces of broken biscuit that he allowed Dylan and the goats to enjoy along with some spilt tea, which hadn't yet been absorbed in the soil. We sipped our drinks and spoke about Miranda.

We talked of the afternoon we'd first met her, when Frances, having been dragged unceremoniously across the field had remarked,

'She was a pet....I suppose children would think this funny.'

'And I suppose,' said Gordon, 'They'd think it positively hilarious to have a goat fighting for chocolate biscuits,' and a clearer picture began to emerge of her way of life and eating habits during the last two years. Well, not so much a clearer picture of what her life was; more of what it was not, and it was not the life of a cared for goat. I just hoped our suspicions were wrong.

The following evening Frances phoned to say that she'd been unable to contact the former owners but that she'd keep trying. 'They may be away. Things still the same I suppose? '

'Well, no; they've changed somewhat. We've found something she likes.'

'What's that?' she asked.

'Chocolate biscuits,' and I related the drama of the day.

There was a silence and I knew Frances was thinking what I was thinking.

'Oh.'

A goat will eat almost anything and the occasional tit-bit is fine when its diet is a correct one, but for one that doesn't know about proper food yet is familiar with the sound of the opening of a biscuit tin, the implications were fairly obvious.

'I feel awful about this,' said Frances. 'Surely it can't be as bad as it seems though. I'll be in touch again as soon as I can,' and 'soon' was the next day.

'I hope you're sitting down. When I asked Mrs Barlow what Miranda had been fed on, she said 'goat meal and maize mostly', but I then said I didn't think that was true and she got a bit huffy but then said 'well, sometimes she did have a few other sorts of food as well. She then had the gall to say 'she does have a sweet tooth, you know.' 'You mean human food?' I said, and goodness how that woman hedged. Eventually it came out.....they were just so busy, their lives so full of work and children and other commitments, for commitments read socialising I suspect, that it was too much bother to go a few miles to the feed merchant. I was so angry and when she'd got over

255

her blustering she said 'well, goats eat anything anyway so what was the difference and the goat was alright when I took her back, wasn't it?' And of course, apart from racing off when I took hold of her collar, there apparently was nothing wrong with her. I'll take her back, Jenny, I feel so bad about it.'

Poor Frances, she obviously felt responsible, yet she had been as unwitting a pawn as we. 'When I sold her,' she continued, 'I knew they wanted her as a companion for the children but they seemed so sensible and kind. I gave them written instructions about feeding and various do's and dont's, even found the whereabouts of their local feed merchant. I visited twice in the early days, just to make sure they were coping and they were certainly doing the right thing by her then. I honestly had no idea how things had worked out. I'll take her back,' she repeated.

'No, you sold her in good faith. I hate to think of her going through another upheaval and I know Gordon would too. Now I know definitely what's wrong I'd like to see if I could do anything for her. I'll discuss it with Gordon but I know what he'll say. I'll call you back in a day or so.'

So Miranda stayed with us and over the weeks she began to eat a little better; not much, but there was a slight improvement, although I didn't think it was due to any cajoling on my part. Her character didn't change one iota and I could never tell whether she was happy or not.

In due course she came into season and although her eating habits were still markedly strange she seemed healthy, and after conferring with the vet and speaking to Frances it was decided to return once more to Worcestershire to acquaint her with Frances's fine male goat. True to form she snored all the way and three weeks later we went to collect her, spent the usual pleasant hour with Frances, although a good deal of the time was taken up discussing what Miranda was now eating and the cruelty of people who deny animals their dignity. Then we bundled our hopefully pregnant goat in the back of the Land Rover and made for home.

Winter passed, and with the first signs of spring we should have noticed her increased girth; but didn't. Was she in kid I wondered every time I looked at her, peering at the front, back and both sides for the telltale swelling. It would fit in with her general outlook to repudiate motherhood and the vision of glorious butter and cream began to fall into the category of wishful thinking. Still, some goats, I had heard, didn't show much, so until events proved otherwise we could still hope. We soon got our evidence although it wasn't what we'd hoped for.

Coming into the kitchen one night after making my last check of the goats at about eleven, I flopped down in a chair feeling exceptionally weary; too weary even to pick up the patchwork quilt I was making, so Gordon made some coffee and we talked about a commission he had just finished and was delivering to Ayelsbury in two days time. We tossed new ideas about and talked of future projects and I became more enthusiastic and less tired. Two hours later we were still talking, although the topic had changed many times and it was at this point that he said, 'I'm just going to check on something I've left drying in the workshop; I'll only be five minutes.'

I put the dirty mugs in the sink, plumped up the cushions, said goodnight to the dogs and was just about to go upstairs when Gordon returned. 'I thought you were going to be a bit longer that that,' I said and immediately saw from his face that something was wrong. 'What's the matter, what's happened?' On his way to the workshop something had prompted him to go into the goat house and looking into Miranda's pen he saw something on the straw, which shouldn't have been there.

'Miranda's aborted.'

I hurried out full of concern for our poor goat but my solicitude was of no consequence. A tiny foetus, very undeveloped for one only three weeks off birth, lay in the straw. Miranda was in her usual position, her chest pushed up against the apex of the wall and the slats that divided her pen from the next. It seemed she hadn't a care in the world but if she hadn't, we had.

The thought of keeping an unproductive goat for a further year was not a happy one and although I felt sorry for her, I felt a good deal more sorry for us. I made a bran mash and put some malt in it but after a perfunctory examination from her it was left to go cold and in the morning Bluebell and Snowdrop polished it off.

The daily opening of the doors and the clattering of buckets always had the Saanan's up on their feet, draped over the wooden partition to oversee the preparation of the first meal of the day, whereas Miranda's response was to ignore me completely, so I wasn't in any way bothered when the following day I put down her bucket and she remained lying down looking at her wall. I scooped up the soiled straw, tidied up around her and brought in fresh water from the tub outside, then having turned Bluebell and Snowdrop out into the meadow repeated the ablutions, tidied the goat house generally before returning to Miranda.

'Come on Miranda,' I said, 'Let's get moving,' and after a tug on her collar she slowly rose to her knees, pausing for a few seconds before jerking to a standing position. Encouraging her to rise, enticing her to sample the contents of the bucket and persuading her to venture outside was standard procedure but this time there was something about her that was different. She looked the same, she behaved the same but I felt something was wrong. I knelt down and stroked her but she turned her head away and I grabbed a handful of hay and wafted it under her nose. I thought for a while and then carefully grasped her head. She resisted with all her might but I held firm.

'Alright old thing, let mother have a look. There's a good girl.'
With the thumb of my other hand I gently pulled up an eyelid, then with difficulty I opened her mouth. What I saw sent me hurrying to the house to summon the vet.

***

Our vet having been appraised of Mirand's culinary habits said 'Well all you can do is try to keep her alive until this stuff works but she's such a fussy devil I'd say it's very much in the balance. There's nothing else I can do.' He looked at the languid creature on the straw as he pocketed the bottle of iron from which he had just given Miranda a shot, hoping to stem the pernicious anaemia. 'The trouble is, some of these Anglo's are so bloody neurotic.'

'I don't think it's the breed. It's something in her' I replied and I wondered about an animal that preferred to look at a wall rather than the world.

'Just give her what she'll eat,' he said in a voice that was a mite too casual for my humour, 'And hope for the best.'

'I've always given her what I know she'll eat, in moderation,' I protested indignantly, 'I've had to. And as for hoping for the best, I've been hoping for that for the past eight months and it just isn't coming.'

I held out my hands in a gesture of frustration. 'This goat and I are not as one. I shall be tripping out here with plates of toast and strawberry jam but if she decides to die all the strawberry jam in the world won't stop her.'

'Well, you could always try her with a few discarded jumpers.' Mr Edmonds had not forgotten the fiasco in the surgery that summer evening when we brought Miranda from Worcestershire.

'I think you'd better go,' I said testily; 'I am not in a humorous vein, and should you be unfortunate enough to be woken from your slumbers tonight, just think of me crossing the yard to feed this animal with midnight feasts of Fair Isle Consommé or Cardigan in Aspic.'

'I've heard of worse things,' he said as he left, pretending to examine his sweater for the most succulent bits and I returned to the goat house.

I felt so sad and helpless. If Snowdrop or Bluebell had been unwell I'd have detected it at once, for they would have given some sign. I knew every nuance of their behaviour and a simple examination would have brought to light either the cause, or the fact that something was wrong.

But Miranda's illness had remained undetected because her attitude to life was one of exaggerated lethargy and over the past weeks I'd never noticed any alteration in her behaviour. All I could do now was to try to keep her alive for the next few days and if I succeeded then maybe I could build her up again. At this stage I wasn't prepared to think how.

I fetched a goat coat from the cupboard and strapped it on her, then went back to the house to set about preparing a meal with such thought that anyone coming into the kitchen would have assumed my favourite aunt was coming to tea. I placed a round of toast spread with apricot jam and cut into squares on a tin tray and flanked it on one side with sliced apples and sultanas and currants on the other. A wedge of shortbread and two Cornish Farings broken in half were placed next to the apples and half a dozen red grapes alongside a few orange segments completed the meal. The appetizing array was garnished with pieces of orange peel. Even at this stage I drew the line at chocolate biscuits. It looked quite tempting but as goats are not appreciative of the aesthetic side of the culinary arts I went into the

259

goat house with my fingers crossed, hoping that something there would entice her.

'Here you are girlie.'

She turned to look at the tray as I set it down beside her and leaned over slightly in order to give it a general once-over, then moving a step backwards attacked the toast and apricot jam with vigour. Within short order it vanished, then she drifted her nose across the remaining food, daintily sampling apples, biscuits, cereal and dried fruit in turn and for the first time in our acquaintance she looked straight at me and I could have sworn she was thinking at last she's got the message.

I patted her and left to get on with the morning's work which was now far behind and when I returned the food had all gone except for the sultanas, which apparently did not measure up to the gourmet goat tray and had been scattered as she picked her way through.

Four hours later I again prepared her tray, this time substituting marmalade sandwiches for the jammy toast and omitting the sultanas. Everything met with her approval, only a few biscuit crumbs remaining as proof of the feast. I noticed that the sandwiches and toast were always the first things to be eaten so I increased the amount during the day, varying what I spread on them and feeling my hand metaphorically slapped when I slipped in some marmite! I set the alarm for three o'clock and went to bed hoping I'd soon be asleep.

That night I sat in the straw beside her, drinking coffee and eating honey sandwiches, listening to intermittent scuffles as a swallow rearranged itself in a nest in the eaves and the occasional movement from the stall next door. I tried to focus my mind on what seemed an insurmountable problem; a goat that as far as eating habits went didn't know it was a goat, but my thoughts were fuzzy and repetitive and no inspiration came.

I don't know how long I sat there dozing, huddled up with my arms round my knees, occasionally reaching out to stroke Miranda but I awoke to find myself very cold with my head leaning painfully against the wooden partition. I got up, full of aches and stiffness, straightened her goat coat, checked the water bucket and left. It was just starting to get light and a ground mist was coming up as I hurried across the yard. Oh, the joy of feeling the warmth as I stepped into the kitchen. I made some more coffee, wrapped a plaid rug round my shoulders and pulled a chair up close to the Rayburn. Although it was too early to tell, I was beginning to feel a little more hopeful. There remained, however, the diet problem, which my befuddled thinking of a few hours earlier had done nothing to solve. Until now Miranda had picked at various types of animal feed which she would eat in minute quantities as long as they were laced with broken biscuits, wholemeal bread, diluted honey and suchlike. Throughout the winter there was nothing of any nourishment in the meadow and she ate little of our hay. Two things alone sustained her; variety and sweetness. 'But I can't be making up a la carte menus every day,' I moaned, as I made yet another coffee. Indeed, was I prepared to?

My hands warmed as I hugged the mug and I considered the situation.

1. We could keep Miranda in the 'favourite aunt manner' for the rest of her life.

2. I could try to build her up when she'd recovered from the anaemia and mate her again but there was no guarantee that any kid would be female. What if a male kid was produced? Did we keep her another year and through another mating process and possibly still have no female kid? If we did get a female kid then Miranda would be put down and goat keeping would return to normal. Not really normal though, I thought. I'd feel guilty every time I looked at her daughter. You're a fool, I said to myself. She wouldn't know, and her daughter wouldn't know. What alternative is there? You can't palm her off on Frances, it wouldn't be fair. You can't afford to keep her as she is eating all this ridiculous food that isn't doing her any good, and you can't let anyone else have her because you'd be worried sick about how she was being treated. For goodness sake see reason. But reason isn't always easy to see and my tears dropped into the coffee, and Dylan, sensing my unhappiness, got down from his bed and came over to settle on my foot to comfort me in his doggy way.

During the course of the day I placed a handful of flaked maize on the tray but it was passed over to remain in isolation after the rest had been eaten. Another time I put out plain bread and butter but that was not touched either although after re-hashing it with marmalade it was acceptable. For two days and nights Miranda put away such dishes every four hours, these being interspersed with buckets of warm milk. But I had no illusions that she was not a very sick goat.

261

I talked to her constantly, trying to encourage her, trying to get through to her, although I wondered why I bothered since I'd been encouraging and talking and trying to get through to her since she came to us with no result. Her attitude when she wasn't eating was exactly the same as it had always been, except that now, when I arrived, she sometimes looked up but would then turn away to stare at the wall in her usual hypnotic state. She showed no sign of being better or worse. The third day progressed as the previous two had done but when I visited her at eleven o'clock that night with warm milk and goodies she showed little of her former interest, only nuzzling about for a few seconds. I tempted her with dried fruit and toast but she would have none of it.

With all this disturbed sleep I was very tired, but I had to make an early check on her, so I set the alarm for one o'clock and at that hour staggered out of bed barely awake, to feel my way down the stairs because it seemed too much effort to open my eyes. I crept out into the night carrying some warm milk laced with honey but she took very little. I knelt in the straw talking to her but my soft words and the arm I put over her back meant nothing. I went back to the house to collect the plaid rug, an oil lamp and some matches, then made my way to the barn to search for a fold-up garden chair. The light from a full moon streamed through the huge open doors lighting up the north end. I pulled away planks of wood, old doors and various other items which we'd accumulated over the winter and dumped there, probably neither knowing nor caring that the fold-up chairs were there first. Eventually I found them, picked up the nearest, dusted off several cobwebs and insects and returned to the goat house, lit the lantern preferring its soft glow to the electric light, hung it from a beam, and wrapping the blanket round me settled in the chair. Miranda seemed to be asleep and it wasn't long before I was too.

I woke up shortly before four, chopped up some apple and made jam sandwiches for her and some coffee for me. Her future, I decided, had to be in the lap of the Gods. If she was still living by seven o'clock I would phone the vet. He'd said that the iron he'd given her would take a few days to get through her system, but...... but what? What would I say? If it took a few days, it took a few days and there was nothing anyone could do about it.....the vet; me; no-one. But yes, I'd phone.

262

I leaned over to stroke her behind the ears, then I fell asleep.

***

As soon as I awoke I knew. Her head was resting on the tray, her nose a few inches from the adored strawberry jam; a sad but fitting end to a goat whose appetite was limited to refined concoctions.

I thought again about the people who had owned her but never loved her; who had treated her so carelessly using her purely for their own amusement, a plaything for their children to be discarded when the novelty wore off and I felt sick and angry. For some reason my mind fixed on the scenes when we'd run round the meadow, with Bluebell, Snowdrop and Blossom prancing skittishly, leaping high and showing off their prowess as gymnasts. If we sat down they'd come running over, twisting as they jumped as goats do in their carefree way, to ransack pockets as they nuzzled against us. Not so Miranda; she had always stayed outside the family, preferring to gaze into space while the fun was going on. We were always spurned. Her dependence on me, such as it was, purely material. She had nothing to give and I'd never been able to give anything to her. How sad.

For the last two days Gordon had been working in Aylesbury so he was unaware of her death. He was, in fact, due home that very day and I hoped he'd get back early so that Miranda could be buried with as little delay as possible. Late morning he arrived and after rest, refreshment and appraisal of what had been happening we heaved Miranda's weighty carcass onto a wheelbarrow and pushed it up the hill to a corner of the paddock. Later he dug a deep grave and laid her in it. We replaced the soil and I placed some dandelions on the red earth. Goodbye Miranda.

But Miranda wasn't going so easily.

In spite of the fact that she never became one of the family; in spite of her inability to adapt to a proper lifestyle, and although she was almost completely devoid of personality, her memory didn't just linger; it loomed menacingly whenever our funds got near the danger level because some weeks after her demise Gordon jotted down on a sheet of paper several headings:

Cost....petrol....vet....board....service.

We worked out the figures beginning from the first hundred and twelve mile round trip when we bought her, incurring the memorable vet's bill on the return journey. We added the cost of the trips taking and collecting her after her visit to the male goat, her winter keep, both eaten and wasted and the last series of vet's bills, although in deference to recent memory we did not include the cost of the numerous a la carte meals consumed during her last days.

Of course, we'd had milk from her when she'd first arrived, as I'd been curious to sample Anglo-Nubian milk, so yes, we'd had milk; lovely rich creamy milk half filling a half-pint jug on two consecutive mornings before I dried her off. This we put in the credit column. We added up the amounts and found that she had cost us a staggering one hundred and ninety two pounds thirteen pence......or put another way, her milk had cost that much for half a pint. It does help to have a sense of humour.

SHOW WILLING

On many a summer's weekend, rather than rise with the first chink of dawn to organize animals in a frenzy of washing, brushing and powdering, then box them and travel miles to parade them for inspection at some country show, I preferred to remain on our hillside and in such anonymity quietly enjoy their charm and industry. This was probably due to laziness, so it was just as well that the show-world had no appeal. Occasionally I would almost feel guilty at my selfishness, as though if I wasn't prepared to go to the trouble of exhibiting them, I had no right to possess animals of such quality but the fact was that I didn't care a hoot whether someone approved of our stock or not. Certainly as far as the goats were concerned, the telling was in the milking pail.

Quite early in my goat-keeping life I had been speaking on the phone to a woman steeped in the world of goats, and having concluded our business she asked, 'What line are your goats?'

'Langdale Prometheus,' I told her, following with a brief resume of their maternal line.

'They are sure to be very good,' she observed in a very confident voice, 'but I don't recognise your name. Which shows do you go to?'

'I don't go to shows.'

'Really?' She seemed very surprised at this and after a pause said in a voice conveying a mixture of command and condemnation, 'But you should. Of course I've not seen your goats but I'm sure you'd be well up the line. It's great fun you know, well no you obviously don't, but apart from anything else you have the possibility of finding a suitable stud goat for future use as well as seeing the sort of stock other people have.' It occurred to me that these last two could be viewed without having my own stock in tow but I forbore to comment. 'You really should show them.'

'It doesn't appeal.' I countered.

'But you'd do well,' she persisted. 'It might take a little time because there's quite an art to showing but you'd get the hang of it soon enough.' Then in a smiley, sing-song voice, which sounded as though she was trying to humour a two-year old, added, 'and then you'd find it would be worth it.'

'Worth what?'

She was clearly becoming irate and said in a voice slightly louder than before, 'Worth all the time and effort put into it when your goats are placed.'

'But that's why I don't show them; I can't be bothered with all that.'

She was not however, a woman to give up easily and in a reversal of attitude said in a honeyed tone, 'it's all such fun and so interesting. One learns so much and once you've taken the plunge and done your first show you'd just want to keep on. I know you would and I'm sure that with a pedigree like your goats have they'd soon be noticed.'

'You mean that they might win rosettes and things?'

'Well as I said before,' her voice changed to a very soothing tone presumably because she thought that at long last I'd got the message, 'I've not seen your goats but I know the blood-lines and I think there'd be little doubt that sooner or later a judge would put them in the running.'

I was getting a bit fed up with this woman telling me how to run my life, telling me that I should enjoy what she enjoyed doing. If I'd been interested in showing I'd have already been doing it, so if she was trying to encourage me she was going about it in quite the wrong way. She was I felt, being a bit intrusive, so it was now my turn to persist.

'Really? Now why should that be? Why would a judge put them in the running?'

Her patience with my stupidity foundered at this. She stressed her next words so that even an idiot would get their meaning loud and clear.

'Because.....with such a pedigree they are obviously very good goats.'

'But,' I replied laying equal stress as she had done, "I already know they're very good goats.'

At this, the lady kind of heart but a mite too pushy gave up, and said in a tone of controlled exasperation 'Well, I suppose you know your own mind,' and having come to the conclusion that we were not on the same wavelength, made some remark appertaining to the origin of our conversation, and then, after the usual civilities rang off.

I would not dream of denying the value of shows. As the woman said they are the breeders' shop window, the public reason to improve stock, the place where a future mate might be selected or the name of a herd noted. They're where prospective owners can see the very best and talk to breeders and, particularly in the case of goats, where the uninitiated so often fall in love with these enchanting creatures. I am thankful that so many people are enthusiastic about shows. Owners work terribly hard beautifying their animals and I'm sure winning that first rosette must do a power of good for their morale, spurring them on to further heights; but it's not for me. I enjoy looking at our animals and sometimes wish I had the spirit of competitiveness which drives the exhibitors on but I cannot conjure up one iota of enthusiasm for joining them, and after looking at the trade stands, and probably bumping into a few acquaintances we've not seen for some time, we are glad to return to the solitude of our hill. Everyone else seems to have such a glorious time so I'm sure the loss is ours. Still, that's how we are and it's not something I fret about.

Yet when Bessie's fine foal, Saracen, was five months old we did take him and his mother to a country show. It wasn't our idea.

In a moment of stupidity we weakened at the insistence of a friend who was show mad but at the time hadn't anything he considered suitable and couldn't bear the thought of arriving at a highly rated show minus his horse-box.

'Bess doesn't like being boxed' I said, 'She can be very difficult.'

A dismissive gesture of the hand wafted our objections away.

'No problem. I've tussled with all sorts of bloody-minded horses. They always go in eventually.'

Reluctantly we agreed to go; just this once, on condition that if Bess refused to enter the box that would be that. We didn't want the foal upset. So the entry form for the appropriate mare and foal class was filled in and posted and the Friday evening before the show Louise and Angela washed and groomed Bess.

That night I went to bed hoping that I would somehow by-pass the next day and wake on Sunday knowing that the whole thing had been a horrible dream, but Saturday dawned with the alarm shrilling and seconds later a similar demanding noise came from Angela's room. I turned over and buried my head in my pillow but after a few minutes listening to Angela bustling about downstairs, nagging guilt had me on the move. I couldn't let my daughter see to everything, although she knew a great deal more about the necessary preparations than I. If nothing else, moral support was a good thing to have at five o'clock in the morning.

At the appointed time our friend arrived in his smart cream Range Rover and to our amazement, and my private horror, Bess made few objections to being boxed. After a couple of tentative steps onto the ramp and a hesitation, she followed her foal inside. We closed up the end and were on our way, I forcing myself to appear enthusiastic, for in spite of our earlier affirmations that showing was not our idea of a great day our friend really thought he was doing us a favour.

We arrived at the show field to find it thronging with activity and a voice from a loud-speaker system, manned in a very smart van at the edge of the main ring, directed participants. We got Bess and Saracen out and the girls did some last minute grooming and general titivating. We had plenty of time and one by one wandered off to admire the other horses. It was obvious that the majority of people were old hands at this game. I noticed one or two who seemed to be rushing about on some urgent mission or shouting rather loudly to some underling to fetch or do something but generally the scene was of calmness and efficiency, of people getting on with the job; doing what they enjoyed doing.

It had been agreed that Angela should lead Saracen and I should take Bess. Then hearing the announcement that all entries for our class should make their way towards the main ring we set off, Bess and I going first. We stationed ourselves several yards from the entry gate and I thought how lovely Bess looked in her highly polished leather head collar dark against her cream coat, her main and tail, dark grey mingling with cream falling luxuriantly. Saracen kept close to his mother, very woolly looking and his short back proclaiming his Arab sire.

Foals and their dams were on either side of us, all very orderly with some of the owners putting finishing touches to already beautifully groomed animals. Clapping announced the previous class over and within seconds the proud winner, followed by the runners up and the not so successful, trotted their ponies towards the gate where we were waiting. Joy showed in some faces, disappointment in others and resentment in one or two. That's show business!

Third out of the ring was a large woman wearing very yellow jodhpurs and matching jumper, leading an equally bright chestnut pony, with, appropriately, a yellow rosette attached to its bridle. Someone near us caught her eye and in a voice which would have been heard above massed brass bands in the Albert Hall, she stopped and screamed, "Hello there," at which her pony in alarm, leapt into the air, flung itself anti-clockwise in front of her and landed with its posterior a couple of feet away from where Angela was standing with Saracen. The woman took no notice of it and began to regale her acquaintance with the experiences of the previous twenty minutes.

I was a bit concerned regarding the proximity of the pony to our foal and wished the woman would move away as did Angela whose face registered positive fury. Ponies and people already hemmed us in to left and right; with the ring rope and straw bales behind us, and this neurotic chestnut thing was in front tossing its head up and down. I didn't like the look in its eye either and although third in the child's riding pony class it might have been but I wouldn't have trusted it with a rag doll. Bessie's ears had gone back but I knew she wouldn't do anything which might endanger Saracen and I was just about to hiss to the woman to move her animal when she terminated her chat, gave a sudden tug on the leading reign, and the pony, not liking this rough treatment lowered its head to the ground whilst shooting its backend skywards, its hind legs swivelling past me. Bess, sensing the danger snorted, a frightened whinny issued from Saracen and a chorus of high-pitched foal squeals and neighing from their anxious dams was joined by "Oh's' and 'Look out's' from irate owners.

Angela bent down to study Saracen's near-hind leg, looked at me and shrugged. Her face wrinkled in a perplexed frown. 'I think that thing may have caught him but I can't see anything. Maybe he's alright.' The yellow rosette woman was clearly not aware of the upheaval she had caused, nor of the aggrieved atmosphere that remained as several owners soothed their excited mares and bemused foals, for by the time Angela had finished examining our foal's leg, she had raced off through the crowd, no doubt eager to let all and sundry know of her success. Only ten seconds ago all had been orderly and quite enjoyable; now I felt exhausted, albeit through mental fury rather than anything else, and in my imagination I took swipes at the yellow woman with a riding crop.

'Inconsiderate bitch,' I muttered to no-one in particular as I stroked Bessie's neck and the young woman next to me, also consoling her mare said 'What a ghastly woman.'

The voice over the tannoy came again.

'Class twenty-three; mares under fourteen hands with foals at foot. Class twenty-three in the ring please.'

We moved into the ring. The fleeting moment when I'd found myself relaxed about the show had evaporated and the awfulness of it all had now really set in. I looked at the people ahead of me and found it impossible to believe that this was anybody's idea of a fun day. I assumed that the incident with the pony was fairly unusual although I was pretty sure that awful things did happen from time to time but all I wanted to do now was go home. I walked on round the ring following the pony in front of me, working myself into state of chronic self-pity and we'd nearly completed a full circuit when from behind, I heard Angela, in a loud whisper call, 'Mum, Saracen's lame.'

Bringing Bessie to a halt I watched as Angela examined his leg on which an almost infinitesimal swelling had begun to appear.

'That wretched woman. I could kill her. Let's get out of the way; we can't stay here.' Those behind passed us by and a steward came hurrying over to see what was up. 'How unfortunate,' he said. 'Well, why don't you join the end of the line as they come round again and then you can just pop out at the gate? You've only a few yards to go.' I looked at Angela who screwed up her face in disappointment, but said 'O.K.' and we slipped in behind the last of the twenty or so mares and foals that were just completing their second circuit of the perimeter. I again mentally lashed out at the wretched woman and for good measure rammed the yellow rosette down her throat.

Having regard for Saracen's injury we dawdled along, thereby creating an ever widening gap between us and the animal in front and were within a couple of yards of the gate, when one of the judges, smartly tweedy and bowler-hatted, who had been standing close by, bore down on us. In a tone which, in my sensitive mood I imagined as being imperious and accusing, although it was probably nothing of the sort, he enquired, 'Are you aware that your foal is lame?'

So that did it.

That was my one and only entry as an exhibitor on the show field.

Angela poured water on a bandage and wrapped it round Saracen's leg and I thought now, we can go home, but first everyone had to be consulted. Shall we go or would you rather stay and picnic here? Gordon didn't need to answer; our friend said he thought it was a bit early to leave; Louise and Jessica were happy to go as they had other things they could do and Angela would go along with whatever was decided.

But even that idea was thwarted for Bessie refused to enter the box. We encouraged, bribed, pulled and pushed. Two strong men joined us and put a leather surcingle round her back end below her quarters and standing one on each side of the ramp, pulled with all their might. But she dug her heels in and leant back comfortably on the leather and dared them to do more. She was quite content that her son should be inside the trailer but she was not prepared to join him and after a couple of minutes we thanked the two stalwarts. They were loath to give up the battle but I felt a respite was needed even if others enjoyed this sort of thing, so after tethering Bessie and bringing her son out of the box, we sat down on plaid rugs to enjoy a good, if somewhat early lunch.

Bessie enjoyed some salad made into a sandwich and when given a couple of crisps threw back her head, curled up her lips and laughed with pleasure. Spurning the water poured into a bucket for her but well-practised in the art of drinking tea, she drank a mugful of ours and having been thus wined and dined, her humour mellowed, as had mine, for after we'd boxed Saracen again, Louise untied Bess's leading rein and walked up into the box, Bess amiably following. Before she had time to change her mind we heaved up the ramp and secured the bolts.

'That's it. Has everybody finished?' and without waiting for an answer I scrambled everything back into the picnic basket, fastened the straps and pitched it and the rugs into the back of the Range Rover.

'You really can't wait to leave, can you?' commented our friend as we swayed over the uneven ground towards the gate. 'You got yourself into quite a lather earlier on. I'd always seen you as a sensible sort but you genuinely hate it, don't you?' and after ruminating on this hitherto undiscovered aspect of my character, added to himself, 'very odd.'

271

'No, I don't hate it,' I protested, 'It gives me great pleasure to see all these beautifully groomed animals and I admire the justified pride with which their owners exhibit them, but even if I knew that I was going to walk away with ten first prizes I just couldn't be bothered.' And it was true. Neither Gordon nor I could think of a better way to enjoy our animals than leaning on the gate watching them in the meadow among the buttercups and clover doing what animals like to do best; playing, running, leaping, dozing; just enjoying themselves. That's my idea of heaven.

***

However, all was not lost for us on the showground scene because we were able to enjoy some of the glory of showing by a method which suited us very well...... proxy.

It happened like this. When a domestic problem arose necessitating fairly frequent journeys to the south coast, we sold two of our goatlings. We had intended keeping them but with the general upheaval going on it seemed more sensible to have less stock.

When I advertised them they were five months old, still having a bottle morning and night and growing very well. We had several calls in the next couple of days: one from a man who jokily said that he wanted a 'lawn-mower.' I asked him if he realised that everything in sight would also be 'mown' to which he replied, 'Well, it'd be tethered of course.' Shortly after that call a most delightful sounding young woman rang. She had a small paddock, in which was an old pigsty that her husband was in the process of refurbishing for its future occupant, and she wanted a goat for milking. This sounded promising, until I said I really wanted them to go together as goats are sociable creatures and one would be lonely, and I would reduce the price for the two. She thought for some seconds then said hesitantly, 'Well, I don't think I really want two. From what you say there'd be too much milk. I'm not into the cheesey, buttery thing. I'd really only want one. We've got a couple of cats and the children would love it to death.'

Uh-uh! I said something about waiting to see if I could find someone to take the two of them, thanked her for calling, but didn't ask for her number.

The following morning a goat-keeper from somewhere near Ludlow rang and immediately asked about bloodlines.

'That sounds very good. The trouble is I've seen your advert at the wrong time. We're having a lot of work done in the yard; a proper milking parlour and an extension to the goat house so I couldn't possibly take on any more stock for several weeks but I am very interested. Could I come down to see them? I'll give you a deposit if they're what I want.'

'Of course,' I replied, as visions of the kids enjoying life at the' Ludlow Hilton filled my mind, 'what day would you like to come?'

'Well, er' I could hear mutterings and page turnings as she consulted her diary, 'I can't really do anything until a week on Monday. Would that be alright with you?'

I thought quickly. This was ten days away and in the meantime another suitable purchaser might contact us. I didn't think she was the sort who would let me down but if, when she saw them she didn't want them, time would have been wasted.

'Can I take your number?' I asked, and went on to explain my reasons. 'I'll call you if I have to cancel your visit.' She was a most understanding woman. 'Why did the builders have to be there right now,' I mused, wondering at the same time if we'd get any more enquiries. And we did.

Mr Gregory phoned.

Mr Gregory wanted a goat. A quality goat.

'Were our goats quality goats; goats that would give plenty of milk?' he asked.

I assured him on both points and he said would it be all right if he came the following day at about four o'clock. Sure enough he and his wife arrived as he said they would, just a few minutes after four.

What a pleasure it was to do business with them. They bred German Sheperds, and only the previous year had been in the ribbons at Crufts, so when it came to 'class' they knew a thing or two, even though they claimed ignorance regarding goats. They wanted a good kid to eventually produce milk for the kennels. They already had one goat but in-whelp bitches and young stock drank a lot of milk and there would always be a market amongst their doggy chums for the milk when they didn't need it.

As soon as they saw the kids they knew they were looking at quality and stood in the yard for nearly an hour trying to make up their minds which one to take. Several times they came to a decision, announcing, 'Yes, we've made up our minds' only to hesitate and begin weighing the odds of one against the other all over again. We didn't mind; they were so nice, and we knew that whichever one they chose would be going to a good home, although it left me with the task of making sure the remaining one had companionship wherever it went, as I had really wanted to sell the two together. Maybe we'd have to keep one after all.

These deliberations were fuelled by offerings of refreshment from the kitchen, gratefully although sometimes absentmindedly received when the pressure of selection was reaching fever pitch, and periodically our expertise was called upon.

'Which one now, which one would you say was the best?'

'Lupin' I'd say for the umpteenth time, 'She is, I think, the best. Her mother gives fractionally more milk and is the finer goat but there's hardly anything in it.'

Time passed and I milked the goats to an audience, which I found very strange as having their own goat to milk there couldn't have been anything novel about watching me doing the same thing. A chill began to creep in on the air but still the Gregory's debated while they, and sometimes we, watched the kids hurling themselves into space from the bank or the garden wall, leaping sideways down the yard and landing with all four feet touching the ground simultaneously. Then taking off in the same four-feet-together way, twisting and turning in mid-air for the sheer joy of it. And all the time the deliberations continued. The trouble was that I'd pointed out Clover as a real character and the little charmer demonstrated this by constantly leaving the game with her half-sister, to run over to one of us and leaping up, stand with her forelegs pressed against someone's body whilst gazing lovingly into their face. This was very hard to resist and was definitely what prolonged the Gregory's choice. Eventually Clover was chosen and I was happy to know that she wouldn't want for companions with another goat and dogs installed. I said I'd post her pedigree in the next couple of days, and with Mrs Gregory sitting in the back of the car cuddling a very lucky kid, they drove down the track and away home.

'Well Lupin,' I said as she ran off towards her mother and aunt in the meadow, 'it seems you are going to stay with us'.

I was rather surprised when early the following morning Mr Gregory rang.

It appeared that an elderly man who knew a thing or two about goats lived in a village close to where Mr and Mrs Gregory lived and hearing about the new arrival took a stroll, that evening, in their direction. After studying the kid for a short while he pronounced judgement. 'I'll wager that kid has Prometheus blood in it,' he told Mr Gregory, who, on making enquiries as to who or what Prometheus was, realized that they might have acquired a kid which had the blood of one of the finest sires of milking Saanens in the country, coursing through its veins. So when I picked up the phone he came straight to the point.

'Has this kid got Prometheus blood in it?

'Yes,' I was happy to tell him, 'Langdale Prometheus is her grandfather.'

'Have you still got the other one?'

'We have.'

'We'll be up for her tomorrow if that's alright.'

We were delighted.

***

'Why didn't you tell us about her grandfather?' Mr Gregory asked on arrival the following day.

'I did say their grandfather was the father of champion milkers. I don't suppose his name would have meant anything to you.'

'Oh, I expect we were so engrossed in the kids we probably missed a fair bit of what you were saying.' That's true I thought, picturing the scene of the previous day with all the examining, considering, prevarication and discussion.

So Clover and Lupin stayed together after all and we did our showing by proxy because Mr and Mrs Gregory, already experts in the dog world, became hooked on goats, and the following summer, along with thousands of others throughout the country, rose early on many a week-end morning when the dew was still heavy on the ground, to wash, brush and make generally beautiful, Lupin and Clover, before

275

setting off for the show-ring. Their efforts were well rewarded and we looked forward to hearing Mr Gregory's happy voice when he rang from time to time to let us know of the latest successes and of the number of people who asked where his goats had come from. They did all the hard work and showed in style, while we shared their pleasure and pride without moving from our hillside.

For us, a marvellous way to show.

THE END OF THE ROAD

It was hardly likely that the long line of stationary traffic in which we found ourselves one August Bank Holiday Saturday was an isolated incident. At various trouble spots around Britain, motorists eager to get to their destination would be immobile on crowded roads waiting for the vehicles in front of them to crawl forward a few more feet; but there was I reflected, a difference between their situation and ours.

The morning had boded ill when we got up, the sky filled with dark lowering clouds, and I'd just managed to collect several armfuls of greenery for the goats in lieu of the browsing which I knew would shortly be denied them, when the heavens opened and torrential rain hammered down on the yard and clattered brassily on the concrete outside the big kitchen. Hens quickly bedraggled by the sudden onslaught appeared from all corners, scurrying for the shelter of the barn which was always a more popular gathering place than the hen house, where after a good deal of ostentatiously shaking their feathers some pottered over to the wood pile to search for a few juicy tit-bits. But most stood in small groups, muttering to each other or themselves while observing the watery world outside.

Water came coursing down the old cart track which separated our land from the fields above and flowed into the yard where over the centuries it had created a shallow gully. It bubbled over any large stones in its way and taking a host of smaller ones with it piled them in an ever growing heap at the edge of the duck-pond. It then surged out the other side of the pond and down the steep track towards the meadow gate.

We had planned to go to a farm sale in the early afternoon, although by lunchtime we were having second thoughts. Gordon tapped the barometer and I said I thought the sky seemed to be getting a bit lighter. Certainly by half-past one the rain had lessened so we donned waterproofs and wellies and splashed out to the Land Rover. We drove either climbing, with the water from the fields rushing towards us, or going downhill with it racing past us, straining our eyes through the windscreen while the wipers fought a losing battle. After twenty minutes a gradual easing off finally ended in a drizzle as small patches of blue appeared in the sky, enlarging as the clouds dispersed.

We didn't know where the farm we were seeking was but headed along several miles of narrow lanes in what we knew to be the general direction until a large sign pointing to an even narrower lane on the left, announced in big letters, 'TO THE SALE'. Familiar with the wayward twists of Welsh byways we carried on until brought to a halt by a long line of stationary vehicles stretching round a bend so that we couldn't see how far they extended. We waited a few minutes, speculating on the reason for the stoppage and idly watched a few people wandering about as though not knowing what to do, until becoming impatient I climbed out and joined some of them.

'There's a blockage further up,' said a man standing by the car in front, 'Some silly bugger's left a van there and nobody knows who it belongs to. Someone's gone to find them but if we don't move soon we'll miss the sale.' As there seemed nothing anyone could do about it we chatted for a minute or so then I moved back to the Land Rover, opened the door, and leaning in relayed the information about the rogue van.

'Well, if that's the case, I can't see any point in waiting here,' said Gordon, We might as well walk.' But it was evidently going to be quite a long walk, for we were told the farm was over a mile away. The lane was awash with muddy water and debris pouring off the hill, and cars, vans, Land Rovers and a couple of lorries had hemmed us in from behind, vanishing from sight round a corner where, judging by the large number of people walking towards us, it stretched to infinity. Everyone wanted to know why they couldn't drive to the farm, and on finding out, discussed at length the stupidity, lack of courtesy, thoughtlessness, even the degenerate morality of the sort of person who would cause such confusion. It flashed through my mind that if no one had examined the van inside, this stupid, discourteous, thoughtless, morally bereft individual could be lying bound and gagged on the floor; even dead; but it seemed a bit bizarre, so I kept the idea to myself.

I turned to catch up with Gordon who'd gone on ahead and was waving to me from where people appeared to be vanishing into the hedge, taking a short cut I assumed. Hurrah! We were going to make the auction after all. When I reached him I saw a narrow path, awash of course, sloping down into a small wood. An ancient individual not much more than five feet tall with a sou'wester pulled well down on his head and wearing a voluminous raincoat which almost reached to the mud on which he was standing, had stationed himself at this junction. In a high-pitched voice and with obvious enthusiasm he directed us down the squelchy path, telling us that it would save us walking all the way along the road. He also gave a running commentary on the weather in general, the effect of such weather on the lane we had just walked, on the woods we were about to slither through, on the stream we were going to cross, along with his deeply considered opinion as to why the van had been abandoned in the lane. It was clearly a great occasion for him and as I drew nearer his oration was made more fascinating by the frantic flexing of his jaw muscles, evidently necessary in order to prevent his lower teeth flying out as he spoke. He didn't seem at all disconcerted by his restless dentures, for no bardic orator ever thrilled to an audience more than the little man on the back lane that wet Bank Holiday Saturday as he gestured us towards the wood, all the while his jaws manipulating the cavity of his mouth constantly seeking a better grip on the pearly plastic within. This was his moment, and by golly, he was going to make the most of it.

We thanked him for his directions and slithered with others down the path to join a group at the edge of what would normally have been a shallow stream but was now a swollen, racing reddish-brown cascade. To my horror I saw that across this was a bridge consisting of two eight-inch wide planks joined end to end in the middle by some unseen method and spanning the eight feet or so width of this perilous stream. I didn't have much confidence in this arrangement because as soon as someone got onto the first plank and moved a couple of feet it began to sag ominously, and where the planks were joined they were so obviously out of alignment that I thought whatever was holding them together couldn't possibly do so for much longer. By the time the centre was reached the whole thing was bouncing up and down a few inches above the water as though it was being dangled on a piece of elastic.

A length of thick rope served as a handrail, tied with baling twine at one end to a tree and at the other to a pole stuck in the muddy bank and I watched with growing terror as the numbers in front of me dwindled. One by one people stepped onto the plank, and with varying degrees of confidence reached the other side. If any of the men were apprehensive they weren't going to show it. The women were either laughing nervously or grimly determined, and probably like me, more scared of being thought chicken-hearted if they turned away, rather than foolish if they fell off. Everyone was helped along with encouraging words from those who'd gone before (contemplating the imminent future had a quieting effect on those of us about to grasp this particular nettle) reaching for an outstretched hand at the near completion of their journey, being clapped and cheered on each safe arrival

I grasped the rope and gingerly placed my right foot on the plank. I moved my left foot alongside it and began to shuffle along crabwise a few inches at a time, terrified that the rope might swing away from me and feeling a close affinity with a 17th century ancestor who sailed the Atlantic to the New world. I concentrated on putting my feet in the right places, all the while hearing calls of encouragement and instructions but I was so scared. I seemed to have been suspended over this torrent for ages, watching and listening to it angrily rushing inches below me, knowing I was getting closer to the centre and the spot where the two pieces of bouncing plank joined. I closed my eyes and had just decided I was going to be sea sick, when Gordon's voice, very close by said 'Reach out, take my hand,' and I found myself putting a foot on terra that was more slippery than firma, but was very, very welcome.

'You alright?' I nodded my head but nonetheless stayed where I was for a few seconds regaining my composure, before we began to follow those ahead, climbing up yet another muddy track eventually reaching the edge of a field within sight of the farm a quarter of a mile further on. Chatting away, the general consensus was that it would have been easier and without any anxiety to have walked along the lane rather than attempt this unusual access and it crossed my mind that the little old man with the high-pitched voice, seeking the opportunity to enjoy a day of high drama, might have engineered the whole episode.

We were surprised to see how few vehicles had reached the parking field before the stationary van had prevented further access. Just two lorries, a van and half a dozen cars. I guessed they were glad they'd got in but wondered if they were sure about getting out! None of my business though and we wandered into the squelching sale field determined to enjoy the day, thankful that a weak sun had come out. We arrived late but as the auction had begun with the heavy machinery and livestock in which we had no interest, we moved into the yard where a surprising number of small implements in which Gordon was interested, were set out. Most of them looked very old and I couldn't tell what possible use some of them could have had been but I recognised several dairying artefacts. It was a jolly time. Everyone chatting to whoever was standing near them, and my questions to an elderly woman about some of the unusual looking items had her reminiscing about how such things had been in regular use in her younger days. I heard several snatches of conversation about the hair-raising episode crossing the bridge, although now it was a source of pride rather than of fear and was regarded as quite an adventure, which indeed it was.

I could hear the voice of the auctioneer as he intoned his mantra. Leaving Gordon I wandered off.

One of the beast houses had been set aside as a bar-cum-tea-room and was packed to bursting, with farmers, identifiable by their uniform dress for such weather of tweed cap, oil-skins and green wellies, and several dealers amongst the crowd. Those unable to get inside the barn were shouting their orders which were relayed to the bar, and the drinks then passed back in chain-gang fashion but in spite of the pandemonium the barman remained unfazed and whatever else happened at the sale, there was no doubt that the bar was a rattling success.

At one end of the barn a number of household items were set around the walls and I hoped I might find a wardrobe there but was out of luck. However, an Edwardian dressing table and two washstands caught my eye. The first washstand was a real little dolly, in pine with a white marble top and ten patterned tiles in a mushroom colour on white in two rows along the back. Delicate brass handles ornamented a long shallow drawer and below it was a small centre cupboard, just large enough to hold two chamber pots, one above the other. The dressing table matching it had a pretty shield-shaped swing mirror above two tiny drawers, which sat centrally on the main chest of four drawers and I thought how pretty they would look in Tironnen. The second washstand was combined with a dressing table, a marble topped cupboard with tiles behind making one half, and a slightly

281

higher chest of drawers and mirror making the other. I'd not seen such a piece before so imagined it to be fairly unusual, which would mean it would fetch more than I could afford. A pity, but I reckoned I stood a fair chance with the other two and when Gordon arrived with mugs of tea we examined all three pieces and found them sound. We settled on a limit and prepared to hang around until the auctioneer had finished selling the livestock. Not of course, that we had much choice about hanging around. Practically everyone we bumped into cheerfully informed us that the driver of the last car in the lane was flat on his face in the bar, and we'd be lucky to be away by nightfall.

'We'll have a party,' shouted one man, inclining his head towards the barn. 'I expect they'd serve breakfast in there.'

'Got your eye on that bed then have you, Gwyn?'

There was much laughter all round but whoever Gwyn was he was up to form.

'Don't need it man, there's plenty of hay about.'

Another voice joined in.

'It's the auctioneer's fault; he should've had the sale in the village.'

'He should be taught a lesson.'

'Let's string 'im up.'

'Aw man, what are you on about. Look at the extra drinking time you've got.'

'Ay, but the missis won't believe I've been held up by a bloody van,' and the speaker, evidently working on the principle of 'in for a penny in for a pound,' made off in the direction of the bar amid the cheers of his neighbours, many of whom I did not doubt were thinking much the same thing.

The humorous sallies continued until the auctioneer, unaware that his blood was being called for, came round from the cattle pens and marched purposefully into the yard, announcing as he did so that he would sell the household goods in the yard rather than in the barn, so would all interested parties please come into the yard. He mounted a wooden box that would serve as a dais and repeated his announcement. Gordon had disappeared and I was standing near the door of the bar, which was still packed to capacity but the noise from within precluded the auctioneer from being heard. Someone near the door yelled that if anyone was interested in the sale they'd better come out now and the noise dwindled and then stopped.

'Sale starting now,' yelled the man, and the auctioneer, realizing that at last he had everybody's attention said loudly 'Move along ladies please, I'm holding the household sale now.'

I looked towards the bar door as the crowd surged forward. From where I was I could see tweed caps and bare male heads in plenty but of 'ladies' there were not so many, in fact there were only five yet still the polite tones of the auctioneer still rang out, trying to jostle the crowd to greater speed in order to get the last lap of the sale under way.

'Outside, ladies please.'

I could hardly believe my eyes as the inheritors of the land of Llywelyn ap Gruffydd meekly shuffled forward. Surely to be addressed in such lowly terms was enough to make even the mildest Welshman, to my knowledge a rare species, pour forth in venomous harangue, but not a sound of rebuke was heard as the patient auctioneer encouraged them into the sunshine. What had happened I wondered, to the fisticuffs, the threatened lynching, the superior sex? I wasn't alone in my thoughts. A lilting female voice close by called clearly, 'Funny looking lot of ladies aren't they?' and a roar of derisive laughter rose from the males in the yard, but those issuing from the bar suddenly didn't seem to have the stomach for violence.

I bought the wash-stand with the mushroom coloured tiles for one pound and the matching dressing table for ten but the bids for the combined piece soared way above our limit and as the hammer came down I walked towards the gate through which we would have driven several hours earlier. The idea of tracing my steps over the stream had no appeal and I followed the lane up to a bend at the head of the valley, where it turned quite sharply to meander for about half a mile before approaching the van which had caused all the trouble, and judging by the group of people around it was still the subject of speculation. Rust surrounded numerous small holes on the bonnet and on jagged edges to the wheel arches. Mid-blue in colour, it didn't need a close inspection to know that it had been painted, and badly painted at that, in fact the paint seemed to have been slapped on any old how for I could see the original black paint beneath in places.

'Do you think it belongs to anyone at the auction?'

'Well, they've kept very quiet about it if it does,' replied Gordon.

'Indeed they have.'

283

'If they came in a van, they were probably going to buy quite big things but how could they get them away when the van was down here?' was one inspired observation. No one said anything.

'I don't think they're at the farm at all,' drawled a tall angular man in his early fifties. 'There weren't many cars in the car park, were there? I counted them. There were six cars,' and after a pause, repeated with great emphasis, 'Six,' as though by concentrating on the word the mystery was halfway to being solved. 'Probably all of them belonged to people to do with the auction, then this van drives up the lane but no-one sees it. So I think that this happened very early; very early indeed and that this vehicle,' here ensued a pause of such length that if it hadn't been for the fact that his eyes were scanning each and every one of us I'd have thought he'd fallen asleep, 'that this vehicle,' we waited with baited breath...... 'has broken down.'

Sherlock Holmes had spoken.

There was silence for a few seconds, then several people coughed into their hands, a few giggled and some just seemed rooted to the spot. I clamped my hand over my mouth in an effort to subdue my chuckles but a woman standing nearby caught my eye and we both hurriedly turned away before our mirth became too visible. I walked quickly, knowing my shoulders were heaving as I heard in my head the tall man's soliloquy complete with pauses, emphases and inflections. How wonderful to be so uninhibited I thought, to announce publicly and with such confidence what had been as clear as daylight to anyone who'd seen the few cars in the car park. I carried on along the lane, the voice in my head repeating over and over the man's oration, when the laughing woman caught up with me.

'What a funny man,' I said. 'Do you know who he is?'

'Oh, yes, that's Peter the Pint, he's...'

'Peter the Pint?' I interjected disbelievingly. 'Peter the Pint?' I'd heard many descriptive names while living in Wales but this was a new one.

'Yes,' she laughed, 'He came from Carmarthen way several years back and I think before that from somewhere in the south of England. I don't know him myself except to nod to and only that because he turns up at all sorts of places. People say he's very nice and a good neighbour. He can't hold his beer though; just one or two drinks and he gets all pompous,' and she began to giggle again. 'He's been known to say some very strange things.'

'You mean he was tipsy back there?'

'Oh, yes, six sheets to the wind.'

'He didn't look it. Didn't sound like it either.'

'But that's how he is. Just gets pompous and says odd things.'

'Peter the Pint,' I muttered, 'Peter the Pint; oh, I love that." And after a pause enquired, "I bet you weren't laughing when you crossed the stream.'

'Oh, that was scary wasn't it? All that water and so fast too. I was convinced I'd never reach the other side,' she said.

'Same here. I don't know whether I was more nervous about the planks or the handrail. But were you surprised when you did get across? Did you think you were still near the centre?'

'Funny you should ask that because I really thought I'd still some way to go. So, yes, I was surprised. And glad! That so-called bridge must have been there for years and years.'

'And not seen much in the way of maintenance!'

Our conversation ended when we reached her Land Rover and turning a bend I saw Gordon standing beside a car two back from ours, in conversation with two strangers. I joined him and his companions, and after introductions were made I gave a colourful rendition of the diversion by the van.

The people whose car we were standing by were from Stratford, on their way home after a few days touring and meandering along the back lanes they had seen the 'sale' sign. Never having attended a country sale before they thought it might be an interesting experience, which with much animation they were now proclaiming it to be. They were going to be much later getting home than they'd planned. As yet there was no indication that they would get home at all and they couldn't wait to tell their friends what had happened, the only trouble being that probably no one would believe them!

By this time a few more people were dribbling past, but with thirty or so vehicles to move before we could, there was nothing to do but enjoy the stories that were being bandied about, the view, and the general good humour. I said I'd take a walk further down the lane and my new companion said she'd come too and we chatted about families and activities as we went until we came to a field gate which afforded

285

us relaxed leaning with a good view of whatever was happening over at the farm on the other side of the valley and whether the number of people there seemed to be lessening, indicating that more folk were making for the lane…unless of course, they were making for the bar!

A small, neat man with a business like air stopped beside us and producing a note book from his breast-pocket, flicked it open with an expert flourish and appearing to read from it demanded in mock seriousness, 'Are you the red Anglia, the blue Cortina or the Land Rover LEU613S?' then spoilt the effect by collapsing into explosive mirth. No one seemed to mind waiting and nearly everyone who passed repeated the tale about the driver of the last car being out for the count and each time we all roared with laughter, although it was beginning to sound a bit forced.

Nearly another hour passed and everyone was a bit weary, when we thought we heard the sound of an engine starting up. People looked at one another with hopeful expressions then the sound came again, and again. Time-passing chat was brought to an end as we all hurried to our vehicles, glad to be getting away. Our companions bid us goodbye and began their journey back to Stratford with memories that they would never have dreamed of having. We climbed into the Land Rover, reversing in convoy until we reached a T-junction, then, suddenly very tired, headed for home.

***

The following morning we were off early to collect our furniture. We passed the place of the previous day's sojourn where imprints of great tractor tyres lay in the mud that covered the lane. The herbage for some way alongside was crushed and mangled where the van had been dragged along before it was finally towed into a field some twenty yards away. We weren't the first arrivals. Three men were already heaving a heavy iron chaff cutter onto a trailer, while a representative of the auction house stood by writing on a clipboard. A few of the big things had already gone, taken the previous day by those who must have stayed around until the removal of the van allowed them access to the farm.

A small melancholy looking man of about fifty, standing by the group with the chaff cutter broke away to come over to us. We told him who we were and what we'd come for and learned that he was the farmer on whose land we were. He helped us load the furniture and we said we thought he must be very sad to be leaving such a lovely place. We didn't want to pry, just let him know that whatever the reasons for his departure we understood just a little of the unhappiness he would be feeling. But he seemed to want to talk and told us how his family had farmed this land for four generations, that his ill health had forced him to give up farming, and with no sons or daughters to take over he had no choice other than to sell. Oh, that poor man.

He looked towards the head of the valley and across to where the steep hill opposite seemed as though it might fold over to engulf the neat buildings, then to the familiar wooded slopes behind the house.

'It's all gone now,' he sighed, in a voice so low we could barely hear. 'Everything gone; the house; the furniture; the land; the stock; everything.' His voice faded even more as he whispered, 'All gone.' Did I imagine his eyes misting over?' But when he spoke again it was in a normal voice. 'I've bought a nice bungalow in Llandovery.'

I can't bear this, I thought. Here we are, carting this man's belongings away from this idyllic spot, from his home and he's telling us that he's bought a nice bungalow in Llandovery. It was the word 'nice' that caught me. My heart went out to him as I wondered what part in his life that pretentious little word had ever played before. Here he was, trying to persuade himself that everything would be alright; that the 'niceness' of his new way of life would make up for the loss of all that was dear to him, the only things that had ever mattered, yet knowing, just as we knew, that for him this was the end of the road. He turned and quickly walked away towards the men at the far end of the yard, seeking to spend his last heart-aching days in the companionship from his past rather than with strangers. We had no place there and drove off in silence feeling guilty at being part of such sadness.

***

We stripped down the furniture, sent the mirror away to be re-silvered and removed the lacquer from the brass handles. When they were re-assembled they looked real charmers and we put the washstand in the secret room where I knew it would delight any future

287

guest, placed a flowered wash bowl and jug on the white marble top, then sat on the stairs below the little oak doorway admiring its prettiness and the effect it had on the room. We moved the dressing table into Jessica's room where its honey-coloured wood glowed against the pink stone wall. I sat down on the patchwork-covered bed looking at it, wondering what tales it could tell. For seventy or eighty years it had been in that farmhouse, disturbed only for spring-cleaning until a few weeks ago when it had had a lot number stuck on it and been pushed against the barn wall.

A strange feeling came over me, just as it had that Saturday in August seven years ago when Norman had phoned to tell us that Tironnen was ours, when the future was suddenly a vast jungle of uncertainty, hope and faith in ourselves. Images began to form in my mind of people whose imprint on the world would never make headlines yet whose presence on it had been so great a part of our life here. Visions of the not infrequent terrifying crises when no work was coming in for Gordon came to mind yet somehow we held on without outside help because what we had was so worth fighting for, and to think of capitulation was impossible. I saw us returning from a thousand journeys and felt the familiar cloak of privacy and peace descend, when having driven up from the lane we reached our track and shot home the bolt in the lower gate. My mind's eye followed the great sweep of skyline, along the Beacons upping and downing in a vast stretch from east to west, brilliantly coloured or sombre, sharply etched or smouldering in mist, always changing, always magnificent in their many moods. Dependable and mysterious, they were an integral part of Tironnen's past, of our past and present, and indeed of our future, for was it not here, high on this hillside, that we really had learned the most crucial lessons of life; here that we found out so much about ourselves?

Ours is a good life in our pretty house I thought, as I stood up and ran my hand along the smooth wood of the dressing table and over the shining brass handles of the two tiny drawers beneath the mirror, lifting them and letting them fall to hit the back plate with a sharp chinking sound to bounce out and back again several times in rapid succession. Yes, I thought, the history of our family has been added to this house, the gamut of our emotions have seeped into the very crevices that hold the secrets of three hundred years, and maybe when

288

the time comes for us to leave we will be able to say that in some small measure we tried to repay the contentment we felt here, for our laughter lies thick on the walls of Tironnen.